Mastering Mesos

The ultimate guide to managing, building, and deploying large-scale clusters with Apache Mesos

Dipa Dubhashi

Akhil Das

[PACKT] open source *
PUBLISHING   community experience distilled

BIRMINGHAM - MUMBAI

Mastering Mesos

First published: May 2016

Production reference: 1200516

Published by Packt Publishing Ltd.
Livery Place
35 Livery Street
Birmingham B3 2PB, UK.

ISBN 978-1-78588-624-9

www.packtpub.com

Credits

Authors
Dipa Dubhashi

Akhil Das

Reviewer
Naveen Molleti

Commissioning Editor
Akram Hussain

Acquisition Editor
Sonali Vernekar

Content Development Editor
Onkar Wani

Technical Editor
Hussain Kanchwala

Copy Editor
Shruti Iyer

Project Coordinator
Bijal Patel

Proofreader
Safis Editing

Indexer
Rekha Nair

Graphics
Kirk D'Penha

Production Coordinator
Aparna Bhagat

Cover Work
Aparna Bhagat

About the Authors

Dipa Dubhashi is an alumnus of the prestigious Indian Institute of Technology and heads product management at Sigmoid. His prior experience includes consulting with ZS Associates besides founding his own start-up. Dipa specializes in envisioning enterprise big data products, developing their roadmaps, and managing their development to solve customer use cases across multiple industries. He advises several leading start-ups as well as Fortune 500 companies about architecting and implementing their next-generation big data solutions. Dipa has also developed a course on Apache Spark for a leading online education portal and is a regular speaker at big data meetups and conferences.

Akhil Das is a senior software developer at Sigmoid primarily focusing on distributed computing, real-time analytics, performance optimization, and application scaling problems using a wide variety of technologies such as Apache Spark and Mesos, among others. He contributes actively to the Apache Spark project and is a regular speaker at big data conferences and meetups, MesosCon 2015 being the most recent one.

We would like to thank several people that helped make this book a reality: Revati Dubhashi, without whose driving force this book would not have seen the light of day; Chithra, for her constant encouragement and support; and finally, Mayur Rustagi, Naveen Molleti, and the entire Sigmoid family for their invaluable guidance and technical input.

About the Reviewer

Naveen Molleti works at Sigmoid as a technology lead, heading product architecture and scalability. Although he graduated in computer science from IIT Kharagpur in 2011, he has worked for about a decade developing software on various OSes and platforms in a variety of programming languages. He enjoys exploring technologies and platforms and developing systems software and infrastructure.

www.PacktPub.com

eBooks, discount offers, and more

Did you know that Packt offers eBook versions of every book published, with PDF and ePub files available? You can upgrade to the eBook version at www.PacktPub.com and as a print book customer, you are entitled to a discount on the eBook copy. Get in touch with us at customercare@packtpub.com for more details.

At www.PacktPub.com, you can also read a collection of free technical articles, sign up for a range of free newsletters and receive exclusive discounts and offers on Packt books and eBooks.

https://www2.packtpub.com/books/subscription/packtlib

Do you need instant solutions to your IT questions? PacktLib is Packt's online digital book library. Here, you can search, access, and read Packt's entire library of books.

Why subscribe?

- Fully searchable across every book published by Packt
- Copy and paste, print, and bookmark content
- On demand and accessible via a web browser

Table of Contents

Preface

Apache Mesos abstracts CPU, memory, storage, and other compute resources away from machines (physical or virtual), enabling fault-tolerant and elastic distributed systems to easily be built and run effectively. It improves resource utilization, simplifies system administration, and supports a wide variety of distributed applications that can be effortlessly deployed by leveraging its pluggable architecture.

This book will provide a detailed step-by-step guide to deploying a Mesos cluster using all the standard DevOps tools to write and port Mesos frameworks effectively and in general demystify the concept of Mesos.

The book will first establish the raison d'être of Mesos and explain its architecture in an effective manner. From there, the book will walk the reader through the complex world of Mesos, moving progressively from simple single machine setups to highly complex multi-node cluster setups with new concepts logically introduced along the way. At the end of the journey, the reader will be armed with all the resources that he/she requires to effectively manage the complexities of today's modern datacenter requirements.

What this book covers

Chapter 1, *Introducing Mesos*, introduces Mesos, dives deep into its architecture, and introduces some important topics, such as frameworks, resource allocation, and resource isolation. It also discusses the two-level scheduling approach that Mesos employs, provides a detailed overview of its API, and provides a few examples of how Mesos is used in production.

Chapter 2, *Mesos Internals*, provides a comprehensive overview of Mesos' features and walks the reader through several important topics regarding high availability, fault tolerance, scaling, and efficiency, such as resource allocation, resource reservation, and recovery, among others.

Chapter 3, Getting Started with Mesos, covers how to manually set up and run a Mesos cluster on the public cloud (AWS, GCE, and Azure) as well as on a private datacentre (on premise). It also discuss the various debugging methods and explores how to troubleshoot the Mesos setup in detail.

Chapter 4, Service Scheduling and Management Frameworks, introduces several Mesos-based scheduling and management frameworks or applications that are required for the easy deployment, discovery, load balancing, and failure handling of long-running services.

Chapter 5, Mesos Cluster Deployment, explains how a Mesos cluster can be easily set up and monitored using the standard deployment and configuration management tools used by system administrators and DevOps engineers. It also discusses some of the common problems faced while deploying a Mesos cluster along with their corresponding resolutions.

Chapter 6, Mesos Frameworks, walks the reader through the concept and features of Mesos frameworks in detail. It also provides a detailed overview of the Mesos API, including the new HTTP Scheduler API, and provides a recipe to build custom frameworks on Mesos.

Chapter 7, Mesos Containerizers, introduces the concepts of containers and talks a bit about Docker, probably the most popular container technology available today. It also provides a detailed overview of the different "containerizer" options in Mesos, besides introducing some other topics such as networking for Mesos-managed containers and the fetcher cache. Finally, an example of deploying containerized apps in Mesos is provided for better understanding.

Chapter 8, Mesos Big Data Frameworks, acts as a guide to deploying important big data processing frameworks such as Hadoop, Spark, Storm, and Samza on top of Mesos.

Chapter 9, Mesos Big Data Frameworks 2, guides the reader through deploying important big data storage frameworks such as Cassandra, the Elasticsearch-Logstash-Kibana (ELK) stack, and Kafka on top of Mesos.

What you need for this book

To get the most of this book, you need to have basic understanding of Mesos and cluster management along with familiarity with Linux. You will also need to have access to cloud services such as AWS, GCE, and Azure, preferably running with 15 GB RAM and four cores on the Ubuntu or CentOS operating system.

Who this book is for

The book aims to serve DevOps engineers and system administrators who are familiar with the basics of managing a Linux system and its tools.

Conventions

In this book, you will find a number of text styles that distinguish between different kinds of information. Here are some examples of these styles and an explanation of their meaning.

Code words in text, database table names, folder names, filenames, file extensions, pathnames, dummy URLs, user input, and Twitter handles are shown as follows: "For the sake of simplicity, we will simply run the `sleep` command."

A block of code is set as follows:

```
{
  "args": [
    "--zk=zk://Zookeeper.service.consul:2181/Mesos"
  ],
  "container": {
    "type": "DOCKER",
    "Docker": {
      "network": "BRIDGE",
      "image": "{{ Mesos_consul_image }}:
        {{ Mesos_consul_image_tag }}"
    }
  },
  "id": "Mesos-consul",
  "instances": 1,
  "cpus": 0.1,
  "mem": 256
}
```

When we wish to draw your attention to a particular part of a code block, the relevant lines or items are set in bold:

```
# Tasks for Master, Slave, and ZooKeeper nodes

- name: Install mesos package
  apt: pkg={{item}} state=present update_cache=yes
  with_items:
    - mesos={{ mesos_pkg_version }}
  sudo: yes
```

Any command-line input or output is written as follows:

```
# Update the packages.
$ sudo apt-get update
# Install the latest OpenJDK.
$ sudo apt-get install -y openjdk-7-jdk
# Install autotools (Only necessary if building from git repository).
$ sudo apt-get install -y autoconf libtool
# Install other Mesos dependencies.
$ sudo apt-get -y install build-essential
  python-dev python-boto libcurl4-nss-dev libsasl2-dev maven libapr1
  -dev libsvn-dev
```

New terms and **important words** are shown in bold. Words that you see on the screen, for example, in menus or dialog boxes, appear in the text like this: "Now press the **ADD** button to add a specific port."

> Warnings or important notes appear in a box like this.

> Tips and tricks appear like this.

Reader feedback

Feedback from our readers is always welcome. Let us know what you think about this book—what you liked or disliked. Reader feedback is important for us as it helps us develop titles that you will really get the most out of.

To send us general feedback, simply e-mail feedback@packtpub.com, and mention the book's title in the subject of your message.

If there is a topic that you have expertise in and you are interested in either writing or contributing to a book, see our author guide at www.packtpub.com/authors.

Customer support

Now that you are the proud owner of a Packt book, we have a number of things to help you to get the most from your purchase.

Downloading the example code

You can download the example code files for this book from your account at http://www.packtpub.com. If you purchased this book elsewhere, you can visit http://www.packtpub.com/support and register to have the files e-mailed directly to you.

You can download the code files by following these steps:

1. Log in or register to our website using your e-mail address and password.
2. Hover the mouse pointer on the **SUPPORT** tab at the top.
3. Click on **Code Downloads & Errata**.
4. Enter the name of the book in the **Search** box.
5. Select the book for which you're looking to download the code files.
6. Choose from the drop-down menu where you purchased this book from.
7. Click on **Code Download**.

Once the file is downloaded, please make sure that you unzip or extract the folder using the latest version of:

- WinRAR / 7-Zip for Windows
- Zipeg / iZip / UnRarX for Mac
- 7-Zip / PeaZip for Linux

The code bundle for the book is also hosted on GitHub at https://github.com/PacktPublishing/Mastering-Mesos. We also have other code bundles from our rich catalog of books and videos available at https://github.com/PacktPublishing/. Check them out!

Errata

Although we have taken every care to ensure the accuracy of our content, mistakes do happen. If you find a mistake in one of our books—maybe a mistake in the text or the code—we would be grateful if you could report this to us. By doing so, you can save other readers from frustration and help us improve subsequent versions of this book. If you find any errata, please report them by visiting http://www.packtpub.com/submit-errata, selecting your book, clicking on the **Errata Submission Form** link, and entering the details of your errata. Once your errata are verified, your submission will be accepted and the errata will be uploaded to our website or added to any list of existing errata under the Errata section of that title.

To view the previously submitted errata, go to https://www.packtpub.com/books/content/support and enter the name of the book in the search field. The required information will appear under the **Errata** section.

Piracy

Piracy of copyrighted material on the Internet is an ongoing problem across all media. At Packt, we take the protection of our copyright and licenses very seriously. If you come across any illegal copies of our works in any form on the Internet, please provide us with the location address or website name immediately so that we can pursue a remedy.

Please contact us at copyright@packtpub.com with a link to the suspected pirated material.

We appreciate your help in protecting our authors and our ability to bring you valuable content.

Questions

If you have a problem with any aspect of this book, you can contact us at questions@packtpub.com, and we will do our best to address the problem.

1
Introducing Mesos

Apache Mesos is open source, distributed cluster management software that came out of AMPLab, UC Berkeley in 2011. It abstracts CPU, memory, storage, and other computer resources away from machines (physical or virtual), enabling fault-tolerant and elastic distributed systems to be easily built and run effectively. It is referred to as a **metascheduler** (scheduler of schedulers) and a "distributed systems kernel/distributed datacenter OS".

It improves resource utilization, simplifies system administration, and supports a wide variety of distributed applications that can be deployed by leveraging its pluggable architecture. It is scalable and efficient and provides a host of features, such as resource isolation and high availability, which, along with a strong and vibrant open source community, makes this one of the most exciting projects.

We will cover the following topics in this chapter:

- Introduction to the datacenter OS and architecture of Mesos
- Introduction to frameworks
- Attributes, resources and resource scheduling, allocation, and isolation
- Monitoring and APIs provided by Mesos
- Mesos in production

Introduction to the datacenter OS and architecture of Mesos

Over the past decade, datacenters have graduated from packing multiple applications into a single server box to having large datacenters that aggregate thousands of servers to serve as a massively distributed computing infrastructure. With the advent of virtualization, microservices, cluster computing, and hyperscale infrastructure, the need of the hour is the creation of an application-centric enterprise that follows a software-defined datacenter strategy.

Currently, server clusters are predominantly managed individually, which can be likened to having multiple operating systems on the PC, one each for processor, disk drive, and so on. With an abstraction model that treats these machines as individual entities being managed in isolation, the ability of the datacenter to effectively build and run distributed applications is greatly reduced.

Another way of looking at the situation is comparing running applications in a datacenter to running them on a laptop. One major difference is that while launching a text editor or web browser, we are not required to check which memory modules are free and choose ones that suit our need. Herein lies the significance of a platform that acts like a host operating system and allows multiple users to run multiple applications simultaneously by utilizing a shared set of resources.

Datacenters now run varied distributed application workloads, such as Spark, Hadoop, and so on, and need the capability to intelligently match resources and applications. The datacenter ecosystem today has to be equipped to manage and monitor resources and efficiently distribute workloads across a unified pool of resources with the agility and ease to cater to a diverse user base (noninfrastructure teams included). A datacenter OS brings to the table a comprehensive and sustainable approach to resource management and monitoring. This not only reduces the cost of ownership but also allows a flexible handling of resource requirements in a manner that isolated datacenter infrastructure cannot support.

The idea behind a datacenter OS is that of intelligent software that sits above all the hardware in a datacenter and ensures efficient and dynamic resource sharing. Added to this is the capability to constantly monitor resource usage and improve workload and infrastructure management in a seamless way that is not tied to specific application requirements. In its absence, we have a scenario with silos in a datacenter that force developers to build software catering to machine-specific characteristics and make the moving and resizing of applications a highly cumbersome procedure.

The datacenter OS acts as a software layer that aggregates all servers in a datacenter into one giant supercomputer to deliver the benefits of multilatency, isolation, and resource control across all microservice applications. Another major advantage is the elimination of human-induced error during the continual assigning and reassigning of virtual resources.

From a developer's perspective, this will allow them to easily and safely build distributed applications without restricting them to a bunch of specialized tools, each catering to a specific set of requirements. For instance, let's consider the case of Data Science teams who develop analytic applications that are highly resource intensive. An operating system that can simplify how the resources are accessed, shared, and distributed successfully alleviates their concern about reallocating hardware every time the workloads change.

Of key importance is the relevance of the datacenter OS to DevOps, primarily a software development approach that emphasizes automation, integration, collaboration, and communication between traditional software developers and other IT professionals. With a datacenter OS that effectively transforms individual servers into a pool of resources, DevOps teams can focus on accelerating development and not continuously worry about infrastructure issues.

In a world where distributed computing becomes the norm, the datacenter OS is a boon in disguise. With freedom from manually configuring and maintaining individual machines and applications, system engineers need not configure specific machines for specific applications as all applications would be capable of running on any available resources from any machine, even if there are other applications already running on them. Using a datacenter OS results in centralized control and smart utilization of resources that eliminate hardware and software silos to ensure greater accessibility and usability even for noninfrastructural professionals.

Examples of some organizations administering their hyperscale datacenters via the datacenter OS are Google with the Borg (and next generation Omega) systems. The merits of the datacenter OS are undeniable, with benefits ranging from the scalability of computing resources and flexibility to support data sharing across applications to saving team effort, time, and money while launching and managing interoperable cluster applications.

It is this vision of transforming the datacenter into a single supercomputer that Apache Mesos seeks to achieve. Born out of a Berkeley AMPLab research paper in 2011, it has since come a long way with a number of leading companies, such as Apple, Twitter, Netflix, and AirBnB among others, using it in production. Mesosphere is a start-up that is developing a distributed OS product with Mesos at its core.

The architecture of Mesos

Mesos is an open-source platform for sharing clusters of commodity servers between different distributed applications (or frameworks), such as Hadoop, Spark, and Kafka among others. The idea is to act as a centralized cluster manager by pooling together all the physical resources of the cluster and making it available as a single reservoir of highly available resources for all the different frameworks to utilize. For example, if an organization has one 10-node cluster (16 CPUs and 64 GB RAM) and another 5-node cluster (4 CPUs and 16 GB RAM), then Mesos can be leveraged to pool them into one virtual cluster of 720 GB RAM and 180 CPUs, where multiple distributed applications can be run. Sharing resources in this fashion greatly improves cluster utilization and eliminates the need for an expensive data replication process per-framework.

Some of the important features of Mesos are:

- **Scalability**: It can elastically scale to over 50,000 nodes
- **Resource isolation**: This is achieved through Linux/Docker containers
- **Efficiency**: This is achieved through CPU and memory-aware resource scheduling across multiple frameworks
- **High availability**: This is through Apache ZooKeeper
- **Monitoring Interface**: A Web UI for monitoring the cluster state

Mesos is based on the same principles as the Linux kernel and aims to provide a highly available, scalable, and fault-tolerant base for enabling various frameworks to share cluster resources effectively and in isolation. Distributed applications are varied and continuously evolving, a fact that leads Mesos design philosophy towards a thin interface that allows an efficient resource allocation between different frameworks and delegates the task of scheduling and job execution to the frameworks themselves. The two advantages of doing so are:

- Different frame data replication works can independently devise methods to address their data locality, fault-tolerance, and other such needs
- It simplifies the Mesos codebase and allows it to be scalable, flexible, robust, and agile

Mesos' architecture hands over the responsibility of scheduling tasks to the respective frameworks by employing a resource offer abstraction that packages a set of resources and makes offers to each framework. The Mesos master node decides the quantity of resources to offer each framework, while each framework decides which resource offers to accept and which tasks to execute on these accepted resources. This method of resource allocation is shown to achieve a good degree of data locality for each framework sharing the same cluster.

An alternative architecture would implement a global scheduler that took framework requirements, organizational priorities, and resource availability as inputs and provided a task schedule breakdown by framework and resource as output, essentially acting as a matchmaker for jobs and resources with priorities acting as constraints. The challenges with this architecture, such as developing a robust API that could capture all the varied requirements of different frameworks, anticipating new frameworks, and solving a complex scheduling problem for millions of jobs, made the former approach a much more attractive option for the creators.

Introduction to frameworks

A Mesos framework sits between Mesos and the application and acts as a layer to manage task scheduling and execution. As its implementation is application-specific, the term is often used to refer to the application itself. Earlier, a Mesos framework could interact with the Mesos API using only the libmesos C++ library, due to which other language bindings were developed for Java, Scala, Python, and Go among others that leveraged libmesos heavily. Since v0.19.0, the changes made to the HTTP-based protocol enabled developers to develop frameworks using the language they wanted without having to rely on the C++ code. A framework consists of two components: a) Scheduler and b) Executor.

Scheduler is responsible for making decisions on the resource offers made to it and tracking the current state of the cluster. Communication with the Mesos master is handled by the **SchedulerDriver** module, which registers the framework with the master, launches tasks, and passes messages to other components.

The second component, **Executor**, is responsible, as its name suggests, for the execution of tasks on slave nodes. Communication with the slaves is handled by the **ExecutorDriver** module, which is also responsible for sending status updates to the scheduler.

The Mesos API, discussed later in this chapter, allows programmers to develop their own custom frameworks that can run on top of Mesos. Some other features of frameworks, such as authentication, authorization, and user management, will be discussed at length in *Chapter 6, Mesos Frameworks*.

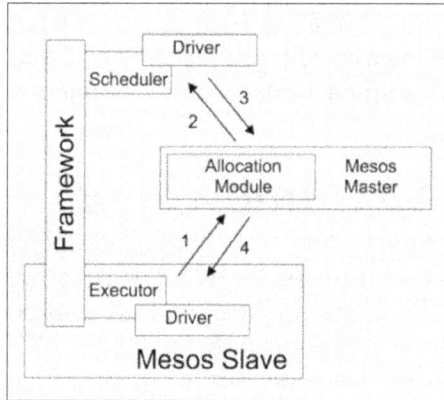

Frameworks built on Mesos

A list of some of the services and frameworks built on Mesos is given here. This list is not exhaustive, and support for new frameworks is added almost every day. You can also refer to http://mesos.apache.org/documentation/latest/frameworks/ apart from the following list:

Long-running services

- **Aurora**: This is a service scheduler that runs on top of Mesos, enabling you to run long-running services that take advantage of the scalability, fault-tolerance, and resource isolation of Mesos.

- **Marathon**: This is a private PaaS built on Mesos. It automatically handles hardware or software failures and ensures that an app is "always on".

- **Singularity**: This is a scheduler (the HTTP API and web interface) for running Mesos tasks, such as long-running processes, one-off tasks, and scheduled jobs.

- **SSSP**: This is a simple web application that provides a "Megaupload" white label to store and share files in S3.

Big data processing

- Cray Chapel is a productive parallel programming language. The Chapel Mesos scheduler lets you run Chapel programs on Mesos.

- Dark is a Python clone of Spark, a MapReduce-like framework written in Python and running on Mesos.

- Exelixi is a distributed framework used to run genetic algorithms at scale.

- Hadoop Running Hadoop on Mesos distributes MapReduce jobs efficiently across an entire cluster.

- Hama is a distributed computing framework based on Bulk Synchronous Parallel computing techniques for massive scientific computations—for example, matrix, graph, and network algorithms.

- MPI is a message-passing system designed to function on a wide variety of parallel computers.

- Spark is a fast and general-purpose cluster computing system that makes parallel jobs easy to write.

- Storm is a distributed real-time computation system. Storm makes it easy to reliably process unbounded streams of data, doing for real-time processing what Hadoop does for batch processing.

Batch scheduling

- Chronos is a distributed job scheduler that supports complex job topologies. It can be used as a more fault-tolerant replacement for cron.

- Jenkins is a continuous integration server. The Mesos-Jenkins plugin allows it to dynamically launch workers on a Mesos cluster, depending on the workload.

- JobServer is a distributed job scheduler and processor that allows developers to build custom batch processing Tasklets using a point and click Web UI.

Data storage

- Cassandra is a performant and highly available distributed database. Linear scalability and proven fault-tolerance on commodity hardware or cloud infrastructure make it the perfect platform for mission-critical data.

- Elasticsearch is a distributed search engine. Mesos makes it easy for it to run and scale.

The attributes and resources of Mesos

Mesos describes the slave nodes present in the cluster by the following two methods:

Attributes

Attributes are used to describe certain additional information regarding the slave node, such as its OS version, whether it has a particular type of hardware, and so on. They are expressed as key-value pairs with support for three different value types—scalar, range, and text—that are sent along with the offers to frameworks. Take a look at the following code:

```
attributes : attribute ( ";" attribute )*

attribute : text ":" ( scalar | range | text )
```

Resources

Mesos can manage three different types of resources: scalars, ranges, and sets. These are used to represent the different resources that a Mesos slave has to offer. For example, a scalar resource type could be used to represent the amount of CPU on a slave. Each resource is identified by a key string, as follows:

```
resources : resource ( ";" resource )*

resource : key ":" ( scalar | range | set )

key : text ( "(" resourceRole ")" )?

resourceRole : text | "*"
```

Predefined uses and conventions

The Mesos master predefines how it handles the following list of resources:

* cpus
* mem
* disk
* ports

In particular, a slave without the cpu and mem resources will never have its resources advertised to any frameworks. Also, the master's user interface interprets the scalars in mem and disk in terms of MB. For example, the value 15000 is displayed as 14.65GB.

Examples

Here are some examples of configuring the Mesos slaves:

- `resources='cpus:24;mem:24576;disk:409600;ports:[21000-24000];bugs:{a,b,c}'`
- `attributes='rack:abc;zone:west;os:centos5;level:10;keys:[1000-1500]'`

In this case, we have three different types of resources, scalars, a range, and a set. They are called `cpus`, `mem`, and `disk`, and the range type is `ports`.

- A scalar called `cpus` with the value `24`
- A scalar called `mem` with the value `24576`
- A scalar called `disk` with the value `409600`
- A range called `ports` with values `21000` through `24000` (inclusive)
- A set called `bugs` with the values a, b, and c

In the case of attributes, we will end up with three attributes:

- A `rack` attribute with the text value `abc`
- A `zone` attribute with the text value `west`
- An `os` attribute with the text value `centos5`
- A `level` attribute with the scalar value `10`
- A `keys` attribute with range values `1000` through `1500` (inclusive)

Two-level scheduling

Mesos has a two-level scheduling mechanism to allocate resources to and launch tasks on different frameworks. In the first level, the master process that manages slave processes running on each node in the Mesos cluster determines the free resources available on each node, groups them, and offers them to different frameworks based on organizational policies, such as priority or fair sharing. Organizations have the ability to define their own sharing policies via a custom allocation module as well.

In the second level, each framework's scheduler component that is registered as a client with the master accepts or rejects the resource offer made depending on the framework's requirements. If the offer is accepted, the framework's scheduler sends information regarding the tasks that need to be executed and the number of resources that each task requires to the Mesos master. The master transfers the tasks to the corresponding slaves, which assign the necessary resources to the framework's executor component, which manages the execution of all the required tasks in containers. When the tasks are completed, the containers are dismantled, and the resources are freed up for use by other tasks.

The following diagram and explanation from the Apache Mesos documentation (http://mesos.apache.org/documentation/latest/architecture/) explains this concept in more detail:

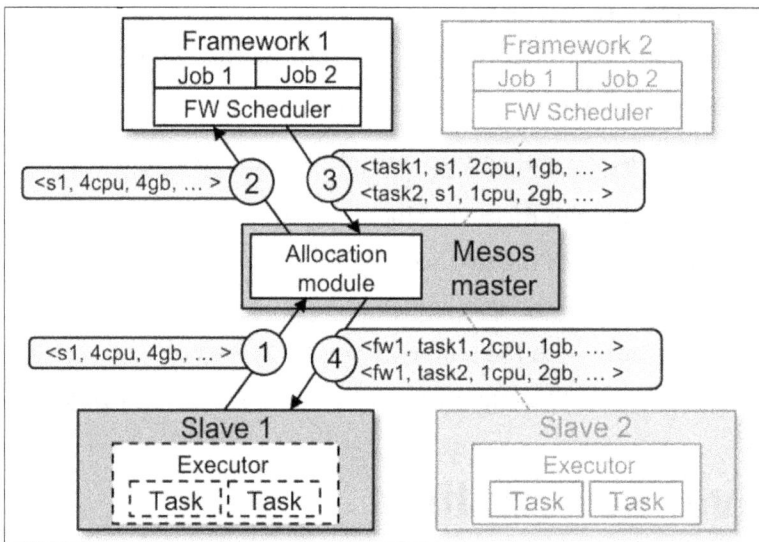

Let's have a look at the pointers mentioned in the preceding diagram:

- **1**: Slave 1 reports to the master that it has four CPUs and 4 GB of memory free. The master then invokes the allocation module, which tells it that Framework 1 should be offered all the available resources.

- **2**: The master sends a resource offer describing these resources to Framework 1.

- **3**: The framework's scheduler replies to the master with information about two tasks to run on the slave using two CPUs and 1 GB RAM for the first task and one CPU and 2 GB RAM for the second task.

- **4**: The master sends the tasks to the slave, which allocates appropriate resources to the framework's executor, which in turn launches the two tasks. As one CPU and 1 GB of RAM are still free, the allocation module may now offer them to Framework 2. In addition, this resource offers process repeats when tasks finish and new resources become free.

Mesos also provides frameworks with the ability to reject resource offers. A framework can reject the offers that do not meet its requirements. This allows frameworks to support a wide variety of complex resource constraints while keeping Mesos simple at the same time. A policy called **delay scheduling**, in which frameworks wait for a finite time to get access to the nodes storing their input data, gives a fair level of data locality albeit with a slight latency tradeoff.

If the framework constraints are complex, it is possible that a framework might need to wait before it receives a suitable resource offer that meets its requirements. To tackle this, Mesos allows frameworks to set filters specifying the criteria that they will use to always reject certain resources. A framework can set a filter stating that it can run only on nodes with at least 32 GB of RAM space free, for example. This allows it to bypass the rejection process, minimizes communication overheads, and thus reduces overall latency.

Resource allocation

The resource allocation module contains the policy that the Mesos master uses to determine the type and quantity of resource offers that need to be made to each framework. Organizations can customize it to implement their own allocation policy—for example, fair sharing, priority, and so on—which allows for fine-grained resource sharing. Custom allocation modules can be developed to address specific needs.

The resource allocation module is responsible for making sure that resources are shared in a fair manner among competing frameworks. The choice of algorithm used to determine the sharing policy has a great bearing on the efficiency of a cluster manager. One of the most popular allocation algorithms, max-min fairness, and its weighted derivative are described in the following section.

Max-min fair share algorithm

Imagine a set of sources (1, 2, ..., m) that has resource demands $x^1, x^2, ..., x_m$. Let the total number of resources be R. We will initially give R/m of the resource to each of the m sources. Now, starting with the source with the least demand, we will compare the allocation to the actual demand. If initial allocation (R/m) is more than the demand requirements of source 1, we will redistribute the excess resources equally among the remaining sources. We will then compare the new allocation to the actual demand of the source with the second-lowest demand and continue the process as before. The process ends when each source gets allocated resources that are less than or equal to its actual demand. If any source gets allocated resources less than what it actually needs, the algorithm ensures that no other source can get more resources than such a source. Such an allocation is called a max-min fair share allocation because it maximizes the minimum share of sources whose demands are not met.

Consider the following example:

How to compute the max-min fair allocation for a set of four sources, *S1, S2, S3*, and *S4*, with demands 2, 2.5, 4, and 5, respectively, when the resource has an overall capacity of 10.

Following the methodology described earlier, to solve this, we will tentatively divide the resource into four portions of size 2.5 each. Next, we will compare this allocation with the actual demand of the source with the least demand (in this case, *S1*). As the allocation is greater than the actual demand, the excess 0.5 is divided equally among the remaining three sources, *S2, S3*, and *S4*, giving them 2.666 each. Continuing the process, we will note that the new allocation is greater than the actual demand of source *S2*. The excess 0.166 is again divided evenly among the remaining two sources *S3* and *S4*, giving them *2.666 + 0.084 = 2.75* each. The allocation for each of the sources is now less than or equal to the actual demand, so the process is stopped here. The final allocation is, therefore, *S1 – 2, S2 – 2.5, S3 – 2.75*, and *S4 – 2.75*.

This works well in a homogenous environment—that is, one where resource requirements are fairly proportional between different competing users, such as a Hadoop cluster. However, scheduling resources across frameworks with heterogeneous resource demands poses a more complex challenge. What is a suitable fair share allocation policy if user A runs tasks that require two CPUs and 8 GB RAM each and user B runs tasks that require four CPUs and 2 GB RAM each? As can be noted, user A's tasks are RAM-heavy, while user B's tasks are CPU-heavy. How, then, should a set of combined RAM and CPU resources be distributed between the two users?

The latter scenario is a common one faced by Mesos, designed as it is to manage resources primarily in a heterogeneous environment. To address this, Mesos has the **Dominant Resource Fairness** algorithm (**DRF**) as its default resource allocation policy, which is far more suitable for heterogeneous environments. The algorithm and its role in efficient resource allocation will be discussed in more detail in the next chapter.

Resource isolation

One of the key requirements of a cluster manager is to ensure that the allocation of resources to a particular framework does not have an impact on any active running jobs of some other framework. Provision for isolation mechanisms on slaves to compartmentalize different tasks is thus a key feature of Mesos. Containers are leveraged for resource isolation with a pluggable architecture. The Mesos slave uses the Containerizer API to provide an isolated environment to run a framework's executor and its corresponding tasks. The Containerizer API's objective is to support a wide range of implementations, which implies that custom containerizers and isolators can be developed. When a slave process starts, the containerizer to be used to launch containers and a set of isolators to enforce the resource constraints can be specified.

The Mesos Containerizer API provides a resource isolation of framework executors using Linux-specific functionality, such as control groups and namespaces. It also provides basic support for POSIX systems (only resource usage reporting and not actual isolation). This important topic will be explored at length in subsequent chapters.

Mesos also provides network isolation at a container level to prevent a single framework from capturing all the available network bandwidth or ports. This is not supported by default, however, and additional dependencies need to be installed and configured in order to activate this feature.

Monitoring in Mesos

In this section, we will take a look at the different metrics that Mesos provides to monitor the various components.

Monitoring provided by Mesos

Mesos master and slave nodes provide rich data that enables resource utilization monitoring and anomaly detection. The information includes details about available resources, used resources, registered frameworks, active slaves, and task state. This can be used to create automated alerts and develop a cluster health monitoring dashboard. More details can be found here:

`http://mesos.apache.org/documentation/latest/monitoring/.`

Network statistics for each active container are published through the `/monitor/statistics.json` endpoint on the slave.

Types of metrics

Mesos provides two different kinds of metrics: counters and gauges. These can be explained as follows:

- **Counters**: This is used to measure discrete events, such as the number of finished tasks or invalid status updates. The values are always whole numbers.

- **Gauges**: This is used to check the snapshot of a particular metric, such as the number of active frameworks or running tasks at a particular time.

The Mesos API

Mesos provides an API to allow developers to build custom frameworks that can run on top of the underlying distributed infrastructure. The detailed steps involved in developing bespoke frameworks leveraging this API and the new HTTP API will be explored in detail in *Chapter 6, Mesos Frameworks*.

Messages

Mesos implements an actor-style message-passing programming model to enable nonblocking communication between different Mesos components and leverages protocol buffers for the same. For example, a scheduler needs to tell the executor to utilize a certain number of resources, an executor needs to provide status updates to the scheduler regarding the tasks that are executed, and so on. Protocol buffers provide the required flexible message delivery mechanism to enable this communication by allowing developers to define custom formats and protocols that can be used across different languages. For more details regarding the messages that are passed between different Mesos components, refer to `https://github.com/apache/mesos/blob/master/include/mesos/mesos.proto`

API details

A brief description of the different APIs and methods that Mesos provides is provided in the following section:

Executor API

A brief description of the Executor API is given below. For more details, visit `http://mesos.apache.org/api/latest/java/org/apache/mesos/Executor.html`.

- `registered`: This can be registered via the following code:

```
void registered(ExecutorDriver driver,
    ExecutorInfo executorInfo,
    FrameworkInfo frameworkInfo,
    SlaveInfo slaveInfo)
```

This code is invoked once the executor driver is able to successfully connect with Mesos. In particular, a scheduler can pass some data to its executors through the `ExecutorInfo.getData()` field.

The following are the parameters:

- `driver`: This is the executor driver that was registered and connected to the Mesos cluster

- `executorInfo`: This describes information about the executor that was registered

- `frameworkInfo`: This describes the framework that was registered

- `slaveInfo`: This describes the slave that will be used to launch the tasks for this executor

- `reregistered`: This can be *reregistered* as follows:

```
void reregistered(ExecutorDriver driver,
    SlaveInfo slaveInfo)
```

This code is invoked when the executor reregisters with a restarted slave.

The following are the parameters:

- `driver`: This is the executor driver that was reregistered with the Mesos master

- `slaveInfo`: This describes the slave that will be used to launch the tasks for this executor

- `disconnected`: This can be disconnected via the following code:

```
void disconnected(ExecutorDriver driver)
```

  The preceding code is invoked when the executor gets "disconnected" from the slave — for example, when the slave is restarted due to an upgrade).

  The following is the parameter:

  ○ `driver`: This is the executor driver that was disconnected.

- `launchTask`: Take a look at the following code:

```
void launchTask(ExecutorDriver driver,
  TaskInfo task)
```

  The preceding code is invoked when a task is launched on this executor (initiated via `SchedulerDriver.launchTasks(java.util. Collection<OfferID>, java.util.Collection<TaskInfo>, Filters)`. Note that this task can be realized with a thread, a process, or some simple computation; however, no other callbacks will be invoked on this executor until this callback returns.

  The following are the parameters:

  ○ `driver`: This is the executor driver that launched the task

  ○ `task`: This describes the task that was launched

- `killTask`: Run the following code:

```
void killTask(ExecutorDriver driver,
  TaskID taskId)
```

  This is invoked when a task running within this executor is killed via `SchedulerDriver.killTask (TaskID)`. Note that no status update will be sent on behalf of the executor, and the executor is responsible for creating a new `TaskStatus` protobuf message (that is, with `TASK_KILLED`) and invoking `ExecutorDriver.sendStatusUpdate (TaskStatus)`.

  The following are the parameters:

  ○ `driver`: This is the executor driver that owned the task that was killed

  ○ `taskId`: This is the ID of the task that was killed

- `frameworkMessage`: Run the following code:

```
void frameworkMessage(ExecutorDriver driver,
  byte[] data)
```

This is invoked when a framework message arrives for this executor. These messages are the best effort; do not expect a framework message to be retransmitted in any reliable fashion.

The following are the parameters:

- `driver`: This is the executor driver that received the message

- `data`: This is the message payload

- `shutdown`: Execute the following code:

```
void shutdown(ExecutorDriver driver)
```

This is invoked when the executor terminates all of its currently running tasks. Note that after Mesos determines that an executor has terminated, any tasks that the executor did not send Terminal status updates for (for example, `TASK_KILLED`, `TASK_FINISHED`, `TASK_FAILED`, and so on), and a `TASK_LOST` status update will be created.

The following is the parameter:

- `driver`: This is the executor driver that should terminate.

- `error`: Run the following:

```
void error(ExecutorDriver driver,
  java.lang.String message)
```

The previous code is invoked when a fatal error occurs with the executor and/or executor driver. The driver will be aborted BEFORE invoking this callback.

The following are the parameters:

- `driver`: This is the executor driver that was aborted due to this error

- `message`: This is the error message

The Executor Driver API

A brief description of the Executor Driver API is given below. For more details, visit `http://mesos.apache.org/api/latest/java/org/apache/mesos/ExecutorDriver.html`.

- `start`: Run the following line:

  ```
  Status start()
  ```

  The preceding code starts the executor driver. This needs to be called before any other driver calls are made.

  The state of the driver after the call is returned.

- `stop`: Run the following line:

  ```
  Status stop()
  ```

  This stops the executor driver.

  The state of the driver after the call is the return.

- `abort`: Run the following line:

  ```
  Status abort()
  ```

  This aborts the driver so that no more callbacks can be made to the executor. The semantics of abort and stop are deliberately separated so that the code can detect an aborted driver (via the return status of `join()`; refer to the following section) and instantiate and start another driver if desired (from within the same process, although this functionality is currently not supported for executors).

  The state of the driver after the call is the return.

- `join`: Run the following:

  ```
  Status join()
  ```

  This waits for the driver to be stopped or aborted, possibly blocking the current thread indefinitely. The return status of this function can be used to determine whether the driver was aborted (take a look at `mesos.proto` for a description of status).

  The state of the driver after the call is the return.

- run: Take a look at the following line of code:

```
Status run()
```

This starts and immediately joins (that is, blocks) the driver.

The state of the driver after the call is the return.

- sendStatusUpdate: Here's the code to execute:

```
Status sendStatusUpdate(TaskStatus status)
```

This sends a status update to the framework scheduler, retrying as necessary until an acknowledgement is received or the executor is terminated (in which case, a TASK_LOST status update will be sent). Take a look at Scheduler.statusUpdate(org.apache.mesos.SchedulerDriver, TaskStatus) for more information about status update acknowledgements.

The following is the parameter:

  ○   status: This is the status update to send.

- The state of the driver after the call is the return.
- sendFrameworkMessage: Run the following code:

```
Status sendFrameworkMessage(byte[] data)
```

This sends a message to the framework scheduler. These messages are sent on a best effort basis and should not be expected to be retransmitted in any reliable fashion.

The parameters are as follows:

  ○   data: This is the message payload.

The state of the driver after the call is the return.

The Scheduler API

A brief description of the Scheduler API is given below. For more details, visit http://mesos.apache.org/api/latest/java/org/apache/mesos/Scheduler.html.

- registered: This can be registered via the following code:

```
void registered(SchedulerDriver driver,
   FrameworkID frameworkId,
   MasterInfo masterInfo)
```

The preceding is invoked when the scheduler successfully registers with a Mesos master. A unique ID (generated by the master) is used to distinguish this framework from others, and `MasterInfo` with the IP and port of the current master are provided as arguments.

The following are the parameters:

- ○ `driver`: This is the scheduler driver that was registered
- ○ `FrameworkID`: This is the `FrameworkID` generated by the master
- ○ `MasterInfo`: This is the information about the current master, including the IP and port.

• `reregistered`: The preceding code can be reregistered as follows:

```
void reregistered(SchedulerDriver driver,
  MasterInfo masterInfo)
```

The preceding code is invoked when the scheduler reregisters with a newly elected Mesos master. This is only called when the scheduler is previously registered. `MasterInfo` containing the updated information about the elected master is provided as an argument.

The parameters are as follows:

- ○ `driver`: This is the driver that was reregistered
- ○ `MasterInfo`: This is the updated information about the elected master

• `resourceOffers`: Execute the following code:

```
void resourceOffers(SchedulerDriver driver,
  java.util.List<Offer> offers)
```

The preceding code is invoked when resources are offered to this framework. A single offer will only contain resources from a single slave. Resources associated with an offer will not be reoffered to this framework until either; (a) this framework rejects these resources (refer to `SchedulerDriver.launchTasks(java.util.Collection<OfferID>, java.util.Collection<TaskInfo>, Filters)`), or (b) these resources are rescinded (refer to `offerRescinded(org.apache.mesos.SchedulerDriver, OfferID)`). Note that resources may be concurrently offered to more than one framework at a time, depending on the allocator being used. In this case, the first framework to launch tasks using these resources will be able to use them, while the other frameworks will have these resources rescinded. (Alternatively, if a framework has already launched tasks with these resources, these tasks will fail with a `TASK_LOST` status and a message saying as much).

The following are the parameters:

- ◦ `driver`: This is the driver that was used to run this scheduler
- ◦ `offers`: These are the resources offered to this framework

- `offerRescinded`: Run the following code:

```
void offerRescinded(SchedulerDriver driver,
  OfferID offerId)
```

This is invoked when an offer is no longer valid (for example, the slave is lost or another framework is used resources in the offer). If, for whatever reason, an offer is never rescinded (for example, a dropped message, failing over framework, and so on), a framework that attempts to launch tasks using an invalid offer will receive a `TASK_LOST` status update for these tasks (take a look at `resourceOffers(org.apache.mesos.SchedulerDriver, java.util.List<Offer>)`).

The following are the parameters:

- ◦ `driver`: This is the driver that was used to run this scheduler
- ◦ `offerID`: This is the ID of the offer that was rescinded

- `statusUpdate`: Take a look at the following code:

```
void statusUpdate(SchedulerDriver driver,
  TaskStatus status)
```

The preceding code is invoked when the status of a task changes (for example, a slave is lost, so the task is lost; a task is finished, and an executor sends a status update saying so; and so on). If, for whatever reason, the scheduler is aborted during this callback or the process exits, then another status update will be delivered. (Note, however, that this is currently not true if the slave sending the status update is lost or fails during this time.)

The parameters are as follows:

- ◦ `driver`: This is the driver that was used to run this scheduler
- ◦ `status`: This is the status update, which includes the task ID and status

- `frameworkMessage`: Take a look at the following code:

```
void frameworkMessage(SchedulerDriver driver,
  ExecutorID executorId,
  SlaveID slaveId,
  byte[] data)
```

The preceding code is invoked when an executor sends a message. These messages are sent on a best effort basis and should not be expected to be retransmitted in any reliable fashion.

The parameters are as follows:

- `driver`: This is the driver that received the message
- `ExecutorID`: This is the ID of the executor that sent the message
- `SlaveID`: This is the ID of the slave that launched the executor
- `data`: This is the message payload

- `disconnected`: Run the following:

```
void disconnected(SchedulerDriver driver)
```

This is invoked when the scheduler becomes disconnected from the master (for example, the master fails and another takes over).

The following is the parameter:

- `driver`: This is the driver that was used to run this scheduler

- `slaveLost`: Execute the following code:

```
void slaveLost(SchedulerDriver driver,
  SlaveID slaveId)
```

This is invoked when a slave is determined unreachable (for example, machine failure or network partition). Most frameworks need to reschedule any tasks launched on this slave on a new slave.

The following are the parameters:

- `driver`: This is the driver that was used to run this scheduler
- `SlaveID`: This is the ID of the slave that was lost

- `executorLost`: Run the following:

```
void executorLost(SchedulerDriver driver,
  ExecutorID executorId,
  SlaveID slaveId,
  int status)
```

The preceding is invoked when an executor is exited or terminated. Note that any running task will have the `TASK_LOST` status update automatically generated.

The following are the parameters:

- ° `driver`: This is the driver that was used to run this scheduler
- ° `ExecutorID`: This is the ID of the executor that was lost
- ° `slaveID`: This is the ID of the slave that launched the executor
- ° `status`: This is the exit status of the executor

- `error`: Run the following code:

```
void error(SchedulerDriver driver,
  java.lang.String message)
```

The preceding is invoked when there is an unrecoverable error in the scheduler or driver. The driver will be aborted *before* invoking this callback.

The following are the parameters:

- ° `driver`: This is the driver that was used to run this scheduler
- ° `message`: This is the error message

The Scheduler Driver API

A brief description of the Scheduler Driver API is given below. For more details, visit `http://mesos.apache.org/api/latest/java/org/apache/mesos/SchedulerDriver.html`

- `start`: Run the following code:

```
Status start()
```

This starts the scheduler driver. It needs to be called before any other driver calls are made.

The preceding returns the state of the driver after the call.

- `stop`: Execute the following code:

```
Status stop(boolean failover)
```

This stops the scheduler driver. If the `failover` flag is set to false, it is expected that this framework will never reconnect to Mesos. So, Mesos will unregister the framework and shut down all its tasks and executors. If `failover` is true, all executors and tasks will remain running (for some framework-specific failover timeout), allowing the scheduler to reconnect (possibly in the same process or from a different process — for example, on a different machine).

The following is the parameter:

  ○ `failover`: This is whether framework failover is expected

This returns the state of the driver after the call.

- `Stop`: Run the following line:

```
Status stop()
```

This stops the scheduler driver assuming no failover. This will cause Mesos to unregister the framework and shut down all its tasks and executors.

This returns the state of the driver after the call.

- `abort`: Execute the following code:

```
Status abort()
```

This aborts the driver so that no more callbacks can be made to the scheduler. The semantics of abort and stop are deliberately separated so that code can detect an aborted driver (via the return status of `join()`; refer to the following section) and instantiate and start another driver if desired from within the same process.

This returns the state of the driver after the call.

- `join`: Run the following:

```
Status join()
```

This waits for the driver to be stopped or aborted, possibly *blocking* the current thread indefinitely. The return status of this function can be used to determine whether the driver was aborted (take a look at `mesos.proto` for a description of `Status`).

This returns the state of the driver after the call.

- `run`: Execute the following:

```
Status run()
```

This starts and immediately joins (that is, blocks) the driver.

It returns the state of the driver after the call.

- `requestResources`: Take a look at the following:

```
Status requestResources(java.util.Collection<Request> requests)
```

This requests resources from Mesos (take a look at `mesos.proto` for a description of Request and how, for example, to request resources from specific slaves). Any resources available are offered to the framework via the `Scheduler.resourceOffers(org.apache.mesos.SchedulerDriver, java.util.List<Offer>)` callback asynchronously.

The following is the parameter:

  ○ `requests`: These are the resource requests.

It returns the state of the driver after the call.

- `launchTasks`: Use the following code:

```
Status launchTasks(java.util.Collection<OfferID> offerIds,
  java.util.Collection<TaskInfo> tasks,
  Filters filters)
```

The preceding code launches the given set of tasks on a set of offers. Resources from offers are aggregated when more than one is provided. Note that all the offers must belong to the same slave. Any resources remaining (that is, not used by the tasks or their executors) will be considered declined. The specified filters are applied on all unused resources (take a look at `mesos.proto` for a description of Filters). Invoking this function with an empty collection of tasks declines offers in their entirety (refer to `declineOffer(OfferID, Filters)`).

The following are the parameters:

  ○ `offerIds`: This is the collection of offer IDs
  ○ `tasks`: This is the collection of tasks to be launched
  ○ `filters`: This is the filters to set for any remaining resources.

It returns the state of the driver after the call.

- `killTask`: Execute the following code:

```
Status killTask(TaskID taskId)
```

This kills the specified task. Note that attempting to kill a task is currently not reliable. If, for example, a scheduler fails over while it attempts to kill a task, it will need to retry in the future. Likewise, if unregistered/disconnected, the request will be dropped (these semantics may be changed in the future).

The following is the parameter:

- ° `taskId`: This is the ID of the task to be killed

    It returns the state of the driver after the call.

- `declineOffer`: Run the following code:

```
Status declineOffer(OfferID offerId,
  Filters filters)
```

This declines an offer in its entirety and applies the specified filters on the resources (take a look at `mesos.proto` for a description of Filters). Note that this can be done at any time, and it is not necessary to do this within the `Scheduler.resourceOffers(org.apache.mesos.SchedulerDriver, java.util.List<Offer>)` callback.

The following are the parameters:

- ° `offerId`: This is the ID of the offer to be declined
- ° `filters`: These are the filters to be set for any remaining resources

    It returns the state of the driver after the call.

- `reviveOffers`: Execute the following:

```
Status reviveOffers()
```

This removes all the filters previously set by the framework (via `launchTasks(java.util.Collection<OfferID>, java.util. Collection<TaskInfo>, Filters)`). This enables the framework to receive offers from these filtered slaves.

It returns the state of the driver after the call.

- `sendFrameworkMessage`: Take a look at the following:

```
Status sendFrameworkMessage(ExecutorID executorId,
   SlaveID slaveId,
   byte[] data)
```

This sends a message from the framework to one of its executors. These messages are sent on a best effort basis and should not be expected to be retransmitted in any reliable fashion.

The parameters are:

   ○ `executorId`: This is the ID of the executor to send the message to

   ○ `slaveId`: This is the ID of the slave that runs the executor

   ○ `data`: This is the message

   It returns the state of the driver after the call.

- `reconcileTasks`: Take a look at the following code:

```
Status reconcileTasks(java.util.Collection<TaskStatus> statuses)
```

This allows the framework to query the status for nonterminal tasks. This causes the master to send back the latest task status for each task in `statuses` if possible. Tasks that are no longer known will result in a `TASK_LOST` update. If `statuses` is empty, the master will send the latest status for each task currently known.

The following are the parameters:

   ○ `statuses`: This is the collection of nonterminal `TaskStatus` protobuf messages to reconcile.

   It returns the state of the driver after the call.

Mesos in production

Mesos is in production at several companies such as Apple, Twitter, and HubSpot and has even been used by start-ups such as Mattermark and Sigmoid. This broad appeal is a validation of Mesos' tremendous utility. Apple, for example, powers its consumer-facing, mission–critical, popular *Siri* application through a large Mesos cluster (allegedly spanning tens of thousands of nodes). One such case study (published on the Mesosphere website) is discussed here.

Case study on HubSpot

Following case study on HubSpot can be found here `https://mesosphere.com/ mesos-case-study-hubspot/`. An excerpt from this link is given below:

HubSpot uses Apache Mesos to run a mixture of web services, long-running processes, and scheduled jobs that comprise their SaaS application. Mesos allows HubSpot to dynamically deploy services, which in turn reduces developer friction and time to deploy, increases reliability, achieves better resource utilization, and reduces hardware costs.

Mesos provides the core infrastructure to build a next-generation deployment system similar to what Heroku provides as a product. On top of Mesos, HubSpot built their own scheduler that is capable of executing both long-running services and scheduled jobs and is the interface through which the development team can view the state of their applications inside the cloud. Building a scheduler framework enables HubSpot to better understand the core concepts inside Mesos, be comfortable with failure modes, and customize user experience.

The cluster environment

Over 150 services run inside Mesos at HubSpot. HubSpot utilizes many hundreds of servers inside Amazon EC2, and the Mesos cluster comprises about 30% of these resources and is aggressively ramping up as more and more services are migrated to Mesos. As Mesos can easily handle large or small server footprints, hundreds of smaller servers are replaced with dozens of larger ones.

Benefits

Mesos provides numerous benefits to both the development team and the company. At HubSpot, developers own the operation of their applications. With Mesos, developers can deploy services faster and with less maintenance. Here are some of the other benefits:

- Developers get immediate access to cluster resources, whether it be to scale or introduce new services.
- Developers no longer need to understand the process of requisitioning hardware or servers, and it is easier to scale up the resource requirements inside Mesos than it is to recreate servers with more or less CPUs and memory.

- Hardware failures are more transparent to developers as services are automatically replaced when tasks are lost or they fail. In other words, developers are no longer paged because of a simple hardware failure.

- Scheduled tasks (cron jobs) are now exposed via a web interface and are not tied to a single server, which may fail at any time, taking the cron job with it.

Mesos also simplifies the technology stack required to requisition hardware and manage it from an operations perspective. HubSpot can standardize server footprints and simplify the base image upon which Mesos slaves are executed.

Lastly, resource utilization is improved, which directly corresponds with reducing costs. Services, which previously ran on overprovisioned hardware now use the exact amount of resources requested.

Additionally, the QA environment runs at 50% of its previous capacity as the HubSpot scheduler ensures that services are restarted when they fail. This means that it is no longer necessary to run multiple copies of services inside QA for high availability.

Challenges

A core challenge behind adoption is introducing a new deployment technology to a group of 100 engineers who are responsible for managing their applications on a daily basis. HubSpot mitigated this challenge by building a UI around Mesos and utilizing Mesos to make the deployment process as simple and rewarding as possible.

Looking ahead

HubSpot sees Mesos as a core technology behind future migrations into other datacenters. As both a virtualization and deployment technology, Mesos has proven to be a rewarding path forward. Additionally, HubSpot hopes to eventually leverage Mesos to dynamically scale out processes based on load, shrink and grow the cluster size relative to demand, and assist developers with resource estimation.

> Detailed steps to download the code bundle are mentioned in the Preface of this book. Please have a look. The code bundle for the book is also hosted on GitHub at https://github.com/PacktPublishing/Mastering-Mesos. We also have other code bundles from our rich catalog of books and videos available at https://github.com/PacktPublishing/. Check them out!

Summary

In this chapter, we introduced Mesos, dived deep into its architecture, and discussed some important topics, such as frameworks, resource allocation, and resource isolation. We also discussed the two-level scheduling approach that Mesos employs and provided a detailed overview of its API. The HubSpot case study at the end was to show how it is used in production and that it is ready for prime time. The objective was to explain what Mesos is and why it is required and provide a high-level overview of how it works.

In the next chapter, we will deep dive into its important features and understand how it contributes to scaling, efficiency, high availability, and extendibility.

2
Mesos Internals

This chapter provides a comprehensive overview of Mesos' features and walks the reader through several important topics regarding high availability, fault tolerance, scaling, and efficiency. Mentioned here are the topics we will cover in this chapter:

- **Scaling and efficiency**
    - Resource allocation (the dominant resource fairness algorithm)
    - Reservation (static and dynamic)
    - Oversubscription
    - Extendibility
- **High availability and fault tolerance**
    - Slave recovery
    - Reconciliation
    - Persistent volumes

Scaling and efficiency

Mesos aims to provide a highly scalable and efficient mechanism to enable various frameworks to share cluster resources effectively. Distributed applications are varied, can have different priorities in different contexts, and are continuously evolving, a fact that led Mesos' design philosophy towards providing for customizable resource allocation policies that users can define and set as per their requirements.

Resource allocation

The Mesos resource allocation module contains the policy that the Mesos master uses to determine the type and quantity of resource offers that need to be made to each framework. Organizations can customize it to implement their own allocation policy, for example, fair sharing, priority, and so on, which allow for fine-grained resource sharing. Custom allocation modules can be developed to address specific needs.

The resource allocation module is responsible for making sure that the resources are shared in a fair manner among competing frameworks. The choice of algorithm used to determine whether the sharing policy has a great bearing on the efficiency of a cluster manager.

One of the most popular allocation algorithms, max-min fairness, works well in a homogenous environment; this is the one where resource requirements are fairly proportional between different competing users, such as the Hadoop cluster. However, scheduling resources across frameworks with heterogeneous resource demands poses a more complex challenge. What is a suitable fair share allocation policy if user A runs the tasks that require two CPUs and 8 GB RAM each and user B runs tasks that require four CPUs and 2 GB RAM each? As can be seen, user A's tasks are RAM-heavy, while user B's tasks are CPU-heavy. How, then, should a set of combined RAM + CPU resources be distributed between the two users?

The latter scenario is a common one faced by Mesos, designed as it is to manage resources primarily in a heterogeneous environment. To address this, Mesos has the **Dominant Resource Fairness algorithm** (DRF) as its default resource allocation policy, which is far more suitable for heterogeneous environments. The algorithm is described in detail in the following sections.

The Dominant Resource Fairness algorithm (DRF)

Job scheduling in datacenters is not limited to only CPUs but extends to other resources, such as the memory and disk, as well. In a scenario where resource demands are varied, some tasks are CPU-intensive, while some are memory- or disk-intensive; this is where the min-max fairness algorithm falls short. Herein lies the need for a resource scheduling mechanism that provides every user in a heterogeneous environment a fair share of the resources most required by it. In simple terms, DRF is an adaptation of the **max-min fairness algorithm** to fairly share heterogeneous resources among users.

Let's consider the following example to understand how the algorithm works.

We will assume that the resources are given in multiples of demand vectors and are divisible.

Consider a case where the total resources available are eight CPUs and 10 GB memory. User 1 runs tasks that require one CPU and 3 GB memory, and user 2 runs tasks that require three CPUs and 1 GB memory. Before we proceed to analyze how the DRF algorithm will allocate tasks, let's understand the concepts of the dominant resource and share:

- **Dominant resource**: This refers to the resource (CPU or memory) that is most required by the user. In this case, user 1 runs tasks that have higher memory requirements (3 GB per task), so the dominant resource for user 1 is memory. On the other hand, user 2 runs computation-heavy tasks (three CPUs per task) and hence has CPU as its dominant resource.

- **Dominant share**: This refers to the fraction of the dominant resource that the user is allocated. Referring to our example, user 1's dominant share is 30% (3/10), while user 2's dominant share is 37.5% (3/8).

The DRF allocation module tracks the dominant share of each user and makes a note of the resources allocated to each user. DRF begins allocation by offering resources (CPU or memory) to the user with the lowest dominant share among all the competing users. The user then has the option to accept the offer if it meets its requirement.

Now, let us look at each step taken by the DRF algorithm to allocate resources for users 1 and 2. For simplicity's sake, we will overlook the resources that get released back into the pool after the completion of small tasks and assume that every resource offer is accepted and that the users run an infinite number of tasks having the resource requirements. Every user 1 task would consume one-eighth of the total CPU and three-tenths of the total memory, making **memory** user 1's dominant resource. Every user 2 task would consume three-eighths of the total CPU and one-tenth of the total memory, making **CPU** user 2's dominant share.

	User 1			User 2			CPU	Memory
User Selected	Resource Share	Dominant Share	Dominant Share %	Resource Share	Dominant Share	Dominant Share %	Total Allocation	Total Allocation
	0/8, 0/10	0	0%	0/8, 0/10	0	0%	0/8	0/10
User 1	1/8, 3/10	3/10	33.33%	0/8, 0/10	0	0%	1/8	3/10
User 2	1/8, 3/10	3/10	**33.33%**	3/8, 1/10	3/8	37.5%	4/8	4/10
User 1	2/8, 6/10	6/10	60%	3/8, 1/10	3/8	**37.5%**	5/8	7/10
User 2	2/8, 6/10	6/10	**60%**	6/8, 2/10	6/8	75%	8/8	8/10

Each row provides the following information:

- **User Selected**: The user that has been offered resources by the algorithm
- **Resource share**: A fraction of the total available resources for each resource type that is allocated to a user in the offer round.
- **Dominant share**: The resource share of the dominant resource
- **Dominant share percentage:** The dominant share expressed as a percentage (%)
- **CPU Total Allocation**: The sum of CPU resources allocated to all users in the current offer round
- **Memory Total Allocation**: The sum of memory resources allocated to all users in the current offer round

[Note: The lowest dominant share in each row is highlighted in yellow.]

To begin with, both users have a dominant share of 0% (as no resource is allocated as yet). We will assume that DRF chooses user 1 to offer resources to first, although had we assumed user 2, the final outcome would have been the same. Here are the steps it will follow:

1. User 1 will receive the required set of resources to run a task. The dominant share for its dominant resource (memory) will get increased to 30%.
2. User 2's dominant share being 0%, it will receive resources in the next round. The dominant share for its dominant resource (CPU) will get increased to 37.5%.
3. As User 1 now has the lower dominant share (30%), it will receive the next set of resources. Its dominant share rises to 60%.
4. User 2 that has the lower dominant share (37.5%) will now be offered resources.
5. The process will continue until there are no more resources to allocate to run the user tasks. In this case, after step 4, the CPU resources will get saturated (highlighted in red).
6. The process will continue if any resources are freed or the resource requirement changes.

Primarily, DRF aims to maximize the minimum dominant share across all users. As in this example, DRF worked with the users to allocate the following:

- Two tasks to user 1 with a total allocation of two CPUs, 6 GB memory, and a dominant share % of 60 (Memory).

- Two tasks to user 2 with a total allocation of six CPUs, 2 GB memory, and a dominant share % of 75 (CPU).

This can be diagrammatically depicted as follows:

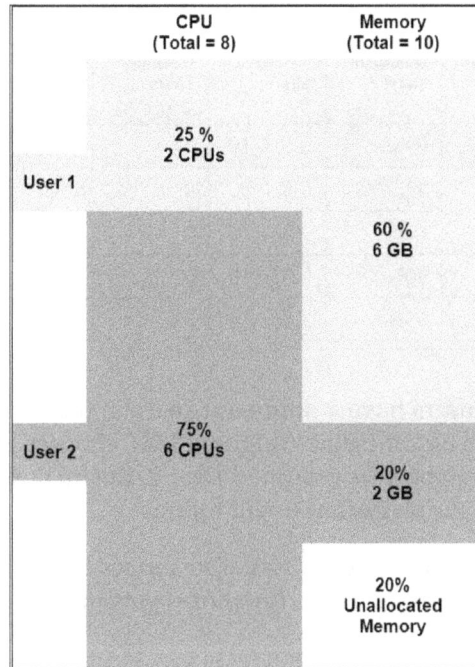

Weighted DRF

We have so far assumed that users have an equal probability of being offered resources. There could also be a modification created in the algorithm, where one user or a set of users is favored over others in terms of resource allocation. This is referred to as Weighted DRF, wherein resources are not shared equally among users. Sharing can be weighted on a per-user and per-resource-level basis, the former being more popular.

Let's consider a per-user weighted computation of the previous example. For every user i and resource j, the weights are stated as $w_{1,j}$ 3 and $w_{2,j} = 1$. This implies that user 1 will have three times the proportion of all the resources compared to user 2 in the system. If both the weights have the value 1, then allocation would be carried out in accordance with the normal DRF algorithm (as described before).

Now, let's look at each step taken by the DRF algorithm to allocate resources for users 1 and 2.

	User 1 (Weightage =3)			User 2 (Weightage =1)			CPU	Memory
User Selected	Resource Share	Dominant Share	Dominant Share %	Resource Share	Dominant Share	Dominant Share %	Total Allocation	Total Allocation
	0/8, 0/10	0	0%	0/8, 0/10	0	0%	0/8	0/10
User 1	1/8, 3/10	3/10	33.33%	0/8, 0/10	0	0%	1/8	3/10
User 1	2/8, 6/10	6/10	60%	0/8, 0/10	0	0%	2/8	6/10
User 1	3/8, 9/10	9/10	90%	0/8, 0/10	0	0%	3/8	9/10
User 2	3/8, 9/10	9/10	90%	3/8, 1/10	3/8	37.5%	6/8	10/10

To begin with, both the users have a dominant share of 0% (as no resource is allocated as yet). We will assume that Weighted DRF chooses user 1 to offer resources to first, although had we assumed User 2, the final outcome would have been the same. Here are the steps that it will follow:

1. User 1 will receive the required set of resources to run a task. The dominant share for its dominant resource (memory) gets increased to 10% (30% divided by 3).

2. User 2's dominant share being 0%, it will receive resources in the next round. The dominant share for its dominant resource (CPU) will get increased to 37.5%.

3. As user 1 now has the lower dominant share (10%), it will receive the next set of resources. Its dominant share will rise to 20% (60% divided by 3).

4. User 1 still has the lower dominant share (20%) and is now offered resources again to make it 30% (90% divided by 3).

5. The process will continues till there are no more resources to allocate to run the user tasks. In this case, after step 4, the memory resources will get saturated (highlighted in red).

6. The process will continue if any resources are freed or the resource requirement changes.

Weighted DRF aims to prioritize resource sharing based on the weight assigned to every user. In this example, Weighted DRF worked with the users to allocate the following:

- Three tasks to user 1 with a total allocation of three CPUs and 9 GB memory
- Only one task to user 2 with a total allocation of three CPUs and 1 GB memory

This can be diagrammatically depicted as follows:

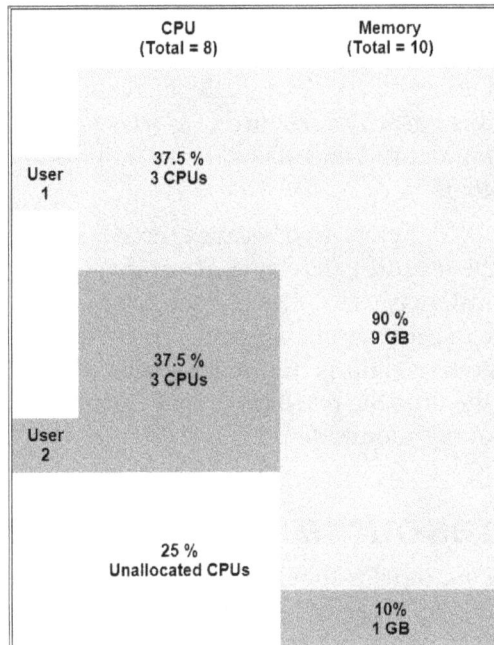

In addition to this, it is possible to create custom modules that cater to an organization or need specific resource allocation. This will be covered later in the same chapter.

Let's now look at some of the important properties that DRF follows/satisfies:

1. **Progressive Filling**: Allocation by progressive filling in DRF increases the dominant shares of all users at the same speed, while other resource allocations of users increase proportionally based on the demand. This continues up to a point at which at least one resource is saturated, after which the allocations of users that require the saturated resource are halted, and these users are eliminated. Progressive filling for other users proceeds in a recursive fashion and ends when there is no user left whose dominant share can be increased.

2. **Share Guarantee**: The DRF algorithm allocates resources to users via "progressive filling", which ensures that every user's dominant share allocation increases at the same rate and continues until one resource gets saturated and the resource allocation is frozen. This indirectly ensures that all users are treated equally and are guaranteed 1/n of at least one resource.

3. **Strategy-proofness**: This property of DRF ensures that users at any given point of time cannot benefit from increased allocation by falsifying their resource demands. In case a user does try to *game* the system by demanding extra resources, the DRF algorithm is such that the allocation of resources may happen in a manner that is deterrent to this user.

4. **Pareto efficiency**: This property of DRF implies that increasing the dominant share of a given user will proportionally decrease the dominant share of other users for this particular resource. Courtesy of the progressive filling algorithm, it is but natural that allocation of more resources to one specific user will hurt others.

5. **Envy-freeness**: DRF is envy-free because there is no need for any user to prefer or envy the resource allocation of another. Envy comes into the picture only when, for instance, user 1 envies user 2, whose dominant share for a particular resource is higher. However, considering that resource allocation is done via progressive filling, dominant shares of both users 1 and 2 will be the same by the time the resource in question is saturated. This *envy* is neither beneficial nor required.

Configuring resource offers on Mesos

A common problem encountered is that sometimes, frameworks do not accept any resource offers due to improper resource configuration settings on the slaves. For example, the Elasticsearch framework requires ports 9200 and 9300, but the default port range configuration in the Mesos slaves is 31000 to 32000.

The slaves must be configured correctly so that the right resource offers are made to frameworks that can then accept them. This can be done as follows:

1. In the `mesos-slave` command, add the necessary resource parameters Here's an example:

    ```
    --resources='ports:[9200-9200,9300-9300]' ...
    ```

2. Create a *file* under /etc/mesos-slave called `resources` whose content is the necessary resource string. Run the following command:

    ```
    $ cat /etc/mesos-slave/resources
    ports:[9200-9200,9300-9300]
    $
    ```

Reservation

Mesos also provides the ability to reserve resources on specified slaves. This is particularly useful in ensuring that important services get guaranteed resource offers from a particular slave (for example, a database may need resource offers only from a particular slave, which contains the necessary data). In the absence of a reservation mechanism, there is the possibility that an important service or job may need to wait for a long time before it gets a resource offer satisfying its filter criteria, which would have a detrimental impact on performance.

On the other hand, misusing the reservation feature can lead to the same kind of problems, such as the resource underutilization that Mesos sought to resolve in the first place. Thus, it is necessary to use this judiciously. The Mesos access control mechanism makes sure that the framework requesting a reservation of resources has the appropriate authorization to do so.

Mesos provides two methods of resource reservations:

1. Static reservation
2. Dynamic reservation

Static reservation

In this type of reservation, specified resources can be reserved on specific slave nodes for a particular framework or group of frameworks. In order to reserve resources for a framework, it must be assigned to a role. Multiple frameworks can be assigned to a single role if necessary. Only the frameworks assigned to a particular role (say, role X) are entitled to get offers for the resources reserved for role X. Roles need to be defined first, then frameworks need to be assigned to the required roles, and finally, resource policies must be set for these roles.

Role definition

Roles can be defined by starting the master with the following flag:

```
--roles = "name1, name2, name3"
```

For example, if we want to define a role called hdfs, then we can start the master using the following:

```
--roles = "hdfs"
```

Alternatively, you can do this by running the following:

```
echo hdfs > /etc/mesos-master/role
```

Now, the master needs to be restarted by running the following:

```
sudo service mesos-master restart
```

Framework assignment

Now, we need to map the frameworks to specific roles. The method to do this varies by the framework. Some, such as Marathon, can be configured using the –mesos_role flag. In the case of HDFS, this can be done by changing `mesos.hdfs.role` in `mesos-site.xml` to the value of `hdfs` defined before.

```
<property>
  <name>mesos.hdfs.role</name>
  <value>hdfs</value>
</property>
```

Custom roles for frameworks can be specified by setting the `role` option within `FrameworkInfo` to the desired value (the default is *).

Role resource policy setting

Resources on each slave can be reserved for a particular role by leveraging the slave's `-resources` flag. Slave-level resource policy setting has its drawbacks as the management overhead can quickly become daunting as the cluster size and number of frameworks being run increases.

If we have eight cores and 24 GB (the number is specified in MBs in Mesos) RAM available on a particular slave and seek to reserve 2 cores and 6 GB RAM for the `hdfs` role, then we can make the following changes on the slave:

```
--resources="cpus:6;mem:18432;cpus(hdfs):2;mem(hdfs):6144"
```

Once this is done, `mesos-slave` with these changed settings can be stopped by executing the following:

```
sudo service mesos-slave stop
```

The older state on these slaves can be removed by the following command. Any running tasks can be manually terminated as the task states will also get removed:

```
rm -f /tmp/mesos/meta/slaves/latest
```

Now, the slave can be restarted with the following command:

```
sudo service mesos-slave start
```

Dynamic reservation

The main drawback of static reservation is that the reserved resources cannot be used by other roles during downtime, nor can they be unreserved and made available as part of the wider pool. This leads to poor resource utilization. In order to overcome this challenge, support for dynamic reservation was added in version 0.23.0, which allows users to reserve and unreserve resources more dynamically as per workload requirements.

For a resource offer, frameworks can send back the following two messages (through the `acceptOffers` API) as a response:

* `Offer::Operation::Reserve`
* `Offer::Operation::Unreserve`

These are described in detail in the following sections. Note that the framework's principal is required for authorization, which will be discussed in more detail in *Chapter 6, Mesos Frameworks*.

Offer::Operation::Reserve

Each framework can reserve resources as part of the offer cycle. As an example, let's say that a resource offer with eight cores and 12 GB RAM unreserved is received by a framework. Take a look at the following code:

```
{
  "id": <offer_id>,
  "framework_id": <framework_id>,
  "slave_id": <slave_id>,
  "hostname": <hostname>,
  "resources": [
    {
      "name": "cpus",
      "type": "SCALAR",
      "scalar": { "value": 8 },
      "role": "*",
    },
    {
      "name": "mem",
      "type": "SCALAR",
      "scalar": { "value": 12288 },
      "role": "*",
    }
  ]
}
```

We can reserve four cores and 6 GB RAM for the framework by specifying the quantity of each resource type that needs to be reserved and the framework's role and principal in the following message:

```
{
   "type": Offer::Operation::RESERVE,
   "reserve": {
     "resources": [
        {
           "name": "cpus",
           "type": "SCALAR",
           "scalar": { "value": 4 },
           "role": <framework_role>,
           "reservation": {
             "principal": <framework_principal>
           }
        },
        {
           "name": "mem",
           "type": "SCALAR",
           "scalar": { "value": 6144 },
           "role": <framework_role>,
           "reservation": {
             "principal": <framework_principal>
           }
        }
     ]
   }
}
```

The next resource offer will include the preceding reserved resources, as follows:

```
{
   "id": <offer_id>,
   "framework_id": <framework_id>,
   "slave_id": <slave_id>,
   "hostname": <hostname>,
   "resources": [
      {
         "name": "cpus",
         "type": "SCALAR",
         "scalar": { "value": 4 },
         "role": <framework_role>,
         "reservation": {
           "principal": <framework_principal>
```

```
      }
    },
    {
      "name": "mem",
      "type": "SCALAR",
      "scalar": { "value": 6144 },
      "role": <framework_role>,
      "reservation": {
        "principal": <framework_principal>
      }
    },
  ]
}
```

Offer::Operation::Unreserve

Each framework can also unreserve resources as part of the offer cycle. In the previous example, we reserved four cores and 6 GB RAM for the framework/role that will continue to be offered until specifically unreserved. The way to unreserve this is explained here.

First, we will receive the reserved resource offer, as follows:

```
{
  "id": <offer_id>,
  "framework_id": <framework_id>,
  "slave_id": <slave_id>,
  "hostname": <hostname>,
  "resources": [
    {
      "name": "cpus",
      "type": "SCALAR",
      "scalar": { "value": 4 },
      "role": <framework_role>,
      "reservation": {
        "principal": <framework_principal>
      }
    },
    {
      "name": "mem",
      "type": "SCALAR",
      "scalar": { "value": 6144 },
      "role": <framework_role>,
      "reservation": {
```

```
        "principal": <framework_principal>
      }
    },
  ]
}
```

We can now unreserve four cores and 6 GB RAM for the framework by specifying the quantity of each resource type that needs to be unreserved and the framework's role and principal in the following message:

```
{
  "type": Offer::Operation::UNRESERVE,
  "unreserve": {
    "resources": [
      {
        "name": "cpus",
        "type": "SCALAR",
        "scalar": { "value": 4 },
        "role": <framework_role>,
        "reservation": {
          "principal": <framework_principal>
        }
      },
      {
        "name": "mem",
        "type": "SCALAR",
        "scalar": { "value": 6144 },
        "role": <framework_role>,
        "reservation": {
          "principal": <framework_principal>
        }
      }
    ]
  }
}
```

In subsequent resource offers, these unreserved resources will become part of the wider unreserved pool and start being offered to other frameworks.

The /reserve and /unreserve HTTP endpoints were also introduced in v0.25.0 and can be used for dynamic reservation management from the master.

/reserve

Let's say that we are interested in reserving four cores and 6 GB RAM for a role on a slave whose ID is `<slave_id>`. An HTTP POST request can be sent to the `/reserve` HTTP endpoint, as follows:

```
$ curl -i \
  -u <operator_principal>:<password> \
  -d slaveId=<slave_id> \
  -d resources='[ \
    { \
      "name": "cpus", \
      "type": "SCALAR", \
      "scalar": { "value": 4 }, \
      "role": <framework_role>, \
      "reservation": { \
        "principal": <operator_principal> \
      } \
    }, \
    { \
      "name": "mem", \
      "type": "SCALAR", \
      "scalar": { "value": 6144 }, \
      "role": <framework_role>,\
      "reservation": { \
        "principal": <operator_principal> \
      } \
    } \
  ]' \
  -X POST http://<ip>:<port>/master/reserve
```

The response can be one of the following:

- 200 OK: Success

- 400 BadRequest: Invalid arguments (for example, missing parameters)

- 401 Unauthorized: Unauthorized request

- 409 Conflict: Insufficient resources to satisfy the reserve operation

/unreserve

Now, if we are interested in unreserving the resources that were reserved before, an
HTTP POST request can be sent to the /unreserve HTTP endpoint, as follows:

```
$ curl -i \
  -u <operator_principal>:<password> \
  -d slaveId=<slave_id> \
  -d resources='[ \
    { \
      "name": "cpus", \
      "type": "SCALAR", \
      "scalar": { "value": 4 }, \
      "role": <framework_role>, \
      "reservation": { \
        "principal": <operator_principal> \
      } \
    }, \
    { \
      "name": "mem", \
      "type": "SCALAR", \
      "scalar": { "value": 6144 }, \
      "role": <framework_role>\
      "reservation": { \
        "principal": <operator_principal> \
      } \
    } \
  ]' \
  -X POST http://<ip>:<port>/master/unreserve
```

The response can be one of the following:

- 200 OK: Success
- 400 BadRequest: Invalid arguments (for example, missing parameters)
- 401 Unauthorized: Unauthorized request
- 409 Conflict: Insufficient resources to satisfy unreserve operation

Oversubscription

Frameworks are generally provided with enough buffer resources by users to be able to handle unexpected workload surges. This leads to an overall underutilization of the entire cluster because a sizeable chunk of resources are lying idle. Add this across frameworks, and you find that it adds up to significant wastage. The concept of oversubscription, introduced in v0.23.0, seeks to address this problem by executing low priority tasks, such as background processes or ad hoc noncritical analytics, on these idle resources.

To enable this, two additional components are introduced:

1. **Resource estimator**: This is used to determine the number of idle resources that can be used by best-effort processes

2. **Quality of Service (QoS) controller**: This is used to terminate these best-effort tasks in case a workload surge or performance degradation in the original tasks is observed

While the basic default estimators and controllers are provided, Mesos provides users with the ability to create their own custom ones.

In addition, the existing resource allocator, resource monitor, and Mesos slave are also extended with new flags and options. The following diagram illustrates how the oversubscription concept works (source: http://mesos.apache.org/documentation/latest/oversubscription/):

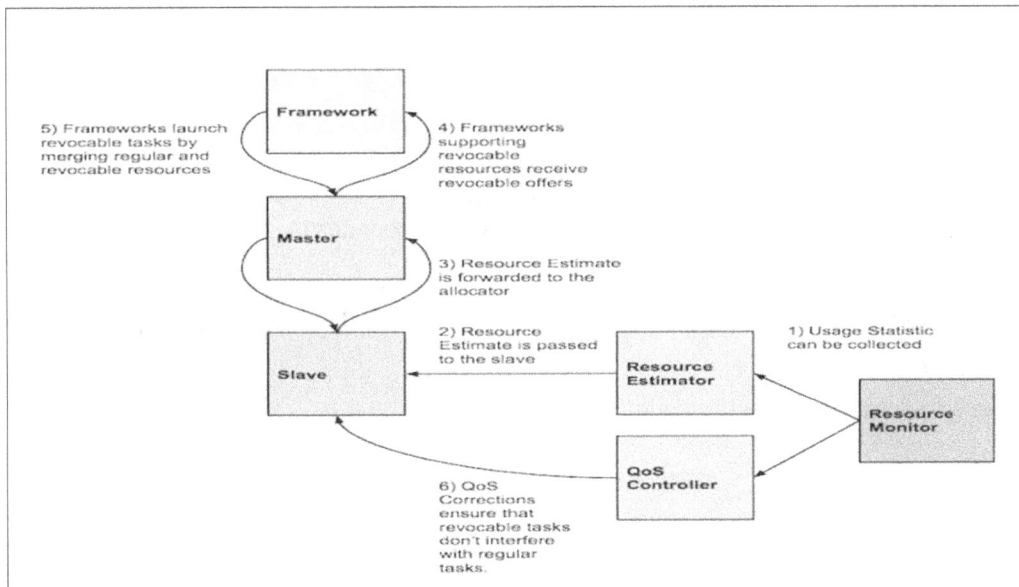

Revocable resource offers

The following steps are followed:

1. The primary step involves collecting the usage statistics and estimating the number of resources that are oversubscribed and available for use by low-priority jobs. The resource monitor sends these statistics by passing `ResourceStatistics` messages to something known as the resource estimator.

2. The estimator identifies the quantity of resources that are oversubscribed by leveraging algorithms that calculate these buffer amounts. Mesos provides the ability to develop custom resource estimators based on user-specified logic.

3. Each slave polls the resource estimator to get the most recent estimates.

4. The slave, then, periodically (whenever the estimate values change) transmits this information to the allocator module in the master.

5. The allocator marks these oversubscribed resources as "revocable" resources and monitors these separately.

6. Frameworks that register with the `REVOCABLE_RESOURCES` set in the `FrameworkInfo` method receive offers of these revocable resources and can schedule tasks on them using the `launchTasks()` API. Note that these cannot be dynamically reserved.

Registering with the revocable resources capability

Run the following code:

```
FrameworkInfo framework;
framework.set_name("Revocable framework");

framework.add_capabilities()->set_type(
    FrameworkInfo::Capability::REVOCABLE_RESOURCES);
```

An example offer with a mix of revocable and standard resources

Take a look at the following code:

```
{
  "id": <offer_id>,
  "framework_id": <framework_id>,
  "slave_id": <slave_id>,
  "hostname": <hostname>,
```

```
  "resources": [
    {
      "name": "cpus",
      "type": "SCALAR",
      "scalar": {
        "value": 4
      },
      "role": "*"
    }, {
      "name": "mem",
      "type": "SCALAR",
      "scalar": {
        "value": 6144
      },
      "role": "*"
    },
    {
      "name": "cpus",
      "type": "SCALAR",
      "scalar": {
        "value": 1
      },
      "role": "*",
      "revocable": {}
    }
  ]
}
```

- The task is launched on the slave when the runTask request is received by it. A container with even a single revocable resource can be terminated by the QoS controller as it is considered a revocable container.

- The original task is also monitored continuously, and the revocable resources are returned to it if any performance deterioration or workload spike is observed. This is known as interference detection.

Currently, the Mesos resource estimator is pretty basic with two default estimators called the **fixed** and **noop** resource estimators. In the first one, a fixed set of resources can be tagged as oversubscribed, while the latter provides a null estimate upon being polled by the slave, effectively saying that no resources are available for oversubscription.

Active work is being done on introducing sophisticated and dynamic oversubscribed resource estimation models (a module called **Project Serenity** by Mesosphere and Intel, for instance) to maximize resource utilization while ensuring no impact on Quality of Service at the same time.

Resource estimator

Run the following code:

```
class ResourceEstimator
{
public:
  virtual Try initialize
    (const lambda::function<process::Future()>& usage) = 0;
  virtual process::Future oversubscribable() = 0;
};
```

The QoS controller

Execute the following code:

```
class QoSController
{
public:
  virtual Try initialize
    (const lambda::function<process::Future()>& usage) = 0;
  virtual process::Future<std::list> corrections() = 0;
};
```

Configuring oversubscription

The slave now has four new oversubscription-related flags available, as shown in the following table:

Flag	Explanation
`--oversubscribed_ resources_ interval=VALUE`	The slave periodically transmits oversubscribed resource estimates to the master. The interval of these updates can be specified via this flag (default: 15 seconds)
`--qos_controller=VALUE`	This is the QoS controller name that needs to be used

Flag	Explanation
`--qos_correction_` `interval_min=VALUE`	The slave polls and carries out QoS corrections, which are performed by the slave from the controller-based on the performance degradation/deterioration levels of the original tasks. This flag controls the interval of these corrections (default: 0 ns)
`--resource_` `estimator=VALUE`	This is the resource estimator name that needs to be used for the determination of oversubscribed resources

Extendibility

Different organizations have different requirements. Also, within the same organization, different users run clusters in different ways with different scale and latency requirements. Users need to deal with application-specific behavior, ensuring that their industry-specific security compliances are met and so on. All this means that Mesos needs to be extremely customizable and extendable if it is to achieve its goal of serving as the OS for the entire datacenter for all organizations. It required a feature that could keep the Mesos core small and lightweight while making it powerful enough to allow as much customization/extendibility as required at the same time.

A number of software systems, such as browsers, support libraries to:

- Extend feature support
- Abstract complexity
- Make development configuration-driven

Mesos modules

Mesos modules, introduced in v0.21.0, build on this concept to allow users to extend the functionality of Mesos through libraries that can be created as well as shared without continuous recompilation. A module in the context of Mesos is an entire component that can be added or replaced by any user. All external dependencies are treated as separate libraries that can be loaded on demand. All users can now develop their experimental features on top of Mesos without needing to understand all the detailed inner workings or impacting other users. Custom allocation logic, custom oversubscribed resource estimation algorithms, and many such use-case-specific customized functionalities can be implemented. Different subsystems, such as load balancers, isolation mechanisms, and service discovery mechanisms can also be configured in a modular way.

Module invocation

The `--modules` cli flag is available for the master and slave to provide a module list that needs to be made available.

The module list can be provided through a file with a JSON-formatted string using `--modules=filepath`. The `filepath` can be of the `/path/to/file` or `file:///path/to/file` type.

To provide a module list inline, use `--modules="{...}"`.

There are two parameters, `name` and `file`; one of these must be provided for every library. The `file` parameter can be an absolute path (for example, `/User/mesos/lib/example.so`), a filename (for example, `example.so`) or a relative path (for example, `lib/example.so`). The `name` parameter is the name of a library (for example, `example`). If this is provided, it gets expanded to the appropriate library name for the current OS automatically (for example, `example` gets expanded to `example.so` on Linux and `example.dylib` on OS X). If both the parameters are provided, then the `name` parameter is ignored.

An example JSON string is given below:

1. Load a library `example.so` with two modules `org_apache_mesos_X` and `org_apache_mesos_Y` as follows:

    ```
    {
      "libraries": [
        {
          "file": "/path/to/example.so",
          "modules": [
            {
              "name": "org_apache_mesos_X",
            },
            {
              "name": "org_apache_mesos_Y"
            }
          ]
        }
      ]
    }
    ```

From the library example, load the `org_apache_mesos_X` module and pass argument A with value B (load the other module `org_apache_mesos_Y` without any parameters) via the following code:

```
{
  "libraries": [
    {
      "name": "example",
      "modules": [
        {
          "name": "org_apache_mesos_X"
          "parameters": [
            {
              "key": "A",
              "value": "B",
            }
          ]
        },
        {
          "name": "org_apache_mesos_Y"
        }
      ]
    }
  ]
}
```

2. To specify modules inline, use the following code:

```
--modules='{"libraries":[{"file":"/path/to/example.so",
  "modules":[{"name":"org_apache_mesos_X"}]}]}'
```

An example `Hello World` module implementation is provided here: `http://mesos.apache.org/documentation/latest/modules/`.

Building a module

The following command assumes that Mesos is installed in the standard location — that is, the Mesos dynamic library and header files are available:

```
g++ -lmesos -fpic -o test_module.o test_module.cpp
$ gcc -shared -o libtest_module.so test_module.o
```

Hooks

Mesos provides another way to extend its capabilities that doesn't involve having to create an entire component from the ground up through something called **hooks**. Hooks do not interfere with processing of a request; instead, they allow users to add features as part of Mesos' life cycle. Some hooks can change the contents of an object while it is in motion. These are called **decorators**.

The currently supported modules

The following are the currently supported modules on Mesos:

- **Allocator**: This is described in more detail in the subsequent section.

- **Authenticator**: This module allows users to create and integrate new custom authentication methods.

- **Isolator**: Through this interface, users can develop bespoke isolators that address a variety of use cases, such as networking (for example, Project Calico).

- **QoS controller**: Using this, a sophisticated logic for revoking best effort tasks launched on oversubscribed resources can be implemented.

- **Resource estimator**: This allows third party developers to experiment with their own revocable resource estimation algorithms for maximizing cluster utilization. Efforts such as Project Serenity are leveraging this module to try and come up with a production quality dynamic resource estimation logic.

The allocator module

The Mesos resource allocation module contains the policy that the Mesos master uses to determine the type and quantity of resource offers that need to be made to each framework. Organizations can customize it to implement their own allocation policy—for example, fair sharing, priority, and so on—which allows for fine-grained resource sharing. Custom allocation modules can be developed to address specific needs. An example is the oversubscription module, which allows revocable resources to be offered, something not supported by the default DRF allocator.

The following steps are required to load a custom allocation module in the master:

- List it in the `--modules` configuration
- Select it using the `--allocator` flag

For example, to run the master with a custom allocator called
`ExternalAllocatorModule`, the following command needs to be run:

```
./bin/mesos-master.sh --work_dir=m/work
  --modules="file://<modules-including-allocator>.json"
  --allocator=ExternalAllocatorModule
```

Now, we shall take a look at how to implement a custom allocator and package it as
a module to load into the master as shown previously.

Implementing a custom allocator module

Allocator modules are implemented in C++ and need to implement the interface
defined in `mesos/master/allocator.hpp` (the methods are listed in the following
table). They can also be developed using other languages via a C++ proxy that
redirects calls to the implementation defined in this other language:

Method	Description
`initialize(flags, offerCallback, roles)`	Allocator initialization

`addFramework(frameworkId, frameworkInfo, usedResources)`
 	
`removeFramework(frameworkId, frameworkInfo, usedResources)`
	Framework addition/removal

`activateFramework(frameworkId)`
 	
`deactivateFramework(frameworkId)`
	Framework activation/deactivation

`addSlave(slaveId, slaveInfo, totalResources, usedResources)`
 	
`removeSlave(slaveId, slaveInfo, totalResources, usedResources)`
	Slave addition/removal

`activateSlave(slaveId)`
 	
`deactivateSlave(slaveId)`
	Slave activation/deactivation

`requestResources(frameworkId, requests)`	Resource request callback
`updateAllocation(frameworkId, slaveId, operations)`	Resource allocation update
`recoverResources(frameworkId, slaveId, resources, filters)`	Resource recovery callback
`reviveOffers(frameworkId)`	Offer revival callback
`updateWhitelist(whitelist)`	Slave whitelist updating

The default hierarchical DRF allocator has a nonblocking actor-based implementation. This can be utilized in the custom allocator by extending the `MesosAllocatorProcess` class defined in `src/master/allocator/mesos/allocator.hpp`. Using the *Sorter* abstraction, the default allocator can be extended, preventing the need to build a new one from the ground up. The sorter API is defined in `src/master/allocator/sorter/sorter.hpp`, and some of its methods are listed in the following table:

Method	Description
`void add(client, weight=1)` `void remove(client)`	This adds/removes client from the allocation process
`void deactivate(client)` `void activate(client)`	This activates/deactivates the client

`void add(slaveId, resources)`
 `void remove(slaveId, resources)`
 `void update(slaveId, resources)`
	This adds/removes/updates the resource quantities to be allocated

`List<string> sort()`	This returns the list of clients sorted based on a specified policy stating how they should receive resources

`void allocated(client, slaveId, resources)`
 `void update(client, slaveId, oldResources, newResources)`
 `void unallocated(client, slaveId, resources)`
	This decides the allocation/updating/deallocation of resources to the specified client

`Map<SlaveId, Resources> allocation(client)`	This returns the allocated resource to the specified client
`bool contains(client)`	This is true if a sorter contains a specified client and is false otherwise
`int count()`	This returns the client count

Once developed, the customized allocator needs to be set up as the allocator to be used for resource allocation instead of the default one. This involves wrapping the custom allocator in an allocator module and then loading it in the master.

The process to wrap a custom allocator (as implemented in `external_allocator.hpp`) into a module called `ExternalAllocatorModule` is described in detail here: `http://mesos.apache.org/documentation/latest/allocation-module/`.

High availability and fault tolerance

High availability, in simple terms, means achieving very close to 100% system uptime by ensuring that there is no single point of failure. This is typically done by incorporating redundancy mechanisms, such as backup processes taking over instantly from the failed ones and so on.

Mastering high availability

In Mesos, this is achieved using Apache ZooKeeper, a centralized coordination service. Multiple masters are set up (one active leader and other backups), with ZooKeeper coordinating the leader election and handling lead master detection by other Mesos components such as slaves and frameworks.

A minimum of three master nodes are required to maintain a quorum for a high availability setting. The recommendation for production systems is however, at least five. The leader election process is described in detail at `http://zookeeper.apache.org/doc/trunk/recipes.html#sc_leaderElection`.

The state of a failed master can be recreated on whichever master gets elected next by leveraging the information stored with the slaves and framework schedulers. Upon the election of the new master, other components are apprised of this development by ZooKeeper, allowing them to now register with this new master and pass along status update messages to it. Based on this data, the newly elected master is able to regenerate the state of the failed master.

Framework scheduler fault tolerance

This is achieved through the registration of multiple schedulers of each framework with the current leading master. In the event of a scheduler failure, the secondary scheduler is asked by the master to take charge. However, the state-sharing implementation between multiple schedulers of each framework needs to be handled by the respective frameworks themselves.

Slave fault tolerance

Mesos has a slave recovery mechanism for fault tolerance, which is discussed at length in the subsequent section. The master monitors the status of all the slaves. The master removes a particular slave node and tries to terminate it if it doesn't respond to the heartbeats sent by it despite several communication attempts.

Executor/task

In case of task or executor failures, the master notifies the corresponding framework scheduler that launched the task. Based on the policies specified in the scheduler's logic, it will handle the execution of the failed task, generally by launching it on new slave nodes that match the resource requirement criteria.

Slave recovery

Slave recovery is a fault tolerance mechanism introduced in v0.14.0 through which tasks can continue to run even if a slave process goes down and also enable slave process to reestablish a connection with the tasks that are running on this slave upon restart. The slave process may go down and need to be restarted during either planned upgrades or following unexpected crashes.

To achieve this, the slaves save information about the tasks being currently executed to the local disk (also known as **checkpointing**). The data that they write out includes task, executor, and status information. To enable this feature, both the slave and the frameworks running on these need to be configured appropriately. If checkpointing is enabled, then the slave restarts post-failure events and can recover data from the most recent checkpoint, reestablish connection with the executors, and continue running the task. When a slave goes down, both the master and executors wait for it to restart and reconnect. As checkpointing involves multiple writes to the local disk, the need for high availability needs to be weighed against the latency overheads caused by these frequent writes.

In addition, improvements have also been made to the executor driver, making it more robust and tolerant of failure events. For instance, the driver caches updates passed to it by the executor during the time a slave is down and resends them to the slave once it reestablishes connection with the executor. This ensures that the executors can continue running the tasks and transmitting messages while not being concerned about the slave process.

Checkpointing also improves reliability by ensuring that messages regarding task updates are passed on to the frameworks even if failures occur. For instance, if a slave and master failed at the same time, frameworks would not receive the required TASK_LOST status update message. Through checkpointing, a slave can now recover information about the tasks from the last checkpointed state and can send the required messages to the framework upon reconnection.

Slave recoverability is important for various reasons, such as ensuring that stateful processes or long-running tasks can restart from the last recorded state, performing seamless cluster upgrades, and reducing maintenance and management overheads.

Enabling slave checkpointing

Slave checkpointing can be enabled in the following way.

> Note that slave checkpointing for all slaves is enabled by default since v0.22.0.

The relevant flags are as follows:

- `checkpoint`: This allows users to specify whether a slave needs to checkpoint information to enable recovery [The default is `true`].

    o   A restarted slave can recover updates and reestablish connection with (`--recover=reconnect`) or terminate (`--recover=cleanup`) executors.

    > Note that this flag will be removed starting v0.22.0 and enabled for all slaves.

- `strict`: This determines whether recovery should be carried out in strict mode or not [the default is `true`].

    o   If `strict=true`, then all the errors related to recovery are treated as fatal.

    o   If `strict=false`, then the state is recovered on a best-effort basis in case of any errors related to recovery, such as data corruption and so on.

- `recover`: This determines whether a slave should reconnect with or terminate old executors [the default is `reconnect`].

    o   If `recover=reconnect`, the slave can reestablish connection with the live executors.

    o   If `recover=cleanup`, the slave terminates the old executors. This option is typically used when performing incompatible upgrades.

    > Note that no recovery is performed if no checkpointed information is present. Upon restart, the slave gets registered as a new slave with the master.

- recovery_timeout: This is the time within which the slave must recover [the default is 15 mins].
  - ° If the slave doesn't recover within the recovery_timeout value specified, the master shuts the slave, which leads to all executors getting terminated as well.

> Note that this is only applicable and available when --checkpoint is enabled.

Enabling framework checkpointing

Frameworks can enable checkpointing by setting the value of the optional checkpointing field included in FrameworkInfo to true (FrameworkInfo. checkpoint=True) before registration. If this option is enabled, then only offers from checkpointed slaves will be received by such frameworks.

Reconciliation

Mesos implements an actor-style message passing programming model to enable nonblocking communication between different Mesos components and leverages protocol buffers for the same. For example, a scheduler needs to tell the executor to utilize a certain number of resources, an executor needs to provide status updates to the scheduler regarding the tasks that are being executed, and so on. Protocol buffers provide the required flexible message delivery mechanism to enable this communication by allowing developers to define custom formats and protocols, which can be used across different languages.

An at-most-once message delivery model is employed for this purpose except for certain messages, such as status updates, a lot of which follow the at-least-once delivery model by making use of acknowledgements. In case of failures, there is a high chance that messages between the master and slaves can get lost leading to state inconsistencies.

For instance, there are multiple scenarios in which a task can be lost whenever a framework issues a request to launch tasks. The master can fail after the request is sent by the framework but before it receives it, or it can fail after a message is received but before it can send it to the slave. The framework can fail after expressing its desire to launch a task but before sending the required message and so on. To tackle the inconsistencies created by such situations, there needs to be a reconciliation mechanism between Mesos and the frameworks. Mesos needs to make sure that the frameworks are aware of the failure events that might occur and when these get resolved. Moreover, it must ensure that the states of all components are in sync with each other once recovery occurs and maintain consistency.

Task reconciliation

A framework needs to explicitly reconcile tasks after a failure as the scheduler doesn't maintain task-related information. There are two kinds of reconciliations available in Mesos:

- The first is "Explicit" reconciliation, in which the scheduler sends details of the tasks for which it wants to know the state and the master sends back the state of each of these tasks

- The second is "Implicit" reconciliation, in which the scheduler doesn't specify the tasks and just sends an empty list to the master for which the master returns the state of all the known tasks

The way to implement this is as follows:

```
message Reconcile {
  repeated TaskStatus statuses = 1; // Should be non-terminal only.
}
```

The master inspects only the compulsory `TaskID` field and an optional `SlaveID` field.

Offer reconciliation

Offers get automatically reconciled. They do not stay beyond the master's life and are no longer valid if a failure occurs. They are reissued every time the framework gets reregistered.

For more information on reconciliation, refer to `http://mesos.apache.org/documentation/latest/reconciliation/`.

Persistent Volumes

Since v0.23.0, Mesos has introduced experimental support for a new feature called **Persistent Volumes**. One of the key challenges that Mesos faces is providing a reliable mechanism for stateful services such as databases to store data within Mesos instead of having to rely on external filesystems for the same.

For instance, if a database job is being run, then it is essential for the task to be scheduled on slave nodes that contain the data that it requires. Earlier, there was no way to guarantee that the task would get resource offers only from the slave nodes that contained the data required by it. The common method to deal with this problem was to resort to using the local filesystem or an external distributed filesystem. These methods involved either network latency or resource underutilization (as the specific data-bearing nodes needed to be statically partitioned and made available only to the frameworks requiring that data) issues.

The two new features that address this problem are:

- **Dynamic reservations**: In addition to the features discussed in the *Reservation* section earlier in this chapter, another advantage of dynamic reservations is the ability of a framework to reserve a persistent store, ensuring that it will always be offered back to it when another task needs to be launched.

- **Persistent volumes**: Mesos now gives the ability to create a persistent volume from disk resources. A volume can be created when a new task is being launched, which resides outside the sandbox of the task. This will remain persisted even after the completion of the task and will be offered to the same framework again so that it can launch another task on the same disk resources.

Note that persistent volumes can only be generated from statically or dynamically reserved disk resources. If a persistent volume is created from dynamically reserved disk resources, then it cannot be unreserved without the destruction of the volume. This provides a security mechanism to prevent sensitive data from being accidentally exposed to other frameworks. Garbage collection mechanisms to delete residual data are in the works.

The interface for the creation of persistent volumes is described here:

- Frameworks can send two messages through the `acceptOffers` API as offer responses: `Offer::Operation::Create` and `Offer::Operation::Destroy`

- The master can manage persistent volumes via the `/create` and `/destroy` HTTP endpoints, which are currently in the alpha stage.

Note that the framework's principal is required for authorization, which shall be discussed in more detail in *Chapter 6, Mesos Frameworks*

Offer::Operation::Create

Volumes can be created by frameworks as part of the regular offer cycle. For instance, let's say a resource offer of a 6-GB dynamically reserved disk is received as follows:

```
{
  "id" : <offer_id>,
  "framework_id" : <framework_id>,
  "slave_id" : <slave_id>,
  "hostname" : <hostname>,
  "resources" : [
    {
      "name" : "disk",
```

```
      "type" : "SCALAR",
      "scalar" : { "value" : 6144 },
      "role" : <framework_role>,
      "reservation" : {
        "principal" : <framework_principal>
      }
    }
  ]
}
```

A persistent volume can now be created from these disk resources by sending the following message. In it, the following need to be specified:

1. A unique role-specific persistent volume ID

2. A relative path within a container where the volume needs to be stored

3. Volume permissions

A persistent volume can now be created from these disk resources by sending the following message:

```
{
  "type" : Offer::Operation::CREATE,
  "create": {
    "volumes" : [
      {
        "name" : "disk",
        "type" : "SCALAR",
        "scalar" : { "value" : 6144 },
        "role" : <framework_role>,
        "reservation" : {
          "principal" : <framework_principal>
        },
        "disk": {
          "persistence": {
            "id" : <persistent_volume_id>
          },
          "volume" : {
            "container_path" : <container_path>,
            "mode" : <mode>
          }
        }
      }
    ]
  }
}
```

The next resource offer will include the persistent volume created before:

```
{
  "id" : <offer_id>,
  "framework_id" : <framework_id>,
  "slave_id" : <slave_id>,
  "hostname" : <hostname>,
  "resources" : [
    {
      "name" : "disk",
      "type" : "SCALAR",
      "scalar" : { "value" : 6144 },
      "role" : <framework_role>,
      "reservation" : {
        "principal" : <framework_principal>
      },
      "disk": {
        "persistence": {
          "id" : <persistent_volume_id>
        },
        "volume" : {
          "container_path" : <container_path>,
          "mode" : <mode>
        }
      }
    }
  ]
}
```

Offer::Operation::Destroy

Currently, persistent volumes need to be explicitly deleted. This can be done in the following way as part of the regular offer cycle. First, the resource offer with the persisted volume will be received. Taking the preceding example, this will be:

```
{
  "id" : <offer_id>,
  "framework_id" : <framework_id>,
  "slave_id" : <slave_id>,
  "hostname" : <hostname>,
  "resources" : [
    {
      "name" : "disk",
      "type" : "SCALAR",
```

```
          "scalar" : { "value" : 2048 },
          "role" : <framework_role>,
          "reservation" : {
            "principal" : <framework_principal>
          },
          "disk": {
            "persistence": {
              "id" : <persistent_volume_id>
            },
            "volume" : {
              "container_path" : <container_path>,
              "mode" : <mode>
            }
          }
        }
      }
    ]
  }
}
```

Next, the persisted volume is destroyed through the `Offer::Operation::Destroy` message, as follows:

```
{
  "type" : Offer::Operation::DESTROY,
  "destroy" : {
    "volumes" : [
      {
        "name" : "disk",
        "type" : "SCALAR",
        "scalar" : { "value" : 6144 },
        "role" : <framework_role>,
        "reservation" : {
          "principal" : <framework_principal>
        },
        "disk": {
          "persistence": {
            "id" : <persistent_volume_id>
          },
          "volume" : {
            "container_path" : <container_path>,
            "mode" : <mode>
          }
        }
      }
    ]
  }
}
```

Note that deleting the persisted volume does not result in the disk resources being unreserved. As such, the following resource offers will still contain them:

```
{
  "id" : <offer_id>,
  "framework_id" : <framework_id>,
  "slave_id" : <slave_id>,
  "hostname" : <hostname>,
  "resources" : [
    {
      "name" : "disk",
      "type" : "SCALAR",
      "scalar" : { "value" : 6144 },
      "role" : <framework_role>,
      "reservation" : {
        "principal" : <framework_principal>
      }
    }
  ]
}
```

Summary

In this chapter, we dived deep into some of the most important features of Mesos that make it efficient, scalable, and fault tolerant. Advanced topics such as Mesos' resource allocation options and production-grade fault tolerance capabilities were explained in detail. With this strong background, the reader will be guided through the more practical aspects of Mesos installation, administration, and framework setup in the subsequent chapters.

In the next chapter, we will discuss how to set up a multi-node Mesos cluster both on a public cloud service as well as on a private datacenter with a discussion on the common issues faced and how to debug and troubleshoot them.

Getting Started with Mesos

3

This chapter covers how to manually set up and run a Mesos cluster on the public cloud (AWS, GCE, and Azure) as well as on a private datacenter (on the premises), and it also discusses the various debugging methods and explores how to troubleshoot the Mesos setup in detail.

In this chapter, we will explore the following topics:

- How to launch instances (virtual machines) on public cloud platforms, such as AWS, GCE, and Azure, and we will cover setting up Mesos on top of this

- How to install a Mesos cluster on a private datacenter

- How to troubleshoot and debug commonly encountered issues faced during the setup process

Virtual Machine (VM) instances

An instance is a **virtual machine (VM)**, which is hosted on a cloud provider's infrastructure. Instances can run Linux and Windows Server images that are provided by your cloud provider or any customized versions of the same. You can also build and run images of other operating systems. Most cloud providers, such as **Google Compute Engine (GCE)**, **Amazon Web Services (AWS)**, **Microsoft Azure**, and so on, also let you specify the machine properties of your instances, such as the amount of RAM and number of CPUs required, which are based on the type of machine that you use. In the following section, we'll take a look at how to set up Mesos on public cloud platforms.

Setting up a multi-node Mesos cluster on Amazon Web Services (AWS)

Please refer to `http://docs.aws.amazon.com/AWSEC2/latest/UserGuide/concepts.html`.

As the name implies, Amazon Web Services (AWS) is a cloud computing platform provided by Amazon. This comprises a wide range of web services operating from 11 physical world regions, which can be accessed remotely. This offers services with usage-based pricing; all of this can be used under one account including **EC2** (computing or processing), **S3** (storage), **CloudWatch**, **RDS**, **DynamoDB**, **EBS**, and so on.

AWS gives you a free tier to get you started with Amazon EC2 services. Once you sign up, you will be able to launch a **micro machine** (a small machine with 700 MB of memory) and run this for a year almost free of cost. You will have to pay for other services, such as launching a bigger machine, or using their storage service, such as Amazon S3. You can find the updated pricing information on the official website.

Account Signup and Creation: Head to `http://aws.amazon.com`, click on **Sign Up**, and follow the instructions to create an account in AWS. One of the steps requires phone verification. Once the signup process is complete, you will get a confirmation e-mail with the account number specified inside it. Make a note of this as this will be required in the next steps.

Key Pairs: By default, AWS uses the public key authentication to log in to your Linux instances, as this is more secure. You can choose the key pair while you launch the instance from a drop-down list, or you can create a new one at the time of launching the instance. If you haven't created a key pair already, you can create one using the Amazon EC2 console. Note that you will need key pair for each region, separately.

Security Groups: Security groups act as a firewall for associated instances. They can control both inbound and outbound traffic on your instance. You will have to enable the rule to accept the connections from your **IP** address to the **SSH** port for you to log in to the machine. You can also add or remove as many rules as you wish; for example, **HTTP** and **HTTPS** can be accessed from anywhere, but SSH connections should only be accessed from your IP address.

Instance types

Virtual servers or machines on AWS are also known as instances. Amazon EC2 provides a wide selection of optimized instance types that are geared towards different requirements. Instance types come with a variety of resource (storage, RAM, CPU, and network capacity) options, providing users with the flexibility to select the right mix for their particular use case. Each instance type includes one or more instance sizes, which permits the scaling of your resources to the requirements of your target workload.

Instance types are grouped based on the resource type that the application seeks to leverage the most; for example, general purpose (for applications that require an even mix of all resources), computer optimized (for CPU-intensive workloads), GPU instances (for applications requiring GPU capabilities), memory optimized (for tasks that need a lot of memory), storage optimized (for applications that deal with large volumes of data), and micro instances (for quick trials or lightweight applications). Instances are created from preconfigured templates with OS and other common software that is already installed, called **Amazon Machine Images** (**AMI**). AMIs are either provided by AWS, or they can be obtained through the AWS Marketplace. Users can also create and share their own AMIs with a wider community.

Launching instances

There are multiple ways that an instance can be launched on AWS. Here, we will use the common option of launching via the Amazon EC2 console using a selected Amazon Machine Image. The steps are as follows:

1. Navigate to the Amazon EC2 console.

2. Click on the **Launch Instance** button from the console as depicted in the following diagram:

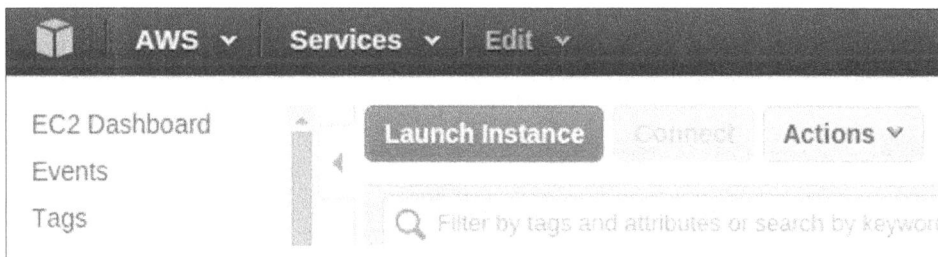

3. Choose **64-bit Ubuntu 14.04 LTS AMI** from the **Choose an Amazon Machine Image (AMI)** page, as follows:

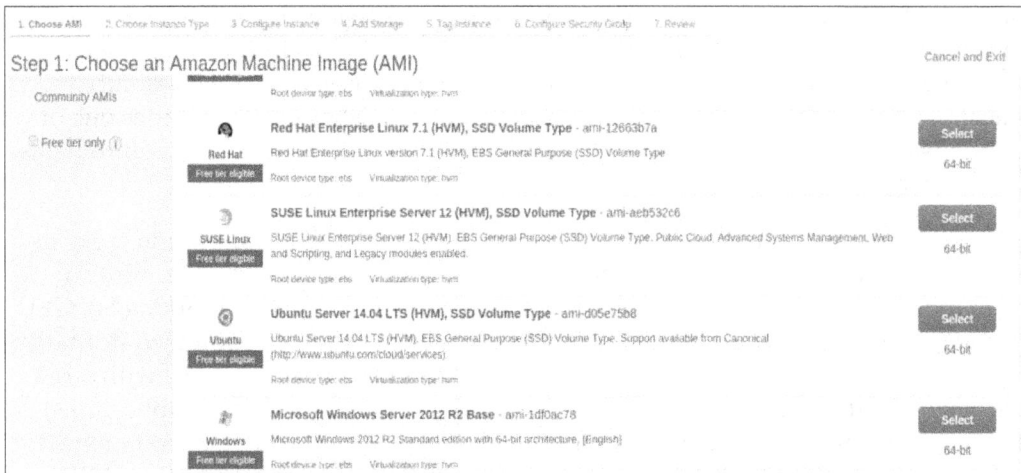

4. On the **Choose an Instance Type** page, select the required instance, which is based on resource requirements (CPU, memory, and so on). For our Mesos cluster, we will use **m4.xlarge** instances having **4** cores and **16** GB of memory on each node:

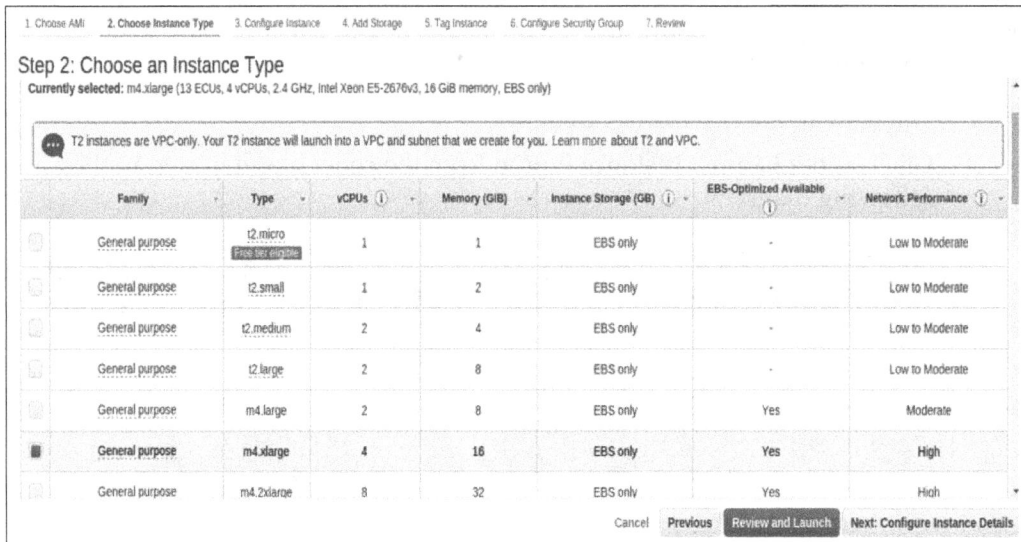

5. On the **Configure Instance Details** page, change the following settings; choose the number of instances as 4 (as we are launching a four node cluster):

6. Click on **Configure Security Group**, add Mesos Web UI port **5050** as **Custom TCP Rule**, and make that sure you set **My IP** as the **Source** address. This option will restrict any other connections, other than your IP address, from attempting to connect to your network:

7. Click on **Review Instance Launch**. We can skip adding storage and tagging instances for now:

| 1. Choose AMI | 2. Choose Instance Type | 3. Configure Instance | 4. Add Storage | 5. Tag Instance | 6. Configure Security Group | 7. Review |

Step 7: Review Instance Launch

▾ Instance Type   Edit instance type ▴

Instance Type	ECUs	vCPUs	Memory (GiB)	Instance Storage (GB)	EBS-Optimized Available	Network Performance
m4.xlarge	13	4	16	EBS only	Yes	High

▾ Security Groups   Edit security groups

| Security group name | launch-wizard-1 |
| Description | launch-wizard-1 created 2015-10-31T13:42:13.407+05.30 |

Type ⓘ	Protocol ⓘ	Port Range ⓘ	Source ⓘ
SSH	TCP	22	0.0.0.0/0

▸ Instance Details   Edit instance details

▸ Storage   Edit storage

▸ Tags   Edit tags

Cancel   Previous   Launch

8. Click on **Launch**.

9. Now, you will be prompted to choose the private key to log in to the machines. You can either choose **Create a new key pair** or use the existing one, and then the machines will be launched:

Select an existing key pair or create a new key pair   ✕

A key pair consists of a **public key** that AWS stores, and a **private key file** that you store. Together, they allow you to connect to your instance securely. For Windows AMIs, the private key file is required to obtain the password used to log into your instance. For Linux AMIs, the private key file allows you to securely SSH into your instance.

Note: The selected key pair will be added to the set of keys authorized for this instance. Learn more about removing existing key pairs from a public AMI.

Create a new key pair   ▾

Key pair name
mesos-cluster

Download Key Pair

💬 You have to download the **private key file** (*.pem file) before you can continue. **Store it in a secure and accessible location.** You will not be able to download the file again after it's created.

Cancel   Request Spot Instances

10. Click on the **Download Key Pair** button and the key pair named
mesos-cluster.pem will be downloaded to your machine. You can
use this file to SSH into the machines that you are launching in AWS.

Installing Mesos

Now log in to all machines:

```
ssh -i  mesos-cluster.pem ec2-54-221-197-122.compute
  -1.amazonaws.com (master)

ssh -i  mesos-cluster.pem ec2-54-221-196-123.compute
  -1.amazonaws.com (slave1)

ssh -i  mesos-cluster.pem ec2-54-221-198-125.compute
  -1.amazonaws.com (slave2)

ssh -i  mesos-cluster.pem ec2-54-221-198-130.compute
  -1.amazonaws.com (slave3)
```

Let's call the first machine from the preceding list as our master machine and rest of
them as slave1, slave2, slave3 for the rest of this chapter.

Now, we can install the dependency libraries and software packages on all four
machines by typing in the following commands:

```
# Following command is used to update the packages.

$ sudo apt-get update


# We will require JDK for deploying java projects over mesos,
  use the following command to install java.
  Here we are using Java version 7.

$ sudo apt-get install -y openjdk-7-jdk


# This step is necessary
  only if you are building from the git repository.
  It will install the autotools.

$ sudo apt-get install -y autoconf libtool


# Now we can install the dependencies for the mesos project.

$ sudo apt-get -y install build-essential
  python-dev python-boto libcurl4-nss-dev libsasl2-dev
  maven libapr1-dev libsvn-dev
```

Now, our environment is ready, and we can start building the Mesos binary.

You can build the Mesos binary from the master machine and then copy the build to the slave machines instead of building from all the machines.

Downloading Mesos

There are two different ways that you can get Mesos:

- Download the latest stable release from Apache (Recommended) at `http://mesos.apache.org/downloads/`. At the time of writing this book, the latest version of Mesos is 0.25.0:

    ```
    ubuntu@ip-10-155-18-106:~$ wget
    http://www.apache.org/dist/mesos/0.25.0/mesos-0.25.0.tar.gz
    ```

    ```
    ubuntu@ip-10-155-18-106:~$ tar -zxf mesos-0.25.0.tar.gz
    ```

    ```
    ubuntu@ip-10-155-18-106:~$ mv mesos-0.25.0 mesos
    ```

- Clone the Mesos git repository (Advanced Users Only):

    ```
    ubuntu@ip-10-155-18-106:~$ git clone
    https://git-wip-us.apache.org/repos/asf/mesos.git
    ```

Building Mesos

We can build Mesos as follows:

```
# Change working directory.
ubuntu@ip-10-155-18-106:~$ cd mesos


# This step is only required if you are building from the git
  repository, or else you can skip this step.
ubuntu@ip-10-155-18-106:~$ ./bootstrap


# Create a build directory. This will contain the compiled Mesos
  binaries. It is a good practice to create the build directory.
ubuntu@ip-10-155-18-106:~$ mkdir build
ubuntu@ip-10-155-18-106:~$ cd build


# Now we can trigger the "configure build" command and "make" command
  followed by it. This step is time consuming and can take some time
  to get executed
ubuntu@ip-10-155-18-106:~$ ../configure
ubuntu@ip-10-155-18-106:~$ make
```

In order to speed up the building and reduce verbosity of the logs, you can append-j <number of cores> V=0 to make:

```
# Once the make command is executed,
  you can test the make by issuing the following command.
ubuntu@ip-10-155-18-106:~$ make check
# The following step is optional,
  you can use it if you are installing it system wide.
ubuntu@ip-10-155-18-106:~$ make install
```

Now, we can copy the build directory from the Mesos master machine to `slave1`, `slave2`, and `slave3` machines:

```
ubuntu@ip-10-155-18-106:~$ rsync -za mesos ip-10-155-18-107:
ubuntu@ip-10-155-18-106:~$ rsync -za mesos ip-10-155-18-109:
ubuntu@ip-10-155-18-106:~$ rsync -za mesos ip-10-155-18-110:
```

Start the Mesos master, as follows:

```
ubuntu@ip-10-155-18-106:~/mesos/build$ ./bin/mesos-master.sh
  --work_dir=/var/lib/mesos
```

Start the Mesos slaves:

```
ubuntu@ip-10-155-18-107:~/mesos/build$ ./bin/mesos-slave.sh
  --master=mesos-master:5050
ubuntu@ip-10-155-18-109:~/mesos/build$ ./bin/mesos-slave.sh
  --master=mesos-master:5050
ubuntu@ip-10-155-18-110:~/mesos/build$ ./bin/mesos-slave.sh
  --master=mesos-master:5050
```

The Mesos Web UI runs on port 5050 on the master machine, and this is where the installation completion status can be checked.

To do this, type in the following URL in your web browser:

```
http://ec2-54-221-197-122.compute-1.amazonaws.com:5050
```

And the Mesos UI will appear as follows:

Using mesos-ec2 script to launch many machines at once

Mesos provides scripts to create Mesos clusters of various configurations on EC2. The mesos-ec2 script, which is located in the ec2 directory allows launching, running jobs, and tearing down the Mesos clusters. Note that we can use this script even without building Mesos, but you will require Python (>=2.6). We can manage multiple clusters using different names.

We will need an AWS key pair to use the ec2 script, and our access and secret key, which we created in the preceding steps:

```
ubuntu@local:~ $ export AWS_ACCESS_KEY_ID=<your-access-key>
ubuntu@local:~ $ export AWS_SECRET_ACCESS_KEY=<your-secret-key>
```

Now, we can use the EC2 scripts that are provided with Mesos to launch a new cluster using the following command:

```
ubuntu@local:~/mesos/ec2 $ ./mesos-ec2 -k <your-key-pair>
  -i <your-identity-file> -s 10 launch mesos-cluster
```

This will launch a cluster named `mesos-cluster` with ten slaves. Once the scripts are done, this will also print the Mesos Web UI link in the form of `<master-hostname>:8080`. We can confirm that the cluster is up by going to the web interface.

The script provides a number of options, a few of which are listed in the following table. We can list all the available options of the script by running `mesos-ec2 --help`:

Command	Use
`--slave` or `-s`	This is the number of slaves in the cluster
`--key-pair` or `-k`	This is the SSH key pair for authentication
`--identity-file` or `-i`	This is the SSH identity file used to log in to the instances
`--instance-type` or `-t`	This is a slave instance type, and this must be 64-bit
`--ebs-vol-size`	This is the size of an EBS volume, which is used to store the persistent HDFS data
`--master-instance-type` or `-m`	This is a master instance type, and this is must be 64-bit
`--zone` or `-z`	This is the Amazon availability zone to launch instances
`--resume`	This flag resumes the installation from the previous run

We can use the login action to log in to the launched cluster by providing a cluster name, as follows:

```
ubuntu@local:~/mesos/ec2 $ ./mesos-ec2 -k <your-key-pair>
  -i <your-identity-file> login mesos-cluster
```

The script also sets up an HDFS instance, which can be used via commands in the `/root/ephemeral-hdfs/` directory.

Finally, we can terminate a cluster using the following command. Be sure to copy any important data before terminating the cluster:

```
ubuntu@local:~/mesos/ec2 $ ./mesos-ec2 destroy ec2-test
```

The script also supports advanced functionalities, such as pausing and restarting clusters with EBS-backed instances. The Mesos documentation is a great source of information for any clarification. It is worth mentioning that Mesosphere (http://mesosphere.com) also provides you with an easy way of creating an elastic Mesos cluster on Amazon EC2, Google Cloud, and other platforms and provides commercial support for Mesos.

Setting up a multi-node Mesos cluster on Google Compute Engine (GCE)

Google Compute Engine (GCE) is Google's **Infrastructure as a Service (IaaS)** offering, which allows users to run their computational workloads on virtual servers that are part of the same infrastructure that powers services, such as Gmail, YouTube, and Google's search engine.

Introduction to instance types

Machine types determine the virtualized hardware resources that are available to your instances, such as the amount of memory, virtual CPU, and the persistent disk limits an instance will have. A single virtual CPU maps to a single hardware hyper-thread on the host CPU that is running your instance.

Machine types are divided into different classes, and they are managed by the Google Compute Engine. Each machine type has its own pricing and is billed separately. For pricing information, review the price sheet.

Available machine types include the following:

- Standard machine types
- High-CPU machine types
- High-memory machine types
- Shared-core machine types

Launching machines

The easiest way to get started with Google Compute Engine is to create a virtual machine instance in the browser tool that Google Cloud Platform offers, the Google Developers Console, which can be found at `https://console.developers.google.com`.

Set up a Google Cloud Platform project

We need to set up a Google Cloud Platform project before we begin to launch the machines:

1. Go to the Google Developers Console. When prompted, select an existing project or create a new project.

> The name you use must be between 1 and 63 characters with a lowercase letter as the first character. You can use a dash, lowercase letter, or digit for the remaining characters, but the last character cannot be a dash. Also, you should be aware that some resource identifiers (such as project IDs) might be retained beyond the life of your project. For this reason, avoid storing sensitive information in resource identifiers.

2. Follow the prompts to set up billing. If you are new to the Google Cloud Platform, you have free trial credit to pay for your instances.

Create the network and firewall rules

After you set up your project and billing, go to the **Networking** section in the Developers Console:

1. Click on **Create network** to create your first network and name it mesos-network:

Create a network

Name

    mesos-network

Description (Optional)

Address range

    10.240.0.0/16

Gateway (Optional)

Firewall rules
Select any of the firewall rules below that you would like to apply to this network. Once the network is created, you can manage all firewall rules on the Firewall rules page.

Name	Source tag / IP range	Allowed protocols / ports	Target tags
mesos-network-allow-icmp	0.0.0.0/0	icmp	Apply to all targets
mesos-network-allow-internal	10.240.0.0/16	tcp:1-65535 2 more ▾	Apply to all targets
mesos-network-allow-rdp	0.0.0.0/0	tcp:3389	Apply to all targets
mesos-network-allow-ssh	0.0.0.0/0	tcp:22	Apply to all targets

Create   Cancel

2. Once the network is added, click on the network and click on the **Add Firewall Rules** button.

3. Add the rules to open TCP 22 and 5050 ports, this is usually a semicolon separated list consisting of `protocol:port`:

Create a firewall rule

By default, incoming traffic from outside your network is blocked. To allow incoming traffic, set up a firewall rule. Firewall rules regulate only incoming traffic to an instance. When a connection is established with an instance, traffic is permitted in both directions over that connection. Learn more

Name

mesos-ssh

Description (Optional)

Network

spark-axhil-network

Source filter

IP ranges

Source IP ranges

0.0.0.0

Allowed protocols and ports

tcp:22;tcp:5050

Target tags (Optional)

Create   Cancel

4. Click on **Create**.

Create the instances

After you set up your project and billing, go to the **VM instances** section in the Developers Console:

1. Click on **Create a new instance** to create your first instance.

2. Set the **Name** field of your instance to `mesos-master`.

3. Under **Boot disk**, click on **Change** and select an **Ubuntu 14.04 LTS** boot disk image if this is not already specified by default. Compute Engine has several other operating systems for you to choose from, but we will use Ubuntu for this example. Save your changes:

Create a new instance

Name

mesos-master

Zone

europe-west1-b

Machine type

n1-standard-4

vCPUs

4

Memory

15 GB

Change

Boot disk

New 10 GB standard persistent disk

Image

Ubuntu 14.04 LTS

Change

Firewall

Add tags and firewall rules to allow specific network traffic from the internet

Allow HTTP traffic

Allow HTTPS traffic

Project access

Allow API access to all Google Cloud services in the same project. Learn more

Management, disk, networking, access & security options

4. Click on **Networking** and choose **mesos-network**, which we created in an earlier step.

5. Click on **Create** to create your instance. The page automatically refreshes after the instance starts.

Once we launch the `mesos-master` machine, now repeat the preceding steps three times to start our `mesos-slave1`, `mesos-slave2`, and for our cluster:

Installing Mesos

By this point, you will have three machines up and running in the Google Compute Cloud named `mesos-master`, `mesos-slave1`, and `mesos-slave2`:

☐	mesos-master	us-central1-a	cloudplan-v2	mesos-network
☐	mesos-slave1	us-central1-a	gerrit, gerrit-git-disk	mesos-network
☐	mesos-slave2	us-central1-a	instance-1	mesos-network

Now, log in to all three machines:

```
mesos-master: ssh 146.148.62.84
mesos-slave1:  ssh 104.197.92.182
mesos-slave2:  ssh 104.197.92.145
```

Now, we can install the dependency libraries and software packages on all three machines by typing in the following commands:

```
# Update the packages.
$ sudo apt-get update
# Install the latest OpenJDK.
$ sudo apt-get install -y openjdk-7-jdk
# Install autotools (Only necessary if building from git repository).
$ sudo apt-get install -y autoconf libtool
# Install other Mesos dependencies.
$ sudo apt-get -y install build-essential
  python-dev python-boto libcurl4-nss-dev libsasl2-dev maven libapr1-
  dev libsvn-dev
```

Now, our environment is ready, and we can start building the Mesos binary.

You can build the Mesos binary from the master machine, and then copy the build to the slave machines instead of building from all the machines.

Downloading Mesos

Follow the steps from the corresponding *Downloading Mesos* subsection under the *Setting up a multi-node Mesos cluster on Amazon Web Services (AWS)* section to download and extract Mesos on the master machine.

Building Mesos

Building Mesos is discussed in the corresponding AWS section. You can follow the instructions listed there to build Mesos on the master machine.

We can now make sure that the installation is complete by looking at the Mesos Web UI running on port 5050 on the master machine.

Open your browser and head to the following URL:

```
http://146.148.62.84:5050
```

And the Mesos Web UI will appear as follows:

Setting up a multi-node Mesos cluster on Microsoft Azure

Microsoft Azure is a cloud computing platform and infrastructure, which is created by Microsoft to build, deploy, and manage applications and services through a global network of Microsoft-managed and Microsoft partner-hosted datacenters. For more information check out https://azure.microsoft.com.

Introduction to instance types

Virtual machines are available in two tiers: basic and standard. Both types offer a choice of sizes, but the basic tier doesn't provide some capabilities, such as load-balancing and autoscaling, which are available in the standard tier. The standard tier of sizes consists of different series: A, D, DS, G, and GS.

Launching machines

To get started with development or test in the cloud, you will need an active Microsoft Azure subscription. If you don't currently have a subscription, you can get a free one-month trial with $200 that you can spend on whatever Azure services you want to use:

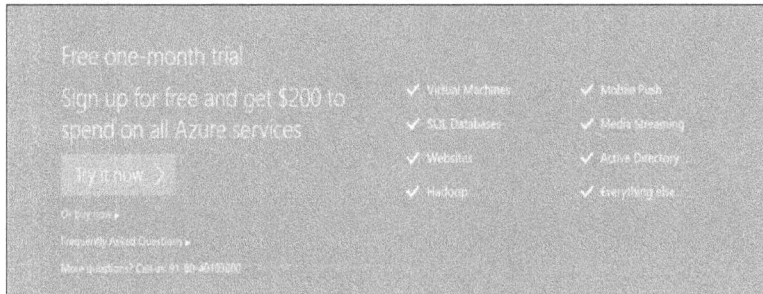

Once you sign-up for Azure, visit the management portal to launch the instances. Azure management portal is available at the following URL: `https://manage.windowsazure.com`

Create a cloud service

A cloud service in Azure gives you a public endpoint to access all the services (VMs and so on) that are running within the cloud service. An endpoint would look something like the following:

```
the-name-you-give.cloudapp.net (e.g: mesos-cluster.cloudapp.net)
```

Following are the steps to create a cloud service:

1. Click on the **CLOUD SERVICES** option from the left-hand side menu panel:

2. Choose **NEW**, then click on **CLOUD SERVICE**, and then click on **QUICK CREATE**:

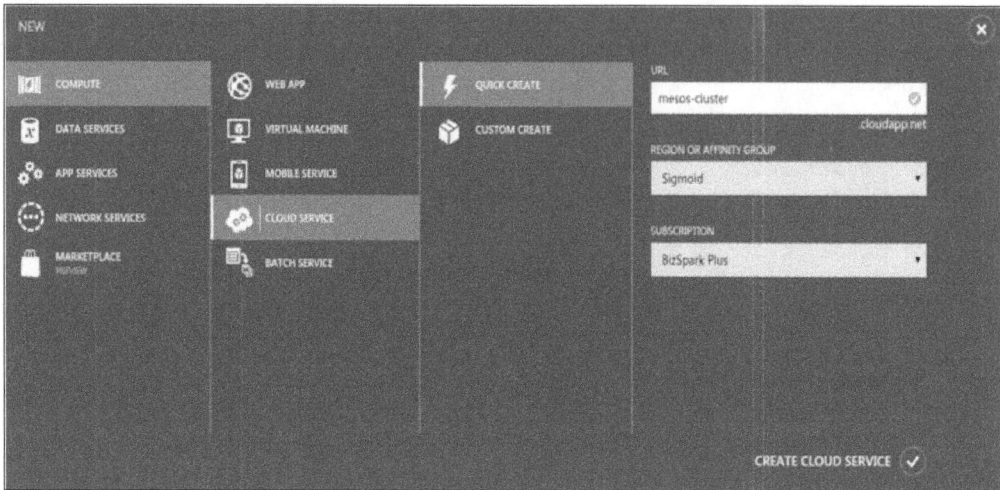

We used the name `mesos-cluster`; hence, the public endpoint to access this service will become `mesos-cluster.cloudapp.net`.

3. Click on **Create Cloud Service**. Once you create the cloud service, you can see it, as follows:

Create the instances

Once you have the cloud service ready, the next thing that you need to do is to start the Virtual machines for our Mesos cluster:

1. Click on **NEW**, then choose **COMPUTE**, and then choose **VIRTUAL MACHINE**:

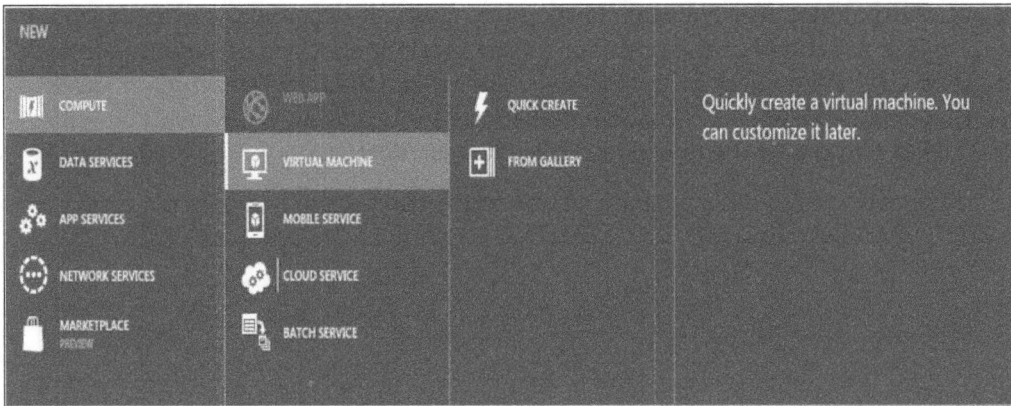

2. Click on **FROM GALLERY**; this options gives us better choices and controls over the machine.

3. **Choose an Image** and click on **UBUNTU**, and then choose the **Ubuntu Server 14.04 LTS** image from the list and click on **Next**:

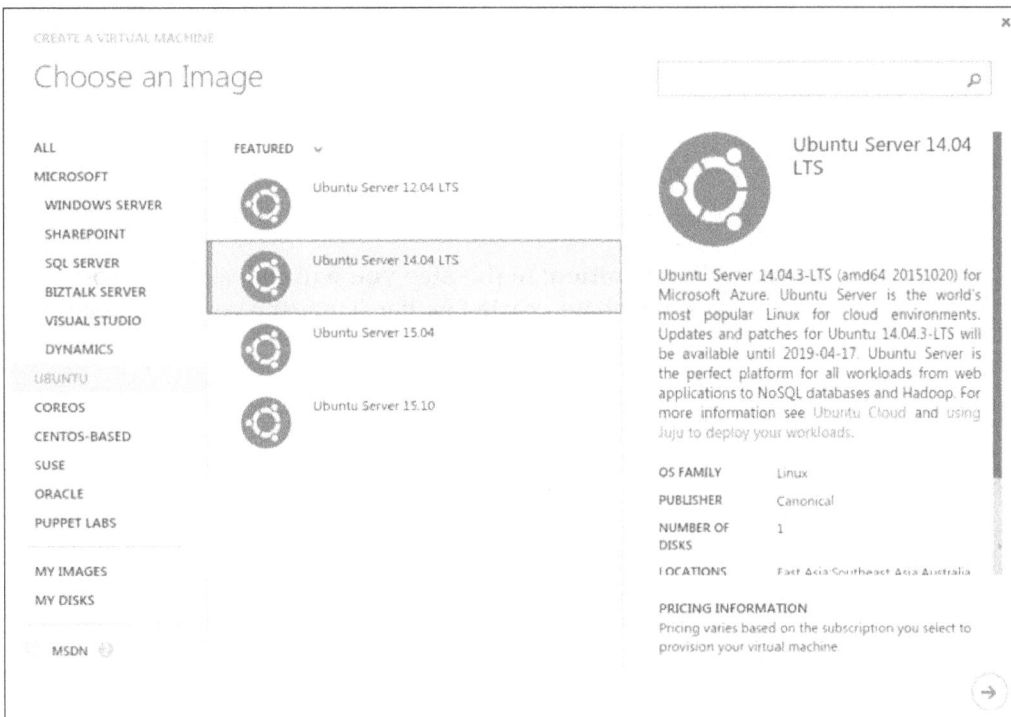

4. **Virtual Machine Naming**: In this step, you will name your virtual machine. This name will be the hostname of the machine that you are about to launch, so we will name it `mesos-master`. Choose the **SIZE** as **D3 (which is the 4 cores 14GB Memory machine)** and type in the password, which you will use to log in to the machine. Now, click on **Next**:

5. **Virtual Machine Configuration**: In this step you will choose the **mesos-cluster** cloud service, which we created earlier. Thus, the very machine that you will be launching for this exercise will fall under the `mesos-cluster` cloud service:

CREATE A VIRTUAL MACHINE

Virtual machine configuration

CLOUD SERVICE

mesos-cluster ▼

CLOUD SERVICE DNS NAME

[   ] .cloudapp.net

REGION/AFFINITY GROUP/VIRTUAL NETWORK

South Central US ▼

STORAGE ACCOUNT

Use an automatically generated storage accoun ▼

AVAILABILITY SET

(None) ▼

ENDPOINTS

NAME	PROTOCOL	PUBLIC PORT	PRIVATE PORT
SSH	TCP	22	22
ENTER OR SELECT A VALUE ▼			

Ubuntu Server 14.04 LTS

Ubuntu Server 14.04.3-LTS (amd64 20151020) for Microsoft Azure. Ubuntu Server is the world's most popular Linux for cloud environments. Updates and patches for Ubuntu 14.04.3-LTS will be available until 2019-04-17. Ubuntu Server is the perfect platform for all workloads from web applications to NoSQL databases and Hadoop. For more information see Ubuntu Cloud and using Juju to deploy your workloads.

OS FAMILY
Linux

PUBLISHER
Canonical

NUMBER OF DISKS
1

PRICING INFORMATION
Pricing varies based on the subscription you select to provision your virtual machine.

← →

6. Click on **Next** and hit the **Finish** button:

CREATE A VIRTUAL MACHINE

Virtual machine configuration

VM AGENT

☑ Install the VM Agent

CONFIGURATION EXTENSIONS

☐ Chef
Published by: Chef Software, Inc | Learn more | Legal terms

Ubuntu Server 14.04 LTS

Ubuntu Server 14.04.3-LTS (amd64 20151020) for Microsoft Azure. Ubuntu Server is the world's most popular Linux for cloud environments. Updates and patches for Ubuntu 14.04.3-LTS will be available until 2019-04-17. Ubuntu Server is the perfect platform for all workloads from web applications to NoSQL databases and Hadoop. For more information see Ubuntu Cloud and using Juju to deploy your workloads.

OS FAMILY
Linux

PUBLISHER
Canonical

NUMBER OF DISKS
1

LEGAL TERMS

By clicking the Submit button, I acknowledge that I am getting this software from Canonical and that the legal terms of Canonical apply to it. Microsoft does not provide rights for third-party software. Also see the privacy statement from Canonical.

PRICING INFORMATION
Pricing varies based on the subscription you select to provision your virtual machine.

← ✓

Now, follow the same steps to launch `mesos-slave1` and `mesos-slave2`.

One thing to note here is that for every new machine that you are going to launch, if you want to access any of these machines from outside of the `mesos-cluster` endpoint, you will have to configure the SSH ports, as follows:

1. In the **Virtual machine configuration** Step, under **ENDPOINTS**, change the **PUBLIC PORT** value to another number:

   ENDPOINTS

NAME	PROTOCOL	PUBLIC PORT	PRIVATE PORT
SSH	TCP	44	22
ENTER OR SELECT A VALUE ∨			

2. Let's say the `mesos-master` public port was `22`; this means that suppose we perform the following:

   ```
   ssh mesos-cluster.cloudapp.net -p 22
   ```

3. This will log in to the `mesos-master` machine. Now if you want to log in to `mesos-slave1`, then you will configure the public port as `44` so that you can log in to `mesos-slave1`, as follows:

   ```
   ssh mesos-cluster.cloudapp.net -p 44
   ```

Configuring the network

For security reasons, whenever you deploy a machine in the cloud, always make sure that you have opened up the necessary ports to the public.

Apart from the SSH port, we also need to open up the Mesos UI port, which runs on `5050`. To do this, perform these steps:

1. From the Azure console, click on the **mesos-master** machine under the VMs provisioned and click on the **End Points**.

2. Now click on the **ADD** button to add a specific port:

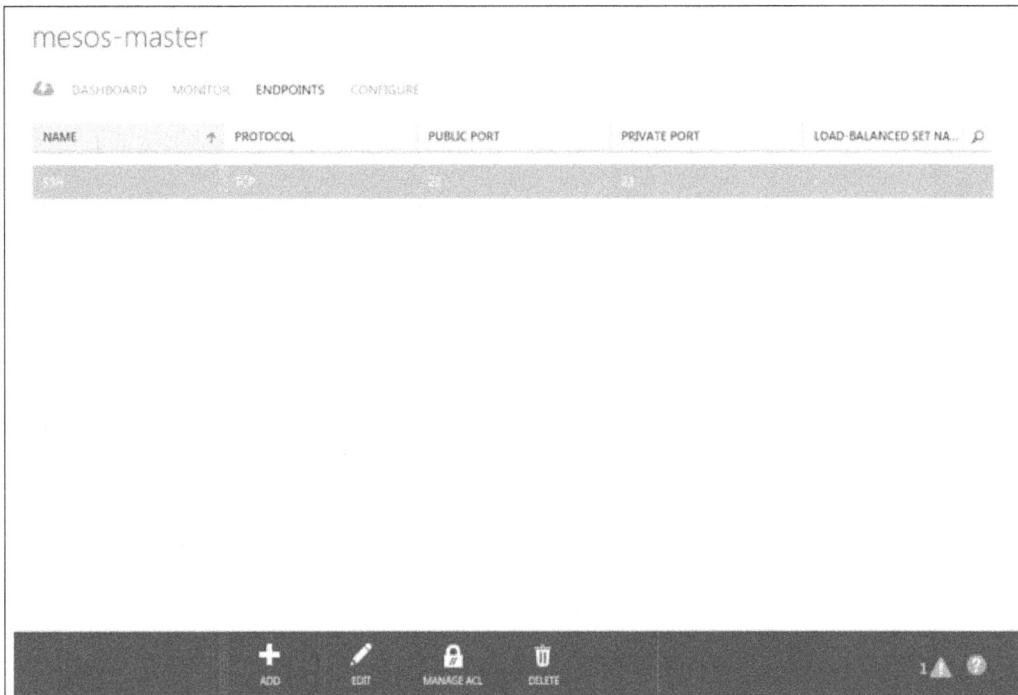

3. Choose the **ADD A STAND-ALONE ENDPOINT** option and click on **Next**:

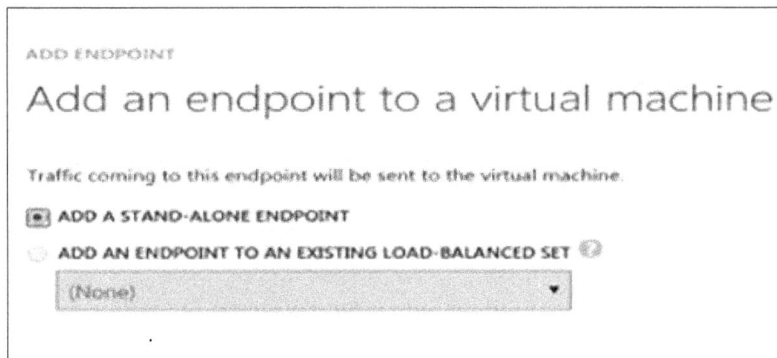

4. Name this `mesos-ui`, choose **TCP** from the protocol list, and use `5050`
   as **PUBLIC PORT**. This will allow you to access it with `http://mesos-cluster.cloudapp.net:5050` and assign port `5050` as **PRIVATE PORT**.
   Click on the **Finish** button:

Installing Mesos

By this point, you will have three machines up and running in the Azure cloud
named `mesos-master`, `mesos-slave1`, and `mesos-slave2`:

Now, log in to all three machines:

```
mesos-master: ssh mesos-cluster.cloudapp.net
mesos-slave1:  ssh mesos-cluster.cloudapp.net -p 23
mesos-slave2:  ssh mesos-cluster.cloudapp.net -p 24
```

It is ideal to use an advanced Linux Terminal, such as **terminator** or **xterm,** to work on multiple machines because these terminals support broadcasting the command. You can type the command on a single window, and it will be executed on all three machines at once, thereby reducing configuration work:

Now, we can install the dependency libraries and software packages on all three machines by typing in the following commands:

```
# Update the packages.
$ sudo apt-get update


# Install the latest OpenJDK.
$ sudo apt-get install -y openjdk-7-jdk


# Install autotools (Only necessary if building from git repository).
$ sudo apt-get install -y autoconf libtool


# Install other Mesos dependencies.
$ sudo apt-get -y install build-essential python-dev python-boto
  libcurl4-nss-dev libsasl2-dev maven libapr1-dev libsvn-dev
```

Now, our environment is ready, and we can start building the Mesos binary. You can build the Mesos binary from the master machine and then copy the build to the slave machines instead of building from all the machines.

Downloading Mesos

Follow the steps from the corresponding *Downloading Mesos* subsection under the *Setting up a multi-node Mesos cluster on Amazon Web Services (AWS)* section to download and extract Mesos on the master machine.

Building Mesos

Building Mesos is discussed in the corresponding *Building Mesos* subsection under the *Setting up a multi-node Mesos cluster on Amazon Web Services (AWS)* section. You can follow the instructions listed there to build Mesos on the master machine.

Once we build this, then we can copy the build directory from the `mesos-master` machine to the `mesos-slave1` and `mesos-slave2` machines:

```
mesos-master:~$ rsync -za mesos mesos-slave1:
mesos-master:~$ rsync -za mesos mesos-slave2:
```

Starting mesos-master

Issue the following command from the master machine to start `mesos-master`:

```
mesos-master:~/mesos/build$ ./bin/mesos-master.sh --work_dir=/var/lib/
mesos
```

After the command, you can see the following logs appearing in the Terminal:

```
I1108 08:26:52.525831 13306 main.cpp:229]
  Build: 2015-11-08 07:26:59 by akhld
I1108 08:26:52.526072 13306 main.cpp:231] Version: 0.25.0
I1108 08:26:52.526406 13306 main.cpp:252]
  Using 'HierarchicalDRF' allocator
I1108 08:26:52.623775 13306 leveldb.cpp:176] Opened db in 97.107324ms
I1108 08:26:52.712013 13306 leveldb.cpp:183]
  Compacted db in 88.081084ms
I1108 08:26:52.712218 13306 leveldb.cpp:198]
  Created db iterator in 72800ns
I1108 08:26:52.712327 13306 leveldb.cpp:204]
  Seeked to beginning of db in 25401ns
```

```
I1108 08:26:52.712745 13306 leveldb.cpp:273]
   Iterated through 3 keys in the db in 342201ns
I1108 08:26:52.713101 13306 replica.cpp:744]
   Replica recovered with log positions 5 -> 6 with
   0 holes and 0 unlearned
I1108 08:26:52.716048 13321 recover.cpp:449]
   Starting replica recovery
I1108 08:26:52.716660 13306 main.cpp:465]
   Starting Mesos master
..........
I1108 08:26:52.776047 13306 master.cpp:376]
   Master 090c9618-090f-49bd-aa95-265ec5f423d5 (100.73.76.103)
   started on 100.73.76.103:5050
```

The output here lists the build version, various configurations that the master has used, and the master ID of the cluster. The slave process should be able to connect to the master. The slave process can specify the IP address or the hostname of the master by the --master option.

Start mesos-slaves

Issue the following commands on the slave machines to start the slave service:

```
mesos-slave1:~/mesos/build$ ./bin/mesos-slave.sh
   --master=mesos-master:5050
mesos-slave1:~/mesos/build$ ./bin/mesos-slave.sh
   --master=mesos-master:5050


I1108 08:31:18.733666 26975 main.cpp:185]
   Build: 2015-11-08 07:26:59 by akhld
I1108 08:31:18.734257 26975 main.cpp:187]
   Version: 0.25.0
I1108 08:31:18.734724 26975 containerizer.cpp:143]
   Using isolation: posix/cpu,posix/mem,filesystem/posix
I1108 08:31:18.747735 26975 main.cpp:272]
   Starting Mesos slave
I1108 08:31:18.748929 26975 slave.cpp:190]
   Slave started on 1)@100.73.76.129:5051
```

This output confirms the connection to the master and lists the slave resources. Now, the cluster is running with two slaves and is ready to run the frameworks.

We can now make sure that the installation is complete by looking at the Mesos Web UI running on port 5050 on the master machine.

Open your browser and head on to the following URL: http://mesos-cluster. cloudapp.net:5050:

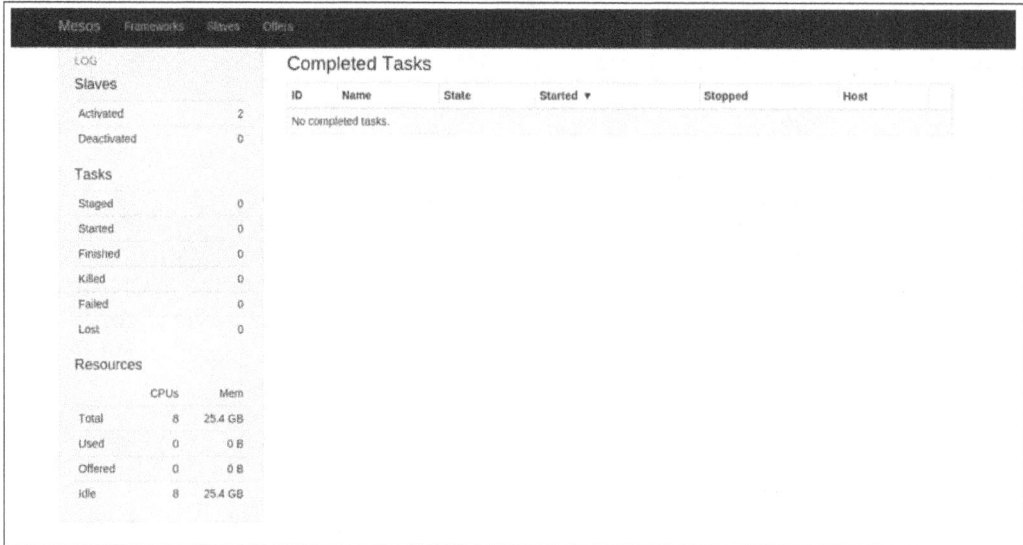

Mesos commands

If you look into the bin directory of Mesos, you can find the following executables, which can be used for various operations as listed here:

Command	Use
mesos-local.sh	This command launches an in-memory cluster within a single process.
mesos-tests.sh	This command runs the Mesos test case suite.
mesos.sh	This is a wrapper script, which is used to launch the Mesos commands. Running without any arguments shows all the available commands.
gdb-mesos-*	This command launches the corresponding processes in debugging mode using gdb.
lldb-mesos-*	This command launches the corresponding processes in debugging mode using lldb.
valgrind-mesos-*	This command launches the corresponding Valgrind instrumentation framework.

Command	Use
`mesos-daemon.sh`	This command starts/stops a Mesos daemon process.
`mesos-start-cluster.sh`	This command starts the Mesos cluster on nodes in the `[install-prefix]`/var/mesos/deploy/masters and `[install-prefix]`/var/mesos/deploy/slaves files.
`mesos-stop-cluster.sh`	This command stops the Mesos cluster on nodes in the `[install-prefix]`/var/mesos/deploy/masters and `[install-prefix]`/var/mesos/deploy/slaves files.
`mesos-start-masters.sh`	This command starts the Mesos masters on nodes listed in the masters file.
`mesos-stop-masters.sh`	This command stops the Mesos masters on nodes listed in the masters file.
`mesos-start-slaves.sh`	This command starts the Mesos slaves on nodes listed in the slaves file.
`mesos-stop-slaves.sh`	This command stops the Mesos slaves on nodes listed in the slaves file.

Testing the installation

We can now test the installation of our cluster by running the simple examples (C++, Java, and Python) that are shipped with Mesos:

```
# Run C++ framework (Exits after successfully running some tasks.).
mesos-master:~/mesos/build$ ./src/examples/test-framework
  --master=mesos-master:5050
```

The output will be as follows:

```
I1108 09:26:45.512217 23136 sched.cpp:164] Version: 0.25.0

I1108 09:26:45.524862 23156 sched.cpp:262]
  New master detected at master@100.73.76.103:5050

I1108 09:26:45.527117 23156 sched.cpp:272]
  No credentials provided.
Attempting to register without authentication

  I1108 09:26:45.531708 23157 sched.cpp:641]
Framework registered with
  5f18729d-c83a-4264-a50b-bd972b2d10f3-0006

Registered!

Received offer 5f18729d-c83a-4264-a50b-bd972b2d10f3-O11 with
  cpus(*):4; mem(*):13000; disk(*):23976; ports(*):[31000-32000]

Launching task 0 using offer
  5f18729d-c83a-4264-a50b-bd972b2d10f3-O11
```

```
Launching task 1 using offer
  5f18729d-c83a-4264-a50b-bd972b2d10f3-011

Launching task 2 using offer
  5f18729d-c83a-4264-a50b-bd972b2d10f3-011

Launching task 3 using offer
  5f18729d-c83a-4264-a50b-bd972b2d10f3-011

Received offer 5f18729d-c83a-4264-a50b-bd972b2d10f3-012 with
  cpus(*):4; mem(*):13000; disk(*):23976; ports(*):[31000-32000]

Launching task 4 using offer
  5f18729d-c83a-4264-a50b-bd972b2d10f3-012

Task 4 is in state TASK_RUNNING

Task 0 is in state TASK_RUNNING

Task 1 is in state TASK_RUNNING

Task 4 is in state TASK_FINISHED

Task 2 is in state TASK_RUNNING

Task 3 is in state TASK_RUNNING

Task 0 is in state TASK_FINISHED

Task 1 is in state TASK_FINISHED

Task 2 is in state TASK_FINISHED

Task 3 is in state TASK_FINISHED

I1108 09:26:45.719132 23154 sched.cpp:1771] Asked to stop the driver

I1108 09:26:45.719321 23154 sched.cpp:1040]
  Stopping framework '5f18729d-c83a-4264-a50b-bd972b2d10f3-0006'

I1108 09:26:45.720949 23136 sched.cpp:1771] Asked to stop the driver
```

```
I1108 09:26:45.531708 23157 sched.cpp:641] Framework registered with 5f18729d-c8
3a-4264-a50b-bd972b2d10f3-0006
Registered!
Received offer 5f18729d-c83a-4264-a50b-bd972b2d10f3-011 with cpus(*):4; mem(*):1
3000; disk(*):23976; ports(*):[31000-32000]
Launching task 0 using offer 5f18729d-c83a-4264-a50b-bd972b2d10f3-011
Launching task 1 using offer 5f18729d-c83a-4264-a50b-bd972b2d10f3-011
Launching task 2 using offer 5f18729d-c83a-4264-a50b-bd972b2d10f3-011
Launching task 3 using offer 5f18729d-c83a-4264-a50b-bd972b2d10f3-011
Received offer 5f18729d-c83a-4264-a50b-bd972b2d10f3-012 with cpus(*):4; mem(*):1
3000; disk(*):23976; ports(*):[31000-32000]
Launching task 4 using offer 5f18729d-c83a-4264-a50b-bd972b2d10f3-012
Task 4 is in state TASK RUNNING
Task 0 is in state TASK RUNNING
Task 1 is in state TASK RUNNING
Task 4 is in state TASK FINISHED
Task 2 is in state TASK RUNNING
Task 3 is in state TASK RUNNING
Task 0 is in state TASK FINISHED
Task 1 is in state TASK FINISHED
Task 2 is in state TASK FINISHED
Task 3 is in state TASK FINISHED
I1108 09:26:45.719132 23154 sched.cpp:1771] Asked to stop the driver
I1108 09:26:45.719321 23154 sched.cpp:1040] Stopping framework '5f18729d-c83a-42
64-a50b-bd972b2d10f3-0006'
I1108 09:26:45.720949 23136 sched.cpp:1771] Asked to stop the driver
akhld@akhldz:/tmp$
akhld@akhldz:/tmp$ cat lol
I1108 09:26:45.527117 23156 sched.cpp:272] No credentials provided. Attempting to register without authent
ication
I1108 09:26:45.531708 23157 sched.cpp:641] Framework registered with 5f18729d-c83a-4264-a50b-bd972b2d10f3-
0006
Registered!
Received offer 5f18729d-c83a-4264-a50b-bd972b2d10f3-011 with cpus(*):4; mem(*):13000; disk(*):23976; ports
(*):[31000-32000]
Launching task 0 using offer 5f18729d-c83a-4264-a50b-bd972b2d10f3-011
Launching task 1 using offer 5f18729d-c83a-4264-a50b-bd972b2d10f3-011
Launching task 2 using offer 5f18729d-c83a-4264-a50b-bd972b2d10f3-011
Launching task 3 using offer 5f18729d-c83a-4264-a50b-bd972b2d10f3-011
Received offer 5f18729d-c83a-4264-a50b-bd972b2d10f3-012 with cpus(*):4; mem(*):13000; disk(*):23976; ports
(*):[31000-32000]
```

You can also look at the status of the tasks from the Web UI:

```
# Run Java framework
  (Exits after successfully running some tasks)
  mesos-master:~/mesos/build$ ./src/examples/java/
  test-framework mesos-master:5050
```

```
# Run Python framework
  (Exits after successfully running some tasks)
mesos-master:~/mesos/build$ ./src/examples/python/
  test-framework mesos-master:5050
```

> To build the example frameworks, make sure that you build the
> test suite by performing the following:
> ```
> make check
> ```

Setting up a multi-node Mesos cluster on your private datacenter

In this section, we will explain how to get Mesos up and running on your fully-managed datacenter. For the sake of simplicity, let's assume you have a datacenter having three machines, and you are going to set up Mesos on top of these. Let's also assume your datacenter VMs are running the **CentOS 6.6** Linux distribution.

Consider that the following machines are opted in to install Mesos:

```
machine-a : 192.168.1.10
machine-b : 192.168.1.11
machine-c : 192.168.1.12
```

We will choose machine-a as the Mesos master machine for our cluster and machine-b, machine-c will be running the slave processes.

Installing Mesos

Below are the steps for installing a multi-node Mesos cluster on your private datacenter.

Preparing the environment

We need to install all the dependencies and libraries for Mesos to run on the CentOS machines. For this to happen we need to log in to all three machines and type in the following commands:

> Note that the following are the instructions for stock CentOS 6.6. If you
> are using a different OS, please install the packages accordingly.

```
# Issue the following command to
  install the wget command for your centos machine
$ sudo yum install -y tar wget
# We will need c++11 support which is available in the devtoolset-2.
  For that you will have to add it to the repo and then issue the
  installation command as follows:
$ sudo wget -O /etc/yum.repos.d/slc6-devtoolset.repo
  http://linuxsoft.cern.ch/cern/devtoolset/slc6-devtoolset.repo
# Import the CERN GPG key.
$ sudo rpm --import
  http://linuxsoft.cern.ch/cern/centos/7/os/x86_64/RPM-GPG-KEY-cern
# Fetch the Apache Maven repo file.
$ sudo wget
  http://repos.fedorapeople.org/repos/dchen/apache-maven/
epel-apache-maven.repo -O /etc/yum.repos.d/epel-apache-maven.repo
# 'Mesos > 0.21.0' requires 'subversion > 1.8' devel package,
# which is not available in the default repositories.
# Add the WANdisco SVN repo file:
'/etc/yum.repos.d/wandisco-svn.repo' with content:

[WANdiscoSVN]
name=WANdisco SVN Repo 1.8
enabled=1
baseurl=http://opensource.wandisco.com/centos/6/
  svn-1.8/RPMS/$basearch/
gpgcheck=1
gpgkey=http://opensource.wandisco.com/RPM-GPG-KEY-WANdisco


# Now we can install the development tools which will contain
  the utilities like make for your our installation
$ sudo yum groupinstall -y "Development Tools"
# Install 'devtoolset-2-toolchain' which includes
  GCC 4.8.2 and related packages.
$ sudo yum install -y devtoolset-2-toolchain
# Now we can install the mesos related dependency for centos.
$ sudo yum install -y apache-maven python-devel
  java-1.7.0-openjdk-devel zlib-devel libcurl-devel openssl-devel
  cyrus-sasl-devel cyrus-sasl-md5 apr-devel subversion-devel
  apr-util-devel
# Now we can enable the devtoolset for the shell.
$ scl enable devtoolset-2 bash
$ g++ --version
# At this point make sure we get the gcc+ version > 4.8.
```

Downloading Mesos

Follow the steps from the corresponding *Downloading Mesos* subsection under the *Setting up a multi-node Mesos cluster on Amazon Web Services (AWS)* section to download and extract Mesos on the master machine.

Building Mesos

We can follow the steps as mentioned in the previous section to build Mesos on the master machine.

Now, we can copy the build directory from `machine-a` to `machine-b` and `machine-c` from the master machine:

```
machine-a:~$ rsync -za mesos machine-b:
machine-a:~$ rsync -za mesos machine-c:
```

Starting mesos-master

Issue the following command from the master machine to start `mesos-master`:

```
machine-a:~/mesos/build$ ./bin/mesos-master.sh --
  work_dir=/var/lib/mesos --ip=192.168.1.10
```

Starting mesos-slaves

Now, we can issue the following command from the slave machines to start the slave services:

```
machine-b:~/mesos/build$ ./bin/mesos-slave.sh
--   master=192.168.1.10:5050
```

```
machine-c:~/mesos/build$ ./bin/mesos-slave.sh
--   master=192.168.1.10:5050
```

We can now make sure the installation is complete by looking at the Mesos Web UI running on port `5050` on the master machine.

Open your browser and head on to the following URL: `http://192.168.1.10:5050`:

Automating the process when you have many machines

We can repeat the previous procedure to manually start `mesos-slave` on each of the slave nodes to set up the cluster, but this is labor-intensive and error-prone for large clusters. Mesos includes a set of scripts in the `deploy` folder that can be used to deploy Mesos on a cluster. These scripts rely on SSH to perform the deployment.

We will set up a cluster with 10 slave nodes (`slave1`, `slave2`, `slave10`) and a master node (master).

Let's configure our cluster to make sure that they have connectivity between them after installing all the prerequisites on all the nodes. The following commands will generate an SSH key and will copy them to all the slaves:

```
master:~ $ ssh-keygen -f ~/.ssh/id_rsa -P ""
```

```
master:~ $ ssh-copy-id -i ~/.ssh/id_rsa.pub slave1
```

```
master:~ $ ssh-copy-id -i ~/.ssh/id_rsa.pub slave2
```

```
master:~ $ ssh-copy-id -i ~/.ssh/id_rsa.pub slave3

master:~ $ ssh-copy-id -i ~/.ssh/id_rsa.pub slave4

master:~ $ ssh-copy-id -i ~/.ssh/id_rsa.pub slave5

master:~ $ ssh-copy-id -i ~/.ssh/id_rsa.pub slave6

master:~ $ ssh-copy-id -i ~/.ssh/id_rsa.pub slave7

master:~ $ ssh-copy-id -i ~/.ssh/id_rsa.pub slave8

master:~ $ ssh-copy-id -i ~/.ssh/id_rsa.pub slave9

master:~ $ ssh-copy-id -i ~/.ssh/id_rsa.pub slave10
```

We need to copy the Mesos build to all the nodes at the same location, as in the master:

```
master:~ $ scp -R build slave1:[install-prefix]
master:~ $ scp -R build slave2:[install-prefix]
master:~ $ scp -R build slave3:[install-prefix]
master:~ $ scp -R build slave4:[install-prefix]
master:~ $ scp -R build slave5:[install-prefix]
master:~ $ scp -R build slave6:[install-prefix]
master:~ $ scp -R build slave7:[install-prefix]
master:~ $ scp -R build slave8:[install-prefix]
master:~ $ scp -R build slave9:[install-prefix]
master:~ $ scp -R build slave10:[install-prefix]
```

Create a masters file in the [install-prefix]/var/mesos/deploy/masters directory with an editor of your choice to list the masters one per line, which in our case will be only the following one:

```
master:~ $ cat [install-prefix]/var/mesos/deploy/masters

master
```

Similarly, the slaves file will list all the nodes that we want to be Mesos slaves:

```
master:~ $ cat [install-prefix]/var/mesos/deploy/slaves
slave1
slave2
slave3
slave4
slave5
slave6
slave7
slave8
slave9
slave10
```

Now, we can start the cluster with the `mesos-start-cluster` script and use `mesos-stop-cluster` to stop it:

```
master:~ $ mesos-start-cluster.sh
```

This in turn calls `mesos-start-masters` and `mesos-start-slaves` that will start the appropriate processes on the master and slave nodes. The script looks for any environment configurations in `[install-prefix]/var/mesos/deploy/mesos-deploy-env.sh`. Also, for better configuration management, the master and slave configuration options can be specified in separate files in `[install-prefix]/var/mesos/deploy/mesos-master-env.sh` and `[install-prefix]/var/mesos/deploy/mesos-slave-env.sh`.

Debugging and troubleshooting

In this section, we will look at how to troubleshoot and debug the common issues faced during setup.

Handling missing library dependencies

Sometimes, when you try to build Mesos on a brand new Linux VM, it may throw up errors in the configure step. An example is a missing `libz-dev` package:

```
configure: error: cannot find libz
-----------------------------------------------------------------
libz is required for Mesos to build.
-----------------------------------------------------------------
```

Whenever you find an error such as the preceding one or something similar to a missing package, the next thing that you need to do is to install these missing packages and execute the `configure` command again.

Here, to resolve the missing `libz` library, you will have to type in the following on the *Ubuntu* machine:

```
$ sudo apt-get install libz-dev
```

For *CentOS* flavors, the command will be as follows:

```
$ yum install zlib-devel
```

Issues with directory permissions

If Mesos is trying to write to `/var/lib/mesos` and if you missed assigning the correct permissions over the directory, this will end up with the following error:

```
mkdir: cannot create directory '/var/lib/mesos': Permission denied
```

To overcome such issues, you will have to assign proper permission to this directory with the following command:

```
$ sudo chown `whoami` /var/lib/mesos
```

Missing Mesos library (libmesos*.so not found)

Whenever you get **libmesos*.so file not found**, then the best thing you can do is to *copy* the `libmesos*.so` from your Mesos installation to the `/lib` directory.

An example of such an error is as follows:

```
/home/akhld/mesos/build/src/.libs/test-executor:
   error while loading shared libraries: libmesos-0.25.0.so:
   cannot open shared object file: No such file or directory
```

Debugging a failed framework

Sometimes, if your cluster is not configured properly or you have a buggy framework, then it will not succeed in its execution. In such a situation, you can open up the Mesos web interface and click on the failed **Framework** under the **Frameworks** tab, as follows:

Here, you can see the tasks marked as **KILLED** for some reason, and your next step is to find out why.

Understanding the Mesos directory structure

On every slave machine, by default, the Mesos work directory lies under `/tmp/mesos`, and under `/tmp/mesos/slaves/` will have `slave id`, which will keep track of the frameworks running under it inside the `frameworks` directory. The framework will contain the number of attempts that it made to execute the given job, and each run attempt's information will be logged in the `runs` directory. You can find the errors and standard output from the `stderr` and `stdout` files located under the runs.

Here's an example directory structure with a single executor instance and multiple frameworks:

```
akhld@mesos-slave2:~/mesos/build$ tree /tmp/mesos/
/tmp/mesos/
├── meta
│   ├── boot_id
│   ├── resources
│   │   └── resources.info
│   └── slaves
│       ├── 63088700-3d5d-4490-a3df-a3f85fe62a01-S1
│       │   └── slave.info
│       └── latest -> /tmp/mesos/meta/slaves/63088700-3d5d-4490-a3df-a3f85fe62a01-S1
├── provisioner
└── slaves
    └── 63088700-3d5d-4490-a3df-a3f85fe62a01-S1
        └── frameworks
            ├── 5f18729d-c83a-4264-a50b-bd972b2d10f3-0000
            │   └── executors
            │       └── default
            │           └── runs
            │               ├── 6c338bdb-9076-477e-a93c-469eed2f307e
            │               │   ├── stderr
            │               │   └── stdout
            │               └── latest -> /tmp/mesos/slaves/63088700-3d5d-4490-a3df-a3f85fe62a01-S1/frameworks/5f18729d-c83a-4264-a50b-bd97
2b2d10f3-0000/executors/default/runs/6c338bdb-9076-477e-a93c-469eed2f307e
            ├── ed4b8897-6c4b-4b14-8575-4a828731785d-0000
            │   └── executors
            │       └── default
            │           └── runs
            │               ├── ceb77308-ce6d-46e0-a7d8-a8557ae236e2
            │               │   ├── stderr
            │               │   └── stdout
            │               └── latest -> /tmp/mesos/slaves/63088700-3d5d-4490-a3df-a3f85fe62a01-S1/frameworks/ed4b8897-6c4b-4b14-8575-4a82
8731785d-0000/executors/default/runs/ceb77308-ce6d-46e0-a7d8-a8557ae236e2
            └── ed4b8897-6c4b-4b14-8575-4a828731785d-0001
```

Now, to track down our issue, you need to go to the corresponding framework ID and look in the `stderr` file, which will log the exact issue that this framework was facing.

Let's take the following example:

```
$ cat /tmp/mesos/slaves/
  63088700-3d5d-4490-a3df-a3f85fe62a01-S1/
  frameworks/ed4b8897-6c4b-4b14-8575-4a828731785d-
  0001/executors/default/runs/latest/stderr

  /var/lib/mesos/: Permission denied
```

Now that you know the issue is with the directory permission, you can fix this using the steps described in the previous section.

Mesos slaves are not connecting with Mesos masters

Issues such as slaves failing to connect with the master can be resolved in two ways:

- Looking at the slave console logs.

  You can look at the console logs while the slave tries to connect to the master, and this will show connection failure messages, such as **Operation timed out**, **Connection refused**, **Network unreachable**, and so on.

- Making sure that the master and slaves bind to the correct network interface.

  Make sure that your master and slaves bind to the correct network interface; it is always safer to use `--ip` option to ensure this.

Launching multiple slave instances on the same machine

If you try to launch multiple slave processes on the same machine, then you will end up with the following exception:

```
Failed to initialize, bind: Address already in use [98]
```

If you need to launch more slave instances on a single machine, there is a way to accomplish this.

You can run one more slave but you have to specify a port and a different `workdir` using the following:

```
./mesos-slave.sh --master=<ipaddr>:<port> --ip=<ip of slave>
  --work_dir=<work_dir other than that of a running slave>
  --port=<another_port>
```

> Can Mesos `master` and `slave` nodes be deployed on the same machines?
>
> You can definitely run `master` and multiple `slave` processes on the same node. You can even run multiple `master` and `slave` processes on the same node, provided that you give them each unique ports, but this works best only for a test cluster.

Summary

In this chapter, we saw how to manually set up and run a Mesos cluster on the public cloud (AWS, GCE, and Azure) as well as on a private datacenter (on the premises). We also discussed common errors that are faced during the setup process and how these can be debugged and resolved efficiently.

In the next chapter, we will explore important scheduling and management frameworks, such as Marathon and Chronos, that often go hand in hand with Mesos and are integral components of the Mesos ecosystem.

4
Service Scheduling and Management Frameworks

This chapter introduces several Mesos-based scheduling and management frameworks or applications that are required for the easy deployment, discovery, load balancing, and failure handling of long-running services. These so-called metaframeworks take care of the *housekeeping* activities of other frameworks and applications, such as **service discovery** (that is, keeping track of the instances on which a particular service is running) and **load balancing** (ensuring an equitable workload distribution among the instances), apart from **configuration management**, **automated job scheduling**, **application scaling**, and **failure handling**. The frameworks that we'll explore here include:

- **Marathon**: This is used to launch and manage long-running applications on Mesos

- **Chronos**: This is a cluster scheduler

- **Apache** Aurora: This is a framework for long-running services and cron jobs

- **Singularity**: This is a platform-as-a-service (PaaS) for running services

- **Marathoner**: This conducts service discovery for Marathon

- **Consul**: This carries out service discovery and orchestration

- **HAProxy**: This is used for load balancing

- **Bamboo**: This is used to automatically configure HAProxy for Mesos and Marathon

In addition, we'll briefly touch upon two very recent open source frameworks, namely **Netflix Fenzo** (a task scheduler) and **Yelp's PaaSTA** (a PaaS for running services).

Using Marathon to launch and manage long-running applications on Mesos

Marathon is a commonly used Mesos framework for long-running applications. It can be considered a replacement for init or upstart in traditional systems or as the init.d of your system.

Marathon has many features, such as controlling a high availability environment, checking the applications' health, and so on. It also comes with **Representational State Transfer (REST)**, such as endpoint, which you can use to start, stop, and scale your applications. It can be used to scale up and down the cluster based on the load, which means that it should be able to start a new instance just in case an available one goes down. Marathon is also designed to run other frameworks on it, such as **Hadoop**, **Kafka**, **Storm**, **Chronos**, and so on. Marathon makes sure that every application that is started through it keeps running even if a slave node goes down.

Marathon runs in a highly available fashion, which implies that there can be multiple schedulers running in the cluster, but at any given point of time, there is only one leader. Whenever an application requests a nonleader, the request will be proxied to the active leader. You can also use HAProxy (explained later in this chapter) for service discovery and load balancing.

Marathon also supports basic authentication mechanisms and uses SSL to encrypt connections.

Installing Marathon

Visit https://mesosphere.github.io/marathon/ to download the latest Marathon release. At the time of writing this book, the latest version is 0.13.0.

Marathon can be downloaded as follows:

```
$ wget http://downloads.mesosphere.com/marathon/v0.13.0/
  marathon-0.13.0.tgz
```

After downloading, extract the files as follows:

```
$ tar xf marathon-0.13.0.tgz
```

You can see the following files once you extract Marathon:

```
akhld@spark-ak-slave:~/marathon-0.13.0$ ls
bin  Dockerfile  docs  examples  LICENSE  README.md  target
akhld@spark-ak-slave:~/marathon-0.13.0$ ls bin/
build-distribution        run-tests-config-template.sh  servicerouter.py
haproxy-marathon-bridge   run-tests-in-loop.sh          start
marathon-framework        run-tests.sh
akhld@spark-ak-slave:~/marathon-0.13.0$
```

There is a development mode for Marathon in which you don't need a distributed Mesos setup. This is called the Marathon local mode. The local mode is for experimental purposes only, and it is not recommended to run it in any production environment. ZooKeeper is required alongside Marathon to store the state.

Installing ZooKeeper to store the state

Marathon requires you to have an Apache ZooKeeper instance up and running for it to be able to save a state. Perform the following steps to install and work with ZooKeeper:

1. Visit `https://zookeeper.apache.org` to download the latest version of ZooKeeper. At the time of writing this book, the current version is 3.4.7.

2. Download ZooKeeper as follows:

    ```
    $ wget https://archive.apache.org/dist/zookeeper/zookeeper-3.4.7/
    zookeeper-3.4.7.tar.gz
    ```

3. After downloading, extract the archive as given here:

    ```
    $ tar xf zookeeper-3.4.7.tar.gz
    ```

4. The next step is to configure ZooKeeper. This can be done as follows:

    Edit the file `conf/zoo.cfg` with the following contents:

    ```
    tickTime=2000
    dataDir=/var/zookeeper
    clientPort=2181
    ```

5. Then, run the following command to start ZooKeeper:

    ```
    $ bin/zkServer.sh start
    ```

You can see the following messages once you start it successfully:

```
akhld@spark-ak-slave:~/zookeeper-3.4.7$ bin/zkServer.sh start
ZooKeeper JMX enabled by default
Using config: /home/akhld/zookeeper-3.4.7/bin/../conf/zoo.cfg
Starting zookeeper ... STARTED
```

Launching Marathon in local mode

The following command launches Marathon in local mode:

```
$ ./bin/start --master local --zk zk://localhost:2181/marathon
```

```
[2015-12-11 18:37:09,366] INFO Binding mesosphere.marathon.api.v2.QueueResource to GuiceManagedComponentProvider with the scope "Singleton" (com.sun.jersey.guice.spi.cont
ainer.GuiceComponentProviderFactory:HttpService$$EnhancerByGuice$$35ed93bd STARTING)
[2015-12-11 18:37:09,371] INFO Binding mesosphere.marathon.api.v2.GroupsResource to GuiceManagedComponentProvider with the scope "Singleton" (com.sun.jersey.guice.spi.con
tainer.GuiceComponentProviderFactory:HttpService$$EnhancerByGuice$$35ed93bd STARTING)
[2015-12-11 18:37:09,372] INFO Binding mesosphere.marathon.api.v2.InfoResource to GuiceManagedComponentProvider with the scope "Singleton" (com.sun.jersey.guice.spi.conta
iner.GuiceComponentProviderFactory:HttpService$$EnhancerByGuice$$35ed93bd STARTING)
[2015-12-11 18:37:09,373] INFO Binding mesosphere.marathon.api.v2.LeaderResource to GuiceManagedComponentProvider with the scope "Singleton" (com.sun.jersey.guice.spi.con
tainer.GuiceComponentProviderFactory:HttpService$$EnhancerByGuice$$35ed93bd STARTING)
[2015-12-11 18:37:09,376] INFO Binding mesosphere.marathon.api.v2.DeploymentsResource to GuiceManagedComponentProvider with the scope "Singleton" (com.sun.jersey.guice.sp
i.container.GuiceComponentProviderFactory:HttpService$$EnhancerByGuice$$35ed93bd STARTING)
[2015-12-11 18:37:09,386] INFO Binding mesosphere.marathon.api.v2.ArtifactsResource to GuiceManagedComponentProvider with the scope "Singleton" (com.sun.jersey.guice.spi.
container.GuiceComponentProviderFactory:HttpService$$EnhancerByGuice$$35ed93bd STARTING)
[2015-12-11 18:37:09,388] INFO Binding mesosphere.marathon.api.v2.SchemaResource to GuiceManagedComponentProvider with the scope "Singleton" (com.sun.jersey.guice.spi.con
tainer.GuiceComponentProviderFactory:HttpService$$EnhancerByGuice$$35ed93bd STARTING)
[2015-12-11 18:37:09,405] INFO Started o.e.j.s.ServletContextHandler@2c99f679{/,null,AVAILABLE} (org.eclipse.jetty.server.handler.ContextHandler:HttpService$$EnhancerByGu
ice$$35ed93bd STARTING)
[2015-12-11 18:37:09,422] INFO Started ServerConnector@40a03845{HTTP/1.1,[http/1.1]}{0.0.0.0:8080} (org.eclipse.jetty.server.ServerConnector:HttpService$$EnhancerByGuice$
$35ed93bd STARTING)
[2015-12-11 18:37:09,424] INFO Started @5954ms (org.eclipse.jetty.server.Server:HttpService$$EnhancerByGuice$$35ed93bd STARTING)
[2015-12-11 18:37:09,425] INFO All services up and running. (mesosphere.marathon.Main$:main)
```

Once it is up and running, the Marathon UI can be seen by pointing your browser to the `8080` port on the server.

Multi-node Marathon cluster setup

To set this up, a high availability Mesos cluster needs to be set up, which will be explained in detail in *Chapter 5*, *Mesos Cluster Deployment*. For the time being, we assume that you already have a high availability Mesos cluster up and running. We'll now take a look at how to install Marathon on all the master machines in the cluster.

Log in to all the Mesos master machines and type in the following commands to set up Marathon.

On *Debain/Ubuntu* machines, run the following command:

```
# Update the repositories
# Setup
$ sudo apt-key adv --keyserver hkp://keyserver.ubuntu.com:80 --recv
E56151BF
$ DISTRO=$(lsb_release -is | tr '[:upper:]' '[:lower:]')
$ CODENAME=$(lsb_release -cs)


# Add the repository
$ echo "deb http://repos.mesosphere.com/${DISTRO} ${CODENAME} main" | \
  sudo tee /etc/apt/sources.list.d/mesosphere.list
$ sudo apt-get update
# Install Marathon
$ sudo apt-get -y install marathon
```

On *RedHat/CentOS* machines, execute the following command:

```
$ sudo yum -y install marathon
```

You can now head to any one of the master machine's 8080 port in the browser and take a look at the Marathon UI:

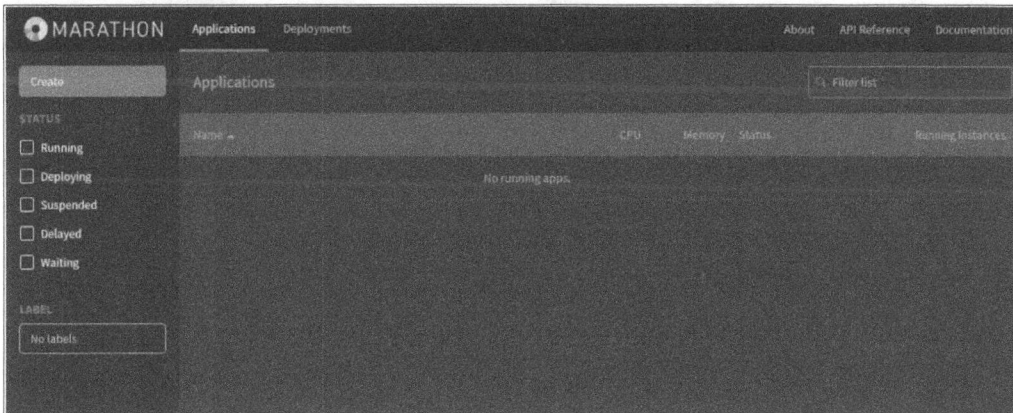

Launching a test application from the UI

An application in Mesos is normally a long-running service that can be scaled to run on multiple instances. Now, we will look at the steps to launch a test application from the user interface:

New Application

ID

```
marathon-test
```

CPUs	Memory (MiB)	Disk Space (MiB)	Instances
1	16	0	1

Command

```
while [ true ] ; do echo 'Hello Marathon' ; sleep 5 ; done
```

May be left blank if a container image is supplied

> Docker container settings

> Environment variables

> Labels

> Health checks

> Optional settings

[+ Create] [Cancel]

1. Click on the **+ Create** button in the upper-left corner.
2. The **ID** can be used to identify the job. Let's name it `marathon-test`.
3. Mention the number of CPUs that are required for the job—say, `1`.
4. Memory is given in MBs, so we will give it `16` MB (which is also the default).
5. The number of instances can be given as 1 for our test application.
6. Write the following bash script in the text box under the command:

   ```
   while [ true ] ; do echo 'Hello Marathon' ; sleep 5 ; done
   ```

If everything is correct, you can see the **marathon-test** test application first with the **Deployed** status, which will finally change to **Running**.

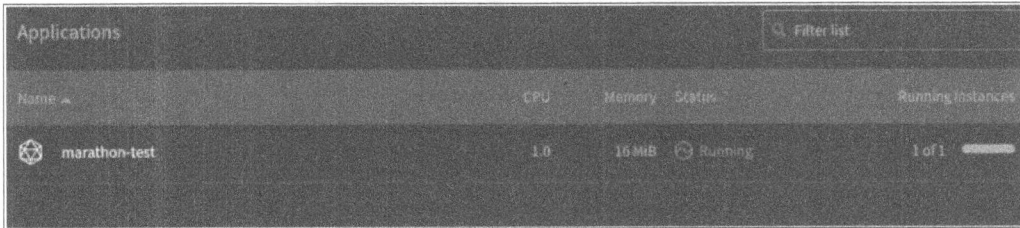

Scaling the application

At the time of creation, we gave 1 as the instance. We can modify the number of instances by clicking on the Scale Application button from the UI. The application will be scaled by launching it on the number of instances specified.

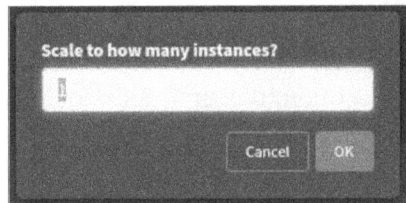

Terminating the application

We can now terminate our marathon-test application by clicking on the application name from the Applications list and then hitting the **Destroy** button.

Destroying the application is an irreversible process and cannot be undone.

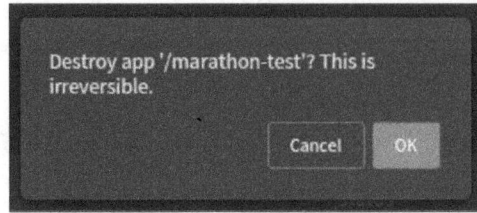

Chronos as a cluster scheduler

One can consider Chronos as a time-based job scheduler, such as **cron** in the typical Unix environment. Chronos is distributed and fully fault-tolerant, and it runs on top of Apache Mesos.

Just like cron, Chronos executes the shell scripts (combined with Linux commands) by default and also supports Mesos executors.

Chronos can interact with systems such as Hadoop or Kafka even if the Mesos worker machine, on which the real execution happens, does not have the system installed. You can use Chronos to start a service or run a script on a remote machine in the background. The wrapper script can have an asynchronous callback to alert Chronos to the job status, such as whether it is completed or failed and so on. For the most part, people use Chronos to run dockerized applications. A detailed explanation of *dockerized applications* is provided in *Chapter 7, Mesos Containerizers*.

Chronos comes with a Web UI in which you can see the job status, statistics of the job's history, job configurations, and retries.

Installing Chronos

Log in to any of the machines (let's say, one of the Mesos master machines) and type in the following commands to set up Chronos.

On *Debain/Ubuntu* machines, run the following:

```
# Install chronos
$ sudo apt-get -y install chronos
# Start the chronos server
$ sudo service chronos start
```

On *RedHat/CentOS* machines, execute the following code:

```
# Install chronos
$ sudo yum -y install chronos
# Start the chronos server
$ sudo service chronos start
```

Once the installation is complete, you can point the browser to the machine's `4400` port to see the Chronos UI, as follows:

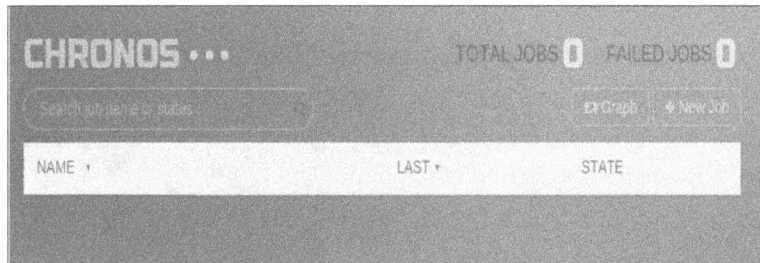

Scheduling a new job

Let's follow the steps mentioned here to schedule a new job:

1. Click on the **+ New Job** button, as seen in the previous screenshot.

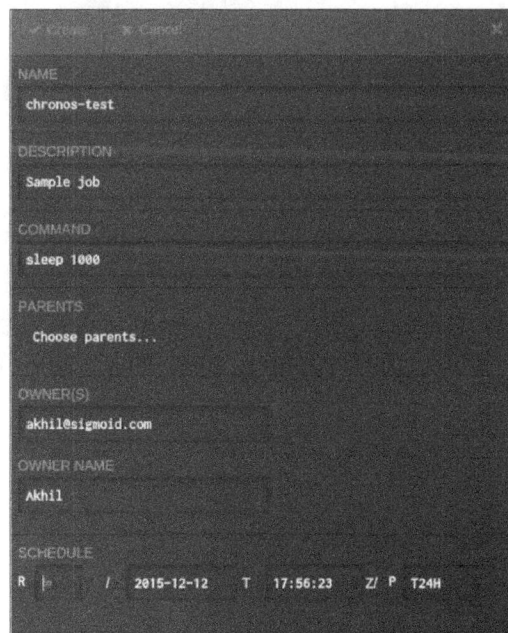

2. Now, fill in the **NAME** and **DESCRIPTION** fields.

3. **COMMAND** is the actual job that will be scheduled to run on the executors. For the sake of simplicity, we will simply run the `sleep` command.

4. In the **OWNER(S)** field, we can fill in the name and e-mail address to which Chronos will send an alert mail in the case of any job failure.

5. Under **SCHEDULE**, we can put in the scheduling frequency at which the job should run. By default, it is empty and infinity. We can set it to any numeric value. For instance, the number of repetitions when the value is set to 0 is only one.

Once the job is created, we can see the summary of the job through the UI, as shown in the following screenshot:

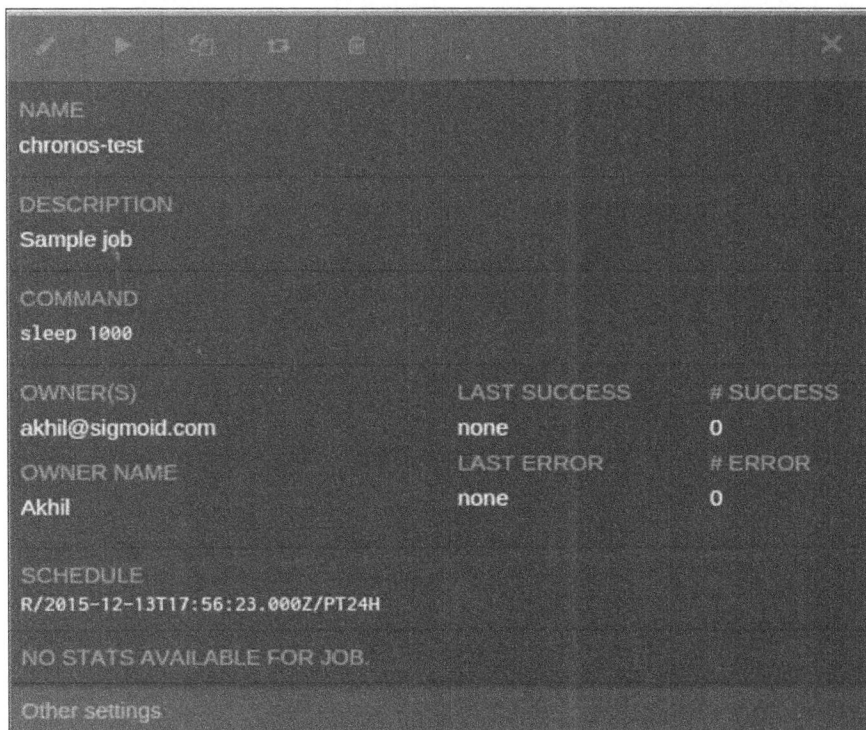

The state of the job can also be seen as in the following screenshot. In this case, we can note that the **chronos-test** job is in the **running** state:

NAME ▾	LAST ▾	STATE
chronos-test	fresh	running

We can head to the Mesos UI (running on the port 5050) and actually see the task being spawned by Chronos.

Active Tasks

ID	Name	State	Started ▾	Host	
ct:1449942983000:0:chronos-test:	ChronosTask:chronos-test	RUNNING	4 minutes ago	100.76.126.34	Sandbox

Chronos plus Marathon

The combination of Chronos and Marathon can be utilized as building blocks to create production-ready distributed applications. You already know that Chronos can be used to fire up tasks at scheduled intervals; cron and Marathon let your jobs run continuously, such as `init` or `upstart`, in typical Linux environments. As mentioned before, both the schedulers come with a REST endpoint that allows the user to manage the jobs. You can use this endpoint to start, manage, and terminate the running jobs. We will now take a look at how this is achieved.

The Chronos REST API endpoint

As mentioned before, you can communicate with Chronos using the REST JSON API over HTTP. By default, those nodes that have Chronos up and running listen at the `8080` port for API requests. This section covers how to perform the following tasks using the REST endpoint:

1. Listing the running jobs
2. Manually starting a job
3. Adding a scheduled job
4. Deleting a job

For more information, visit `http://mesos.github.io/chronos/docs/api.html`.

Listing the running jobs

Using the HTTP GET method on /scheduler/jobs will return a list of currently running jobs in the JSON format.

Here's an example:

```
$ curl -L -X GET localhost:8080/scheduler/jobs
```

The following data is present in the response:

- successCount
- errorCount
- lastSuccess
- lastError
- executor
- parents

Manually starting a job

To start a job manually, send an HTTP PUT request to /scheduler/job with optional parameters that can be added at the end of the command.

Take a look at the following example:

```
$ curl -L -X PUT localhost:8080/scheduler/job/job_a?arguments=-debug
```

Adding a scheduled job

You can send an HTTP POST request to /scheduler/iso8601 with the JSON data to schedule a job. The JSON data that you post to Chronos must contain the following fields:

- name
- command
- schedule
- The number of times to repeat the job;
- Start time of the job in ISO 8601 format;
- Standard ISO 8601 date time format
- scheduleTimeZone
- epsilon
- owner
- async

Take a look at the following example:

```
$ curl -L -H 'Content-Type: application/json'
  -X POST -d '{
  "schedule": "<some_value>", "name": "jab_a", "epsilon"
  : "....", "command": "echo 'FOO'
  >> /tmp/job_a_OUT", "owner": "akhil@sigmoid.com", "async": false
  }' localhost:8080/scheduler/iso8601
```

Deleting a job

To delete jobs, you can use `HTTP DELETE` on `/scheduler/job/<jobName>`, where `jobName` can be obtained from the list of running jobs.

Here's an example:

```
$ curl -L -X DELETE localhost:8080/scheduler/job/job_a
```

Deleting all the tasks of a job

To delete all the tasks of a given job, you can use the `HTTP DELETE` request on `/scheduler/task/kill/<jobName>`.

Take a look at the following example:

```
$ curl -L -X DELETE localhost:8080/scheduler/task/kill/job_a
```

The Marathon REST API endpoint

This section will cover the REST endpoint of Marathon. The following tasks can be performed:

1. Listing the running applications.
2. Adding an application.
3. Changing the configuration.
4. Deleting an application.

Listing the running applications

You can hit the `/v2/apps` endpoint with the `HTTP GET` request to list the running applications that are deployed on Marathon. It also supports a filter that helps you limit the listing to a particular application.

The following are the parameters that the endpoint takes:

- cmd: This filters the apps that contain the given command
- embed: This can be used to specify multiple values multiple times, and it embeds the nested resources that match the supplied path

Here's an example:

```
$ curl -L -X GET "localhost:8080/v2/apps?cmd=sleep 60"
```

You can take a look at the response in a JSON format similar to the following:

```
{
  "apps": [
    {
      "id": "/product/us-east/service/myapp",
      "cmd": "env && sleep 60",
      "constraints": [
        [
          "hostname",
          "UNIQUE",
          ""
        ]
      ],
      "container": null,
      "cpus": 0.1,
      "env": {
        "LD_LIBRARY_PATH": "/usr/local/lib/myLib"
      },
      "executor": "",
      "instances": 3,
      "mem": 5.0,
      "ports": [
        15092,
        14566
      ],
      "tasksRunning": 1,
      "tasksStaged": 0,
      "uris": [
        "https://raw.github.com/Mesosphere/Marathon/master/README.md"
      ],
      "version": "2014-03-01T23:42:20.938Z"
    }
  ]
}
```

Adding an application

To create and start an application from the REST endpoint, you can use the `/v2/apps` endpoint with an HTTP POST request. It takes JSON data as the input, which contains information about the application. The following are the parameters that are required for this call:

- `id`: This is the name of the application
- `cmd`: This is the command to be executed
- `args`: These are optional arguments of the application
- `cpus`: This is the number of CPU cores to be allocated for this application
- `mem`: This is the amount of memory to be allocated for the application
- `ports`: This is to be reserved for the application
- `instances`: This is the number of instances to deploy the application

The following example shows how to launch a simple Python HTTP server as an application in Marathon:

```
$ curl -L -H 'Content-Type: application/json' -X POST -d
'{
  "args": null,
  "backoffFactor": 1.15,
  "backoffSeconds": 1,
  "maxLaunchDelaySeconds": 3600,
  "cmd": "env && python3 -m http.server $PORT0",
  "constraints": [
    [
      "hostname",
      "UNIQUE"
    ]
  ],
  "container": {
    "Docker": {
      "image": "python:3"
    },
    "type": "DOCKER",
    "volumes": []
  },
  "cpus": 0.25,
  "dependencies": [],
  "deployments": [
    {
```

```
          "id": "f44fd4fc-4330-4600-a68b-99c7bd33014a"
      }
   ],
   "disk": 0.0,
   "env": {},
   "executor": "",
   "healthChecks": [
      {
          "command": null,
          "gracePeriodSeconds": 3,
          "intervalSeconds": 10,
          "maxConsecutiveFailures": 3,
          "path": "/",
          "portIndex": 0,
          "protocol": "HTTP",
          "timeoutSeconds": 5
      }
   ],
   "id": "/my-app",
   "instances": 2,
   "mem": 50.0,
   "ports": [
      0
   ],
   "requirePorts": false,
   "storeUrls": [],
   "upgradeStrategy": {
      "minimumHealthCapacity": 0.5,
      "maximumOverCapacity": 0.5
   },
   "uris": [],
   "user": null,
   "version": "2014-08-18T22:36:41.451Z"
}

' localhost:8080/v2/apps
```

Also, note that if the given ID of the application already exists in Marathon, it will throw a duplication error and won't launch the application at all.

Changing the configuration of an application

You can send an HTTP PUT request to the /v2/apps/<appId> endpoint to change the configuration of the given application. The appId value can be obtained using the previous method to list the running applications. Once the request is fired, the currently running tasks will be restarted with this new configuration.

It takes the force parameter, a Boolean value which is false by default. Making it true will override the current deployment if the application's state is affected.

Consider the following example:

```
$ curl -L -X PUT localhost:8080/v2/apps/my_app -d '{
  "cmd": "sleep 55",
  "constraints": [
    [
      "hostname",
      "UNIQUE",
      ""
    ]
  ],
  "cpus": "0.3",
  "instances": "2",
  "mem": "9",
  "ports": [
    9000
  ]
  }
  '
```

Once the update succeeds, it will give us a JSON response containing the following:

```
{
  "deploymentId": "6b2135a6-3326-4e44-9333-554eda6c3838",
  "version": "2015-12-16T12:37:50.462Z"
}
```

Deleting the application

You can use the HTTP DELETE request in /v2/apps/<appId> to destroy the application and the data associated with it.

Take a look at the following example:

```
$ curl -X DELETE localhost:8080/v2/apps/my_app
```

Introduction to Apache Aurora

Apache Aurora is a powerful Mesos framework for long-running services, cron jobs, and ad hoc jobs. It was originally designed at Twitter and was later open sourced under the Apache license. You can turn your Mesos cluster to a private cloud using Aurora. Unlike Marathon, Aurora is responsible for keeping jobs running across a shared pool of resources over a long duration. If any of the machines in the pool fails, then Aurora can intelligently reschedule those jobs on other healthy machines in the pool.

Aurora is not useful if you try to build an application with specific requirements for scheduling or if the job itself is a scheduler.

Managing long-running applications is one of the key features of Aurora. Apart from this, Aurora can be used to provide coarse-grained (that is, fixed) resources for your job so that at any point of time, the job always has a specified amount of resources. It also supports multiple users, and the configuration is templated with **DSL** (**Domain Specific Language**) to avoid redundancy in the configurations.

Installing Aurora

Aurora jobs can be interacted with through the Aurora Web UI and the Aurora command-line utility. To install Aurora, we require the installation of `vagrant`. You can install `vagrant` with the following command:

```
$ sudo apt-get install vagrant
```

Log in to any of the machines on the cluster and clone the Aurora repository with the following command:

```
$ git clone git://git.apache.org/aurora.git
```

Change the working directory to Aurora, as follows:

```
$ cd aurora
```

Then, type in the following command to install Aurora on this machine:

```
$ vagrant up
```

The `vagrant` command will use the configurations shipped with the Aurora distribution to install and start the Aurora services on the virtual machines. It will:

- Download the corresponding Linux virtual machine image
- Configure and start the VM

- Install Mesos and ZooKeeper on the VM along with the build tools

- Compile the Aurora source and build it on the VM

- Start the Aurora services on the VM

This process may take a couple of minutes to complete. If the command fails and complains about VirtualBox not being present on the machine, you can install it with the following command:

```
$ sudo apt-get install virtualbox
```

If everything goes well, you will see the following output on the Terminal:

```
akhld@spark-ak-master:~/aurora$ vagrant up
Bringing machine 'devcluster' up with 'virtualbox' provider...
==> devcluster: Box 'ubuntu/trusty64' could not be found. Attempting to find and install...
    devcluster: Box Provider: virtualbox
    devcluster: Box Version: >= 0
==> devcluster: Loading metadata for box 'ubuntu/trusty64'
    devcluster: URL: https://vagrantcloud.com/ubuntu/trusty64
==> devcluster: Adding box 'ubuntu/trusty64' (v20151208.1.0) for provider: virtualbox
    devcluster: Downloading: https://atlas.hashicorp.com/ubuntu/boxes/trusty64/versions/20151208.
==> devcluster: Successfully added box 'ubuntu/trusty64' (v20151208.1.0) for 'virtualbox'!
==> devcluster: Importing base box 'ubuntu/trusty64'...

Progress: 90%

==> devcluster: Matching MAC address for NAT networking...
==> devcluster: Checking if box 'ubuntu/trusty64' is up to date...
==> devcluster: Setting the name of the VM: aurora_devcluster_1450022994489_98535
==> devcluster: Clearing any previously set forwarded ports...
==> devcluster: Clearing any previously set network interfaces...
==> devcluster: Preparing network interfaces based on configuration...
    devcluster: Adapter 1: nat
    devcluster: Adapter 2: hostonly
==> devcluster: Forwarding ports...
    devcluster: 22 => 2222 (adapter 1)
==> devcluster: Running 'pre-boot' VM customizations...
==> devcluster: Booting VM...
==> devcluster: Waiting for machine to boot. This may take a few minutes...
    devcluster: SSH address: 127.0.0.1:2222
```

Introduction to Singularity

Singularity was originally designed at HubSpot and later open sourced under the Apache license. Singularity acts as an API and web application that can be used to launch and schedule long-running Mesos processes, scheduled jobs, and tasks. One can consider Singularity and the components that come with it as a **PaaS (Platform as a Service)** to the end users. A novice user can use Singularity to deploy tasks on Mesos without having to understand Mesos in detail.

Singularity takes advantages of Apache Mesos features such as fault tolerance, scalability, and resource allocation, and runs as a task scheduler for Mesos frameworks.

Installing Singularity

Before installing Singularity, make sure you have Docker installed on your machine. If you haven't installed it yet, you can do so by following the steps mentioned in the official website at `https://docs.docker.com`.

The first step is to clone the Singularity repository, which can be done as follows:

```
$ git clone https://github.com/HubSpot/Singularity
```

Now, change the working directory to Singularity, as follows:

```
$ cd Singularity
```

Once you have Docker and Docker Compose installed successfully, you can use the Docker Compose `pull` and `up` commands to try Singularity. The commands will set up the following in the container for you:

- The Mesos master and slave
- ZooKeeper
- Singularity
- The Baragon service and Agent

If you wish to install singularity without Docker, the following steps can help you do so:

```
# Compile the source code
$ mvn clean package
```

Once this is done, you can see the Singularity jars being created under the `SingularityService/target` directory.

```
akhld@spark-ak-slave:~/Singularity$ ls SingularityService/target/
classes                      SingularityService-0.4.6-SNAPSHOT.jar
generated-resources          SingularityService-0.4.6-SNAPSHOT-shaded.jar
generated-sources            SingularityService-0.4.6-SNAPSHOT-sources.jar
generated-test-sources       SingularityService-0.4.6-SNAPSHOT-tests.jar
jacoco.exec                  SingularityService-0.4.6-SNAPSHOT-test-sources.jar
maven-archiver               surefire-reports
maven-status                 test-classes
SingularityService
```

We will use **SingularityService-0.4.6-SNAPSHOT-shaded.jar** to run Singularity.

Creating a Singularity configuration file

Singularity configurations are kept in a YAML file. A sample YAML configuration file is explained here.

The port 7099 is used to run SingulartiyService, and the logs will be kept in /var/log/singularity-access.log. Take a look at the following code:

```
server:
  type: simple
  applicationContextPath: /singularity
  connector:
    type: http
    port: 7099
  requestLog:
    appenders:
      type: file
      currentLogFilename: /var/log/singularity-access.log
      archivedLogFilenamePattern:
        /var/log/singularity-access-%d.log.gz

#Mesos configuration, put the content from /etc/Mesos/zk as Mesos
master
mesos:
master:
  zk://100.76.90.36:2181,100.76.126.34:2181,100.72.150.2:2181
  /Mesos
defaultCpus: 1 # number of core that will be used by the job
defaultMemory: 128 # default memory of the job, being 128MB
frameworkName: Singularity
frameworkId: Singularity
frameworkFailoverTimeout: 1000000

Zookeeper: # quorum should be a host:port separated by comma
  quorum: 100.76.90.36:2181,100.76.126.34:2181,100.72.150.2:2181
  zkNamespace: singularity
  sessionTimeoutMillis: 60000
  connectTimeoutMillis: 5000
  retryBaseSleepTimeMilliseconds: 1000
  retryMaxTries: 3

logging:
  loggers:
    "com.hubspot.singularity" : TRACE
```

```
enableCorsFilter: true
sandboxDefaultsToTaskId: false
  # enable if using SingularityExecutor

ui:
  title: Singularity (local)
  baseUrl: http://localhost:7099/singularity
```

Save the preceding configuration as `singularity_config.yaml` and use the following command to start Singularity:

```
java -jar SingularityService/target/SingularityService
  -*-shaded.jar server singularity_config.yaml
```

If everything goes well, you will see the Singularity framework appearing in the Mesos UI under the frameworks tab, as in the following screenshot:

Active Frameworks										
ID ▾	Host		User	Name	Active Tasks	CPUs	Mem	Max Share	Registered	Re-Registered
Singularity	spark-ak-slave.spark-ak-cluster.i6.internal.cloudapp.net		akhld	Singularity	0	2	5.8 GB	14.286%	2 minutes ago	-

You can point the browser to the following URL to access the Singularity UI to `http://ServerIPAddress:7099/singularity/`.

Singularity (local)   Dashboard   Status   Requests   Tasks   Admin ▾   API Docs (beta)

Singularity

Starred requests

No starred requests

Service discovery using Marathoner

Modern distributed applications require a way to communicate with each other, which means that one application should know the presence of the other application when they are on the same network. This is called service discovery. In this section, we will take a look at the service discovery of web services that run on Marathon. One can adopt this approach for most of the stateless applications running on top of Marathon.

We will use the combination of the popular HAProxy TCP/HTTP load balancer along with Marathon's REST API script, which was covered in the previous topics, to regenerate the configuration file of HAProxy for the service discovery of Marathon applications. When a task is spawned on one of the Mesos slaves, they are configured to bind the port to an arbitrary one within the default range of 31,000-32,000.

Service discovery lets the applications running on Marathon communicate with others running alongside Marathon through their configured Marathon application port. For example, you can consider a Python web application that runs on port 80, which can communicate with its Java backend running on port `8080` by connecting to `localhost:8080`.

HAProxy can route the request that it gets to the actual port and host where the instance of the service is running. If, for some reason, it fails to connect to the given host and port, it will try to connect to the next instance where it is configured to run the service.

We will use the HAProxy-Marathon-bridge shell script, which is provided with Marathon, to connect to Marathon and retrieve the hostnames, the ports that the running applications are bound to, and the configured application ports. This script is scheduled to run every 60 seconds through a cron. The script basically checks whether the configuration it generated in the previous run differs from the current configuration and reloads the new configuration in HAProxy if it detects a change. Note that we don't have to restart HAProxy.

The following is a graphical representation of two services, SVC1 and SVC2, running in a cluster, in which they are configured with the applications to run on ports 1111 and 2222, respectively. The Mesos-allocated tasks ports are `31100` and `31200`, respectively. Note that it is the responsibility of HAProxy to route the requests between the user-configured application port and the Mesos-allocated task ports.

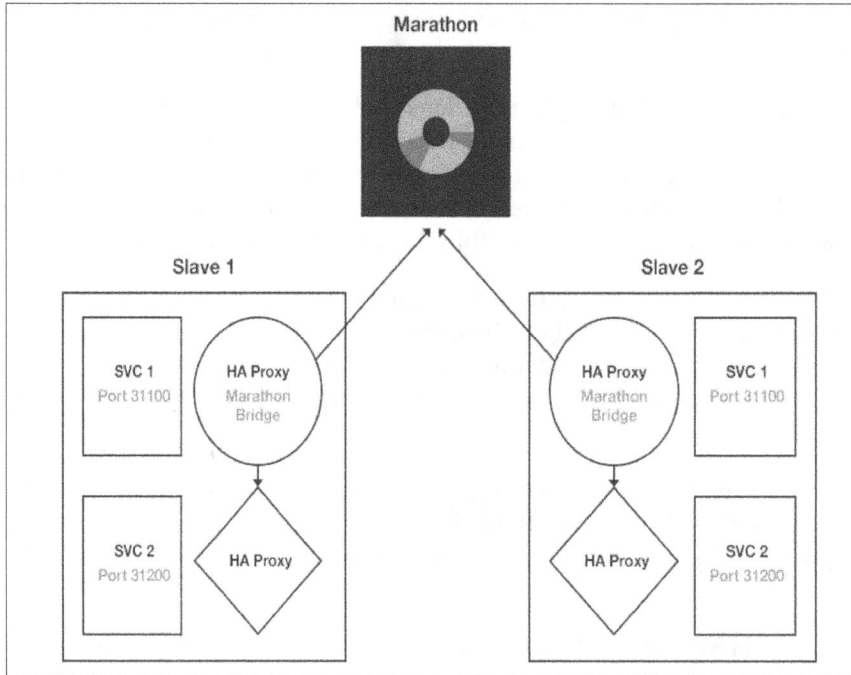

If, for example, SVC2 on Slave 2 tries to connect to SVC1 through `localhost:2222`, HAProxy will route the request to the configured SVC1 instance — that is, the one running on Slave1.

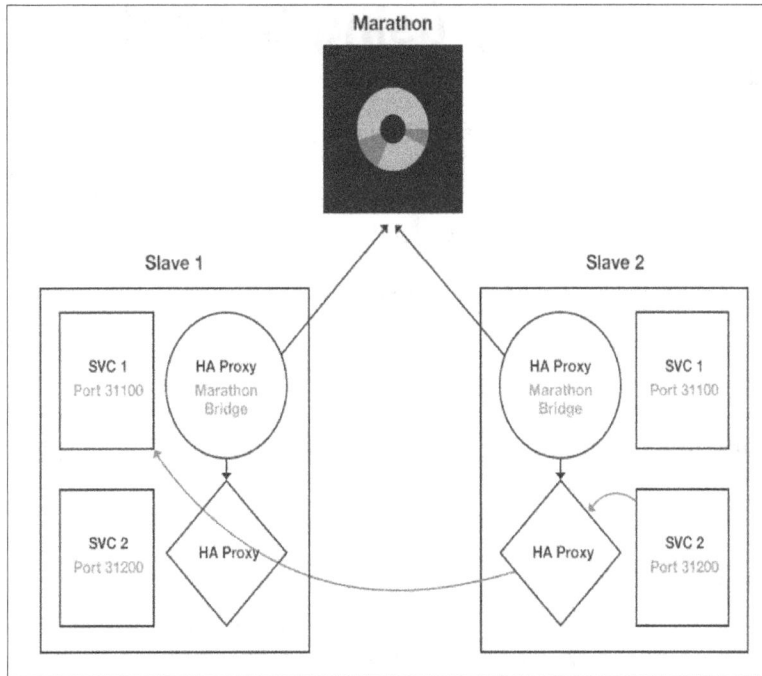

In case Slave 1 goes down, then requests to `localhost:2222` will be routed to Slave 2.

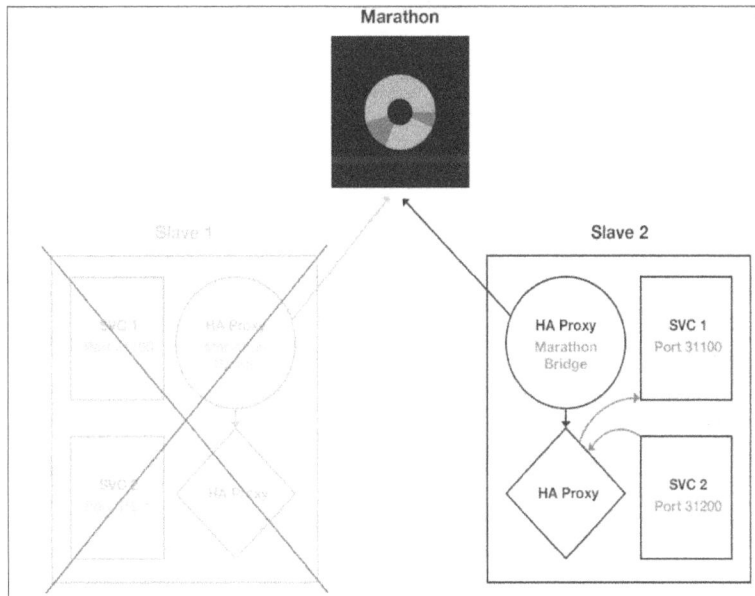

Service discovery using Consul

Mesos-consul is used to register and deregister services that run as Mesos tasks.

For example, if you have a Mesos task called `myapp`, then this program will register the application in Consul, which will expose DNS as `myapp.service.consul`. Consul also does the Mesos leader discovery through the `leader.Mesos.service.consul` DNS, which points to the active leader.

How is this different from other service discovery software?

Mesos-dns is a project similar to Consul. In Mesos-dns, it polls Mesos to get information about the tasks, whereas with Consul, instead of exposing this information via a built-in DNS server, it populates the Consul Service discovery with this information. The services are then exposed by Consul through DNS and its REST endpoint.

Running Consul

You will have to change the values of the environment if your ZooKeeper and Marathon services are not registered in Consul. You can dockerize Consul, and it can be run via Marathon as well.

Consul can be run in the following manner:

```
curl -X POST -d@Mesos-consul.json -H "Content-Type: application/json"
http://Marathon.service.consul:8080/v2/apps'
```

The preceding code is an `HTTP POST` request hitting the Consul API endpoint with the following JSON data in the `Mesos-consul.json` file:

```
{
  "args": [
    "--zk=zk://Zookeeper.service.consul:2181/Mesos"
  ],
  "container": {
    "type": "DOCKER",
    "Docker": {
      "network": "BRIDGE",
      "image": "{{ Mesos_consul_image }}:
        {{ Mesos_consul_image_tag }}"
    }
  },
  "id": "Mesos-consul",
  "instances": 1,
```

```
        "cpus": 0.1,
        "mem": 256
    }
```

Given in the following table are the options supported with the command-line Mesos-consul utility:

Option	Description
version	This prints the Mesos-consul version.
refresh	This refers to the time between the refreshes of Mesos tasks.
Mesos-ip-order	This is a comma-separated list that controls the order in which github.com/CiscoCloud/Mesos-consul searches for a task's IP address. The valid options are netinfo, Mesos, Docker, and host (the default is netinfo,Mesos,host).
healthcheck	This is used to enable health checks for an HTTP endpoint. When this flag is enabled, it serves the health status on 127.0.0.1:24476.
healthcheck-ip	This is the IP for the Health check service interface (the default is 127.0.0.1).
healthcheck-port	This is a port for the Health check service (the default is 24476).
consul-auth	This is the authentication username and password (optional) separated by a colon.
consul-ssl	This uses HTTPS while communicating with the registry.
consul-ssl-verify	This verifies certificates when connecting through SSL.
consul-ssl-cert	Provides the path to an SSL certificate, which it can use to authenticate the registry server.
consul-ssl-cacert	This provides the path to a CA certificate file that contains one or more CA certificates, which it can use to validate the registry server certificate.
consul-token	This is a token for registry ACL.
heartbeats-before-remove	This is the number of times that registration needs to fail before the task is removed from Consul (the default is 1).
zk*	This refers to the Mesos path location in ZooKeeper, the default being zk://127.0.0.1:2181/Mesos.

Load balancing with HAProxy

The HAProxy-Marathon-bridge script is shipped with the Marathon installation. You can also use Marathon-lb for the same. Both of these create a configuration file for HAProxy and a lightweight TCP/HTTP proxy by looking up the running tasks from Marathon's REST API.

HAProxy-Marathon-bridge is a simple script providing a minimum set of functionalities and is easier to understand for novice users. The latter one, Marathon-lb, supports advanced features such as SSL offloading, load balancing based on the VHost, and sticky connections.

Creating the bridge between HAProxy and Marathon

First, you need to create an HAProxy configuration from the running Marathon instance, which, by default, runs on port 8080 of the machine. You can use the HAProxy-Marathon-bridge script for this through the following syntax:

```
$ ./bin/haproxy-Marathon-bridge localhost:8080 >
  /etc/haproxy/haproxy.cfg
```

Note that here we specified localhost:8080 because we ran the Marathon instance and HAProxy on the same machine.

Once you generate the HAProxy configuration, you can simply reload HAProxy without interrupting the existing connections by running the following command:

```
$ haproxy -f haproxy.cfg -p haproxy.pid -sf $(cat haproxy.pid)
```

You can automate the configuration generation and reloading process using a typical cron job. If, for any reason, one of the nodes goes down during the reload process, HAProxy's health check will detect it and stop sending further traffic to this particular node.

You don't have to create the trigger to reload the HAProxy configuration. The HAProxy-Marathon-bridge script already does this for you. It has HAProxy and a cron job that is triggered every minute to pull the configuration from Marathon servers and refresh HAProxy if it detects any changes from the previous version.

You can use the following command to do so:

```
$ ./bin/haproxy-Marathon-bridge install_haproxy_system localhost:8080
```

It will add the pings to Marathon per line in the `/etc/haproxy-Marathon-bridge/` `Marathons` file and the script will be installed at `/usr/local/bin/haproxy-` `Marathon-bridge`. You can find the cron job being installed under `/etc/cron.d/` `haproxy-Marathon-bridge` which will be triggered as root.

Bamboo - Automatically configuring HAProxy for Mesos plus Marathon

Bamboo runs as a web daemon and automatically configures HAProxy for the web services deployed on Mesos and Marathon.

Bamboo comes with the following:

- A Web UI to configure HAProxy **Access Control Limit (ACL)** rules for each of the Marathon applications
- A REST endpoint to do the same
- A preconfigured HAProxy configuration file based on your template, with which you can customize your own template to enable SSL and interface for HAProxy stats or configure strategies for load balancing
- A Healthcheck endpoint if the Marathon application is configured with Healthchecks
- A stateless daemon, which enables scalability and horizontal replication
- No additional dependencies (as it is developed in Golang)
- Integration with StatsD to monitor configuration reload events

Bamboo can be deployed on each of the Mesos slaves with HAProxy. As Bamboo is primarily used for web services deployed on Mesos, the service discovery is as simple as connecting to the localhost or domain you assigned with the ACL rules. However, you can also deploy HAProxy and Bamboo on different machines, which means that you will have to load balance the HAProxy cluster.

The following screenshot shows Bamboo and HAProxy interacting with the Mesos cluster through Marathon:

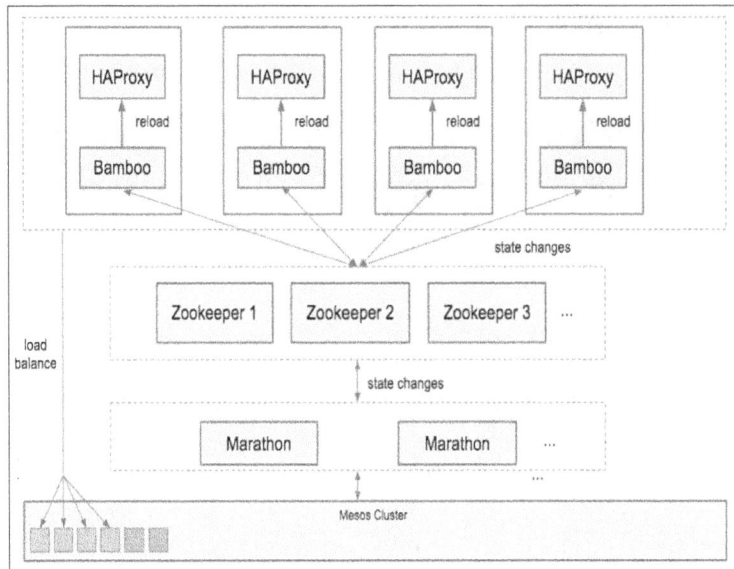

You can install Bamboo with the following commands:

```
# Clone the github repository
$ git clone https://github.com/QubitProducts/bamboo
# Change the working directory
$ cd bamboo
# Install, (make sure you have installed go first)
$ go build bamboo.go; ./builder/build.sh
```

Once you are done with the installation, point your browser to any of the machines where you installed Bamboo on the port 8000, and you will be able see the Web UI as shown in the following screenshot:

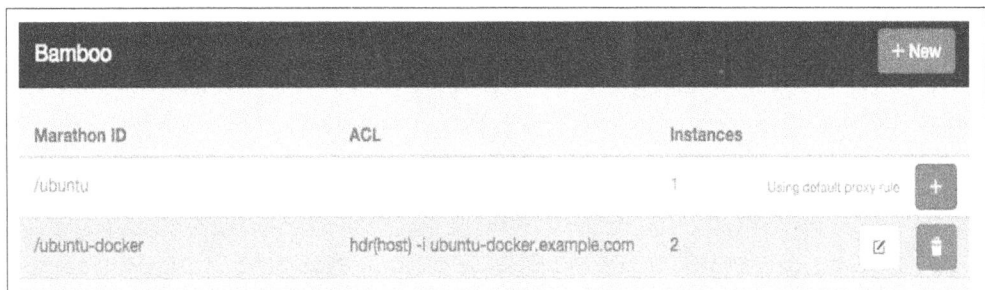

You can configure the ACLs by clicking on the edit icon at the right-hand side end of your Marathon application.

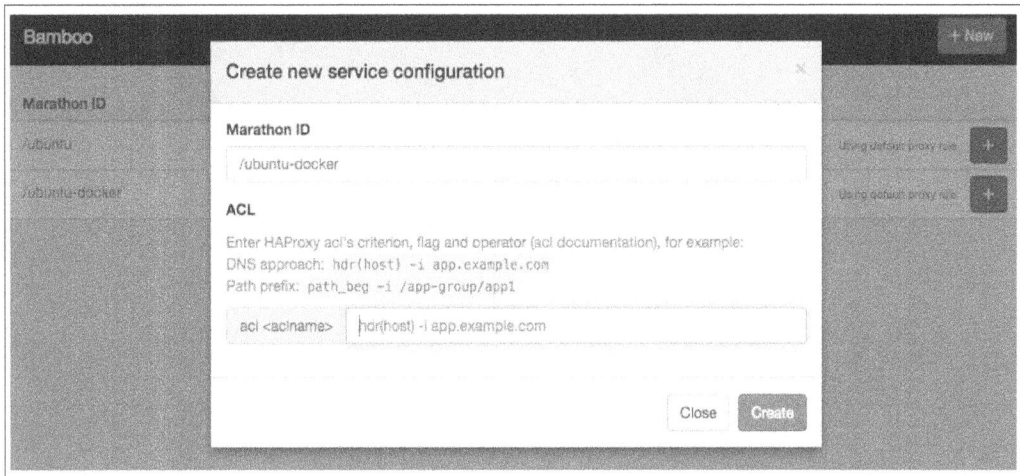

The Bamboo command line accepts a `--config` switch to specify the JSON application configuration file's location. You can find example configuration file templates under the config directory; `config/production.example.json` and `config/haproxy_template.cfg` are two of these. Now, take a look at the following code:

```
{
    // This is where you configure the Marathon instance
    "Marathon": {
        // Since we are running web applications,
        //   give the host:port to the applications
        "Endpoint":"http://Marathon1:8080,
            http://Marathon2:8080,http://Marathon3:8080",
        // Use the Marathon HTTP event streaming feature
        "UseEventStream": true
    },

    "Bamboo": {
        // Bamboo's HTTP address can be accessed by Marathon
        // Used for Marathon HTTP callback and each Bamboo instance
        // must provide a unique Endpoint that is
        //   directly addressable by Marathon
        // (e.g., every server's IP address)
        "Endpoint": "http://localhost:8000",
```

```
     // Proxy setting information is stored in Zookeeper
     // This path is created by Bamboo,
        if it does not already exist

   "Zookeeper": {
       // Make sure that the same setting is used
while running on the same ZK cluster
       "Host": "zk01.example.com:2812,zk02.example.com:2812",
       "Path": "/Marathon-haproxy/state",
       "ReportingDelay": 5
   }
 }

 // Make sure you are using absolute path on production
 "HAProxy": {
   "TemplatePath": "/var/bamboo/haproxy_template.cfg",
   "OutputPath": "/etc/haproxy/haproxy.cfg",
   "ReloadCommand": "haproxy -f /etc/haproxy/haproxy.cfg
-p /var/run/haproxy.pid -D -sf $(cat /var/run/haproxy.pid)",
   // A command that will validate the config
      before you run reload command.
   // '{{.}}' will be expanded to a temporary path
      that contains the config contents
   "ReloadValidationCommand": "haproxy -c -f {{.}}",
   // A command that will always be run after ReloadCommand,
      even if reload fails
   "ReloadCleanupCommand": "exit 0"
 },

 // Enable or disable StatsD event tracking
 "StatsD": {
   "Enabled": false,
   // StatsD or Graphite server host
   "Host": "localhost:8125",
   // StatsD namespace prefix -
   // Label each node if you have multiple Bamboo instances
   // by bamboo-server.production.n1.
   "Prefix": "bamboo-server.production."
 }
}
```

Bamboo maps the following environment variables to the corresponding Bamboo configurations. You can use these in the `production.json` file:

Environment Variable	Corresponds To
MARATHON_ENDPOINT	Marathon.Endpoint
MARATHON_USER	Marathon.User
MARATHON_PASSWORD	Marathon.Password
BAMBOO_ENDPOINT	Bamboo.Endpoint
BAMBOO_ZK_HOST	Bamboo.Zookeeper.Host
BAMBOO_ZK_PATH	Bamboo.Zookeeper.Path
HAPROXY_TEMPLATE_PATH	HAProxy.TemplatePath
HAPROXY_OUTPUT_PATH	HAProxy.OutputPath
HAPROXY_RELOAD_CMD	HAProxy.ReloadCommand
BAMBOO_DOCKER_AUTO_HOST	This sets the BAMBOO_ENDPOINT to $HOST when Bamboo container starts and can be any value
STATSD_ENABLED	StatsD.Enabled
STATSD_PREFIX	StatsD.Prefix
STATSD_HOST	StatsD.Host

Introduction to Netflix Fenzo

Netflix recently open sourced their scheduler library written in Java for Apache Mesos frameworks that supports scheduling optimizations and cluster autoscaling. At the time of writing the book, Fenzo is open sourced and is available in the official Netflix OSS suite repository, which can be found at the following URL: https://github.com/Netflix/Fenzo

There are basically two motivations for developing a framework such as Fenzo. Unlike other schedulers and frameworks discussed earlier, the reasons for building Fenzo are scheduling optimizations and autoscaling the cluster based on the usage.

When there is a huge variation in the amount of data that your cluster handles from time to time, provisioning the cluster for peak usage seems wasteful as most of the time, the resources will be idle. This is the main reason behind autoscaling the application depending on the load—that is, providing more machines to increase the cluster resources when there is peak usage and shutting down these machines when they are idle.

Scaling the cluster up is an easier task. You can have monitoring tools to watch the resource utilization, and when it crosses a threshold, you can go ahead and add more resources to the cluster. On the other hand, while scaling down the cluster, you need to identify whether there are long-running tasks on the machines that you are about to terminate and also whether it will have any impact on the running tasks if you terminate the machine.

Currently, autoscaling in Fenzo is based on the following two strategies:

- The threshold
- Resource shortfall analysis

In threshold-based autoscaling, users can specify rules as per the host group, such as EC2 Auto Scaling, GCE Auto Scaling, and so on. These can be considered as creating host groups to compute intensive, network-intensive, and other workloads. These rules let the new jobs be launched quickly on the preconfigured number of idle hosts.

In the case of resource shortfall analysis, it first calculates the number of hosts that are required to complete the pending workloads. One can also consider this as a predictive autoscaling system that can analyze the workload and spawn up new hosts to satisfy pending workloads. An example of such a system is the Netflix website's Scryer.

The following is a diagram showing how Fenzo can be used by an Apache Mesos framework. Fenzo itself contains a task scheduler that provides the scheduling core without really interacting with Mesos. The framework interfaces with Mesos to get new resource offers and pull task status updates.

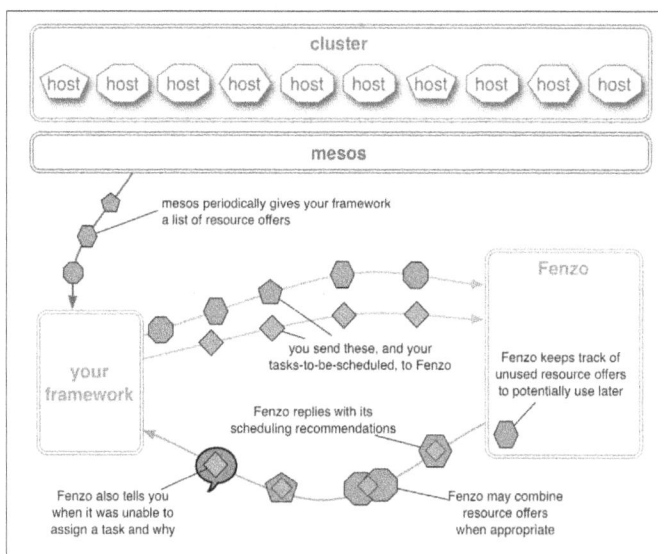

Introduction to PaaSTA

The Yelp's Platform-as-a-service distributed system PaaSTA is highly available and used to build, deploy, and run services using containers such as Docker and Apache Mesos. PaaSTA is designed and developed by Yelp and has been recently open sourced. You can take a look at the open sourced repository at the following URL: `https://github.com/yelp/paasta`

This is a suite for developers to specify how they want their code from their Git repository to be built, deployed, routed, and monitored. Yelp has used PaaSTA for more than a year to power its production-level services. PaaSTA is best suited if you have a strict production environment, such as Yelp, which requires many tiny microservices and where rolling out a new piece of code should be seamless and not disturb production systems. PaaSTA helps automate this entire process.

It comprises the following existing open source components:

- **Docker**: This is used to containerize the code
- **Apache Mesos**: This is used for execution and scheduling
- **Marathon**: This is used to manage long-running applications
- **Chronos**: This is used for scheduling purposes
- **SmartStack**: This is used for service discovery and registration
- **Sensu**: This is used to monitor and alert
- **Jenkins**: This is used for continuous build and deployment (this is optional)

One of the many reasons to have all these components in one place is reusability. You can reuse any of these components to solve different problems in your distributed environment.

A comparative analysis of different Scheduling/Management frameworks

This section will give you a brief comparison and use cases for the different scheduling frameworks that we discussed in this chapter.

Marathon is a PaaS built on Mesos to make sure the job will run forever even if few machines in the cluster go down. It can seamlessly handle the hardware and software failures and ensure the application is always running. These types of frameworks are useful in production environments where your application should always be running and available all the time—for example, a web server hosting a website. In such cases, you can deploy it as a Marathon application that will take care of all these aspects.

Chronos can be considered as a distributed fault-tolerant replacement of the typical Linux cron jobs that are used to fire up scheduled jobs, take periodic backups, check the health of the system, and so on. Both Chronos and Marathon come with a Web UI and a REST endpoint for the management of jobs. We can write wrapper scripts around this and automate the application deployment and job scheduling rather than just using the Web UI.

Aurora and Marathon are very similar in nature in the sense that both are service schedulers. All you have to do is tell Aurora or Marathon how to deploy the application, and they will keep them up and running without failures. Aurora, on the other hand, is a bit difficult to install and work with for a beginner. Unlike Marathon, it doesn't officially support a REST endpoint, which will be available soon. At this time, Aurora exposes a thrift API to make the communication, which means that there is an additional overhead of having to install thrift libraries on the server.

Apache Aurora is designed to handle large-scale infrastructure, such as a datacenter. A typical example is the clusters running on Twitter that consist of thousands of machines and hundreds of engineers accessing and using them for development and production purposes.

Summary

In this chapter, we dived deep into some of the most important frameworks for Mesos that make job scheduling and load balancing much easier and efficient. Frameworks such as Marathon and Chronos and their REST endpoints along with some other tools, such as HAProxy, Consul, Marathoner, Bamboo, Fenzo, and PaaSTA, were explained.

In the next chapter, we'll discuss how system administrators and DevOps professionals can deploy a Mesos cluster using standard tools such as Ansible, Chef, Puppet, Salt, Terraform, and Cloud formation along with monitoring it using Nagios and Satellite.

5
Mesos Cluster Deployment

This chapter explains how a Mesos cluster can be easily set up and monitored using standard deployment and configuration management tools used by system administrators and DevOps engineers. We will explain the steps that are required to set up a Mesos cluster through Ansible, Puppet, SaltStack, Chef, Terraform, or Cloudformation, and how a test environment can be set up using Playa Mesos. We will also talk about some standard monitoring tools, such as Nagios and Satellite that are can be used to monitor the cluster. We will also discuss some of the common problems faced while deploying a Mesos cluster along with their corresponding resolutions.

The topics that will be covered are as follows:

- Deploying and configuring a Mesos cluster using the following:
    - Ansible
    - Puppet
    - SaltStack
    - Chef
    - Terraform
    - Cloudformation

- Creating test environments using Playa Mesos
- Common deployment issues and solutions
- Monitoring the Mesos cluster using the following:
    - Nagios
    - Satellite

Deploying and configuring a Mesos cluster using Ansible

Ansible is one of the popular infrastructure automation tools commonly used by system administrators today and recently acquired by Red Hat. Nodes are managed through **Secure Shell (SSH)** and require only Python support. Ansible has open sourced a lot of playbooks, including an `ansible-mesos` one that we will discuss in this section.

The `ansible-mesos` playbook can be used to install and configure a Mesos cluster with customized master as well as slave setup options. Currently, it supports Ubuntu and CentOS/Red Hat operating system-powered machines. The `ansible-mesos` playbook also supports setting specific slave executors and hence can be run with native Docker support.

Installing Ansible

Ansible installation is only required on a single machine. It does not require a database, nor does it need to keep a daemon running all the time. It uses SSH to manage the cluster and requires Python (versions 2.6 or 2.7) to be installed on the machine. You can even install Ansible on your laptop or personal computer and have it manage the machines running remotely. The machine where Ansible is installed is called the **control machine**. At the time of writing this book, there is no support for Windows machines. The machines that are controlled by the control machine are known as **managed nodes** and require SSH access ability from the control machine as well as Python (version 2.4 or later) installed on them.

Installing the control machine

We can run Ansible without root access as it doesn't require you to install any additional software or database servers. Execute the following code:

```
# Install python pip
$ sudo easy_install pip


# Install the following python modules for ansible
$ sudo pip install paramiko PyYAML Jinja2 httplib2 six


# Clone the repository
```

```
$ git clone git://github.com/ansible/ansible.git --recursive


# Change the directory
$ cd ansible


# Installation
$ source ./hacking/env-setup
```

If everything goes well, then we can see the following output in the Terminal, indicating that the installation was successful. After this, we will be able to use the Ansible command from the Terminal.

By default, Ansible uses the inventory file in /etc/ansible/hosts, which is an INI-like format and could look similar to the following, for example:

```
mail.xyz.com

[webservers]
foo.xyz.com
bar.xyz.com

[dbservers]
one.xyz.com
two.xyz.com
three.xyz.com
```

Here, the group names are indicated in brackets, which can be used to classify the systems that will be controlled.

We can also use the command-line option -i to point it to a different file rather than the one found in /etc/ansible/hosts.

Creating an ansible-mesos setup

Ansible executes a playbook composed of roles against a set of hosts, as described before in the hosts file, which are organized into groups. For more details, visit http://frankhinek.com/create-ansible-playbook-on-github-to-build-mesos-clusters/.

First, let's create a hosts file by pointing to our Mesos master and slave nodes via the following:

```
$ cat hosts
[mesos_masters]
ec2-….compute-1.amazonaws.com zoo_id=1 ec2-….
    compute-1.amazonaws.com zoo_id=2
ec2-….compute-1.amazonaws.com zoo_id=3

[mesos_workers]
ec2-….compute-1.amazonaws.com
ec2-….compute-1.amazonaws.com
```

Here, we created two groups named mesos_masters and mesos_workers and listed the master and slave IP addresses, respectively. For the mesos_masters group, we will also need to specify the ZooKeeper ID as the cluster will run in high availability.

In the following steps, we will take a look at how to deploy Mesos on the machines listed in the hosts file using Ansible:

1. Create a site.yml file with following content:

   ```
   --
   # This playbook deploys the entire
     Mesos cluster infrastructure.
   # RUN: ansible-playbook --ask-sudo-pass -i hosts site.yml

   - name: deploy and configure the mesos masters
     hosts: mesos_masters
     sudo: True

     roles:
   ```

```
    - {role: mesos, mesos_install_mode:
  "master", tags: ["mesos-master"]}

  - name: deploy and configure the mesos slaves
    hosts: mesos_workers
    sudo: True

    roles:
      - {role: mesos, mesos_install_mode:
  "slave", tags: ["mesos-slave"]}
```

2. Now, we can create a group variable file that will be applicable to all the hosts belonging to the cluster, as follows:

$ mkdir group_vars

$ vim all

3. Next, we will put the following contents in all the files:

```
---
# Variables here are applicable to all host groups

mesos_version: 0.20.0-1.0.ubuntu1404
mesos_local_address: "{{ansible_eth0.ipv4.address}}"
mesos_cluster_name: "XYZ"
mesos_quorum_count: "2"
zookeeper_client_port: "2181"
zookeeper_leader_port: "2888"
zookeeper_election_port: "3888"
zookeeper_url: "zk://{{ groups.mesos_masters |
  join(':' + zookeeper_client_port + ',') }}:
  {{ zookeeper_client_port }}/mesos"
```

4. Now, we can create the roles for the Mesos cluster. First, create a roles directory via the following command:

$ mkdir roles; cd roles

5. We can now use the `ansible-galaxy` command to initialize the directory structure for this role, as follows:

$ ansible-galaxy init mesos

6. This will create the directory structure as follows:

```
mesos/
├── defaults
│   └── main.yml
├── files
├── handlers
│   └── main.yml
├── meta
│   └── main.yml
├── README.md
├── tasks
│   └── main.yml
├── templates
├── tests
│   ├── inventory
│   └── test.yml
└── vars
    └── main.yml
```

7. Now, modify the `mesos/handlers/main.yml` file with following content:

```
---
# handlers file for mesos
- name: Start mesos-master
  shell: start mesos-master
  sudo: yes

- name: Stop mesos-master
  shell: stop mesos-master
  sudo: yes

- name: Start mesos-slave
  shell: start mesos-slave
  sudo: yes

- name: Stop mesos-slave
  shell: stop mesos-slave
  sudo: yes

- name: Restart zookeeper
  shell: restart zookeeper
  sudo: yes

- name: Stop zookeeper
  shell: stop zookeeper
  sudo: yes
```

8. Next, modify the tasks from the `mesos/tasks/main.yml` file, as follows:

```
---
# tasks file for mesos

# Common tasks for all Mesos nodes
- name: Add key for Mesosphere repository
  apt_key:
    url=http://keyserver.ubuntu.com/pks/
    lookup?op=get&fingerprint=on&search=0xE56151BF
    state=present
  sudo: yes

- name: Determine Linux distribution distributor
  shell: lsb_release -is | tr '[:upper:]' '[:lower:]'
  register: release_distributor

- name: Determine Linux distribution codename
  command: lsb_release -cs
  register: release_codename

- name: Add Mesosphere repository to sources list
  copy:
    content: "deb http://repos.mesosphere.io/
      {{release_distributor.stdout}}
      {{release_codename.stdout}} main"
    dest: /etc/apt/sources.list.d/mesosphere.list
    mode: 0644
  sudo: yes

  # Tasks for Master, Slave, and ZooKeeper nodes

- name: Install mesos package
  apt: pkg={{item}} state=present update_cache=yes
  with_items:
    - mesos={{ mesos_pkg_version }}
  sudo: yes
  when: mesos_install_mode == "master" or
    mesos_install_mode == "slave"

- name: Set ZooKeeper URL # used for
  leader election amongst masters
  copy:
    content: "{{zookeeper_url}}"
    dest: /etc/mesos/zk
```

```
      mode: 0644
    sudo: yes
    when: mesos_install_mode == "master" or
      mesos_install_mode == "slave"

# Tasks for Master nodes
- name: Disable the Mesos Slave service
  copy:
      content: "manual"
      dest: /etc/init/mesos-slave.override
      mode: 0644
    sudo: yes
    when: mesos_install_mode == "master"

- name: Set Mesos Master hostname
  copy:
      content: "{{mesos_local_address}}"
      dest: /etc/mesos-master/hostname
      mode: 0644
    sudo: yes
    when: mesos_install_mode == "master"

- name: Set Mesos Master ip
  copy:
      content: "{{mesos_local_address}}"
      dest: /etc/mesos-master/ip
      mode: 0644
    sudo: yes
    when: mesos_install_mode == "master"

- name: Set Mesos Master Cluster name
  copy:
      content: "{{mesos_cluster_name}}"
      dest: /etc/mesos-master/cluster
      mode: 0644
    sudo: yes
    when: mesos_install_mode == "master"

- name: Set Mesos Master quorum count
  copy:
      content: "{{mesos_quorum_count}}"
      dest: /etc/mesos-master/quorum
      mode: 0644
    sudo: yes
```

```
    when: mesos_install_mode == "master"

# Tasks for Slave nodes
- name: Disable the Mesos Master service
  copy:
    content: "manual"
    dest: /etc/init/mesos-master.override
    mode: 0644
  sudo: yes
  when: mesos_install_mode == "slave"

- name: Disable the ZooKeeper service
  copy:
    content: "manual"
    dest: /etc/init/zookeeper.override
    mode: 0644
  sudo: yes
  notify:
    - Stop zookeeper
  when: mesos_install_mode == "slave"

- name: Set Mesos Slave hostname
  copy:
    content: "{{mesos_local_address}}"
    dest: /etc/mesos-slave/hostname
    mode: 0644
  sudo: yes
  when: mesos_install_mode == "slave"

- name: Set Mesos Slave ip
  copy:
    content: "{{mesos_local_address}}"
    dest: /etc/mesos-slave/ip
    mode: 0644
  sudo: yes
  when: mesos_install_mode == "slave"

- name: Set Mesos Slave ip
  copy:
    content: "{{mesos_local_address}}"
    dest: /etc/mesos-slave/ip
    mode: 0644
  sudo: yes
```

```
      when: mesos_install_mode == "slave"

    - name: Set Mesos Slave isolation
      copy:
        content: "cgroups/cpu,cgroups/mem"
        dest: /etc/mesos-slave/isolation
        mode: 0644
      sudo: yes
      notify:
        - Start mesos-slave
      when: mesos_install_mode == "slave"

    # Tasks for ZooKeeper nodes only
    - name: Create zookeeper config file
      template: src=zoo.cfg.j2 dest=/etc/zookeeper/conf/zoo.cfg
      sudo: yes
      when: mesos_install_mode == "master"

    - name: Create zookeeper myid file
      template: src=zoo_id.j2 dest=/etc/zookeeper/conf/myid
      sudo: yes
      notify:
        - Restart zookeeper
        - Start mesos-master
      when: mesos_install_mode == "master"
```

This is a standard template to configure the Mesos master slave machines in the cluster. This file also specifies the various configurations that are necessary to install components such as ZooKeeper. The steps are listed as follows:

1. Create the ZooKeeper configuration template as follows:

   ```
   $ vim mesos/templates/zoo.cfg.j2
   ```

2. Then, add the following content:

   ```
   tickTime=2000
   dataDir=/var/lib/zookeeper/
   clientPort={{ zookeeper_client_port }}
   initLimit=5
   syncLimit=2
   {% for host in groups['mesos_masters'] %}
   server.{{ hostvars[host].zoo_id }}={{ host }}:
     {{ zookeeper_leader_port }}:
     {{ zookeeper_election_port }}
   {% endfor %}
   ```

3. Next, enter the following command:

   ```
   $ vim mesos/templates/zoo_id.j2
   ```

4. Finally, add the following content:

   ```
   {{ zoo_id }}
   ```

We can now run this playbook to deploy Mesos on the machines listed in the hosts file. We only need to change the IP addresses from the hosts file to deploy on other machines.

Deploying and configuring Mesos cluster using Puppet

This portion will primarily cover how one can deploy a Mesos cluster with the Puppet configuration management tool using the ZooKeeper and Mesos modules located at the following repositories:

- `https://github.com/deric/puppet-mesos`
- `https://github.com/deric/puppet-zookeeper`

Puppet is an open source configuration management tool that runs on Windows, Linux, and Mac OS. Puppet Labs was founded by Luke Kanies, who produced the Puppet, in 2005. It is written in Ruby and released as free software under the GNU General Public License (GPL) until version 2.7.0 and Apache License 2.0 after that. Using this, system administrators can automate the standard tasks that they need to run regularly. More information about Puppet can be found at the following location:

- `https://puppetlabs.com/puppet/puppet-open-source`

The code will be organized with the profiles and roles pattern, and the node data will be stored using Hiera. Hiera is a Puppet tool to perform a key/value lookup of the configuration data. It allows a hierarchical configuration of data in Puppet, which is difficult to achieve with native Puppet code. Also, it acts as a separator of configuration data and code.

At the end of this module, you will have a highly available Mesos cluster with three masters and three slaves. Along with this, Marathon and Chronos will also be deployed in the same fashion.

We can combine several Puppet modules to manage Mesos and ZooKeeper. Let's perform the following steps:

1. First, create a `Puppetfile` with the following content:

```
forge 'http://forge.puppetlabs.com'
mod 'apt',
  :git => 'git://github.com/puppetlabs/puppetlabs-apt.git',
    :ref => '1.7.0'

mod 'concat',
  :git =>
    'https://github.com/puppetlabs/puppetlabs-concat',
    :ref => '1.1.2'

mod 'datacat',
  :git => 'https://github.com/richardc/puppet-datacat',
    :ref => '0.6.1'

mod 'java',
  :git => 'https://github.com/puppetlabs/puppetlabs-java',
    :ref => '1.2.0'

mod 'mesos',
  :git => 'https://github.com/deric/puppet-mesos',
    :ref => 'v0.5.2'

mod 'stdlib',
  :git =>
    'https://github.com/puppetlabs/puppetlabs-stdlib',
    :ref => '4.5.1'

mod 'zookeeper',
  :git => 'https://github.com/deric/puppet-zookeeper',
    :ref => 'v0.3.5'
```

   Now, we can write the profiles and roles pattern for both Mesos masters and slaves. On the master machines, it will also include managing ZooKeeper, Marathon, and Chronos.

2. Create the following role for the masters:

```
class role::mesos::master {
  include profile::zookeeper
```

```
include profile::mesos::master

# Mesos frameworks
include profile::mesos::master::chronos
include profile::mesos::master::marathon
}
```

3. Next, create the following role for the slaves:

```
class role::mesos::slave {
  include profile::mesos::slave
}
```

Now, we can go ahead and create the reusable profiles that match the include statements listed before in the roles. The profiles will contain the calls to the Mesos and ZooKeeper modules and any other resources that we need to manage. One can consider the roles as the business logic and the profiles as the actual implementation.

4. Create the following profile for ZooKeeper:

```
class profile::zookeeper {
  include ::java
  class { '::zookeeper':
    require => Class['java'],
  }
}
```

5. Create the following profile for Mesos masters:

```
class profile::mesos::master {
  class { '::mesos':
    repo => 'mesosphere',
  }

  class { '::mesos::master':
    env_var => {
      'MESOS_LOG_DIR' => '/var/log/mesos',
    },
    require => Class['profile::zookeeper'],
  }
}
```

6. Next, create the following profile for Mesos slaves:

```
class profile::mesos::slave {
  class { '::mesos':
    repo => 'mesosphere',
  }
  class { '::mesos::slave':
    env_var => {
      'MESOS_LOG_DIR' => '/var/log/mesos',
    },
  }
}
```

These are the basic things we need to launch a Mesos cluster. To manage Chronos and Marathon, the following profiles will also need to be included.

7. Create a profile for Chronos, as follows:

```
class profile::mesos::master::chronos {
  package { 'chronos':
    ensure  => '2.3.2-0.1.20150207000917.debian77',
    require => Class['profile::mesos::master'],
  }

  service { 'chronos':
    ensure  => running,
    enable  => true,
    require => Package['chronos'],
  }
}
```

8. Now, create a profile for Marathon via the following code:

```
class profile::mesos::master::marathon {
  package { 'marathon':
    ensure  => '0.7.6-1.0',
    require => Class['profile::mesos::master'],
  }

  service { 'marathon':
    ensure  => running,
    enable  => true,
    require => Package['marathon'],
  }
}
```

So far, the roles and profiles don't contain any information about the machines that we will use to set up the cluster. This information will come using Hiera. The Hiera data for master would look something similar to this:

```
---
classes:
  - role::mesos::master

mesos::master::options:
  quorum: '2'
mesos::zookeeper:
  'zk://master1:2181,master2:2181,master3:2181/mesos'
zookeeper::id: 1
zookeeper::servers:
  ['master1:2888:3888', 'master2:2888:3888',
  'master3:2888:3888']
```

As we are setting up a highly available cluster, the master machines are named master 1, master 2, and master 3, respectively.

9. Hiera data for slave would look something similar to the following:

```
---
classes:
  - role::mesos::slave

mesos::slave::checkpoint: true
mesos::zookeeper:
  'zk://master1:2181,master2:2181,master3:2181/mesos'
```

Now, we can initiate a Puppet run on each of the machines to install and configure Mesos, ZooKeeper, Chronos, and Marathon.

The installation of the module is the same as for any Puppet module, as follows:

```
$ puppet module install deric-mesos
```

Once executed successfully, we can expect that the Mesos package will be installed and the `mesos-master` service will be configured in the cluster.

Deploying and configuring a Mesos cluster using SaltStack

The SaltStack platform, or Salt, is a Python-based open source configuration management software and a remote execution engine. This module explains how we can use SaltStack to install a Mesos cluster with Marathon and a few other tools in production. SaltStack is an alternative to Puppet, Ansible, Chef, and others. As with the others, it is used to automate the deployment and configuration of software on multiple servers. The SaltStack architecture consists of one node as the SaltStack master and other nodes as the minions (slaves). There are also two different roles: one master role to perform cluster actions and a slave role to run the Docker containers.

The following packages will be installed for the role master:

- ZooKeeper
- The Mesos master
- Marathon
- Consul

The slave role will have the following packages installed:

- The Mesos slave
- Docker
- cAdvisor (used to export metrics to prometheus)
- Registrator (used to register services with Consul)
- Weave (provides an overlay network between containers)

Now, let's take a look at how these components look in the cluster. The following figure shows all these components connected together in the cluster (source: `https://github.com/Marmelatze/saltstack-mesos-test`):

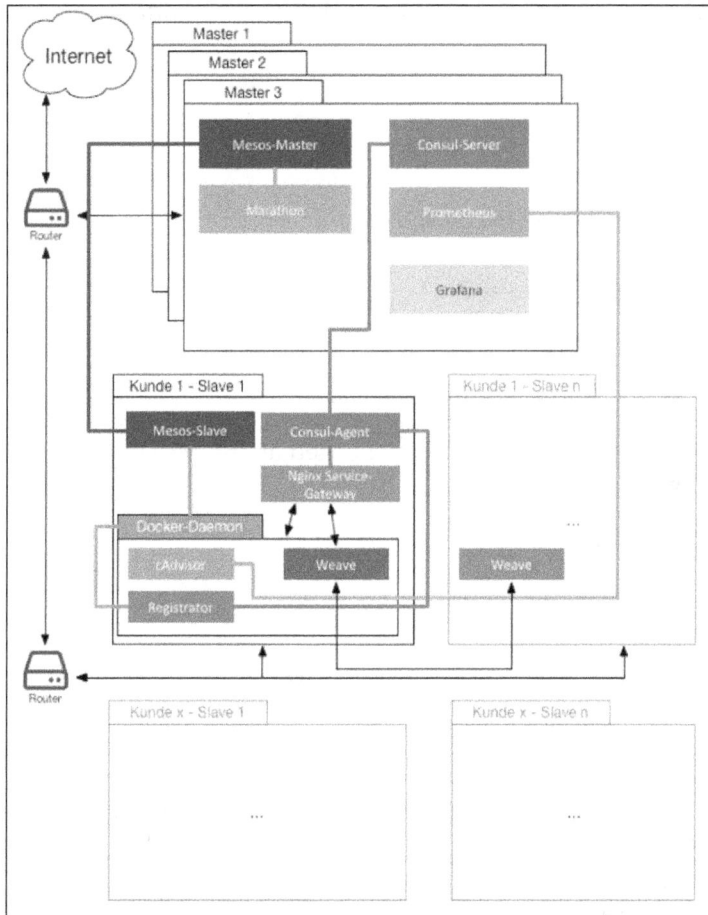

SaltStack installation

We need to install the Salt-Master to coordinate all the Salt-Minions. SaltStack requires the masters to be an odd number. One of these masters can be used as the Salt-Master, and the others will then become the minions. Let's follow the steps mentioned here to install SaltStack:

1. Execute the following command to set up the master and minion:

```
$ curl -L https://bootstrap.saltstack.com -o install_salt.sh
$ sudo sh install_salt.sh -U -M -P -A localhost
#Clone the repository to /srv/salt this is
  where the configurations are kept.
$ sudo git clone
  https://github.com/Marmelatze/saltstack-mesos-test /srv/salt
```

2. Edit the `/etc/salt/master` file and change the configurations, as follows:

```
file_roots:
  base:
    - /srv/salt/salt

# ...
pillar_roots:
  base:
    - /srv/salt/pillar
```

Now restart the master:

```
$ sudo service salt-master restart
```

3. Edit the minion configuration file located at `/etc/salt/minion` via the following code:

```
# ...
mine_interval: 5
mine_functions:
  network.ip_addrs:
    interface: eth0
  zookeeper:
    - mine_function: pillar.get
    - zookeeper
```

4. Now, edit the `salt-grains` file located at `/etc/salt/grains` by executing the following code:

```
# /etc/salt/grains
# Customer-Id this host is assigned to (numeric)-
customer_id: 0
# ID of this host.
host_id: ID

 # ID for zookeeper, only needed for masters.
zk_id: ID

# Available roles are master & slave. Node can use both.
roles:
- master
- slave
```

5. Then, replace the ID with a numerical value starting from 1; this ID is similar to the ZooKeeper ID that we used earlier.

   Now, restart the minion via the following command:

   ```
   $ sudo service salt-minion restart
   ```

6. Public key authentication is used for authentication between the minion and the master. Execute the following command to do so:

   ```
   $ sudo salt-key -A
   ```

7. Once we are done with the preceding steps, we can run SaltStack with the following command:

   ```
   $ sudo salt '*' state.highstate
   ```

If everything is successfully executed, then Mesos services will be up and running in the cluster.

Deploying and configuring a Mesos cluster using Chef

Chef is both the name of a company and the name of a configuration management tool written in Ruby and Erlang. It uses a pure Ruby domain-specific language (DSL) to write system configuration "recipes". This module will explain how to install and configure the Apache Mesos master and slave using the Chef cookbook. Chef is a configuration management tool to automate large-scale server and software application deployments. We will assume that the reader is already familiar with Chef. The following repository will be used for reference:

```
https://github.com/everpeace/cookbook-mesos.
```

The Chef cookbook version at the time of writing this book supports the Ubuntu and CentOS operating systems. The CentOS version is experimental and is not recommended for use in a production environment. Ubuntu 14.04 or higher is required to make use of the cgroups isolator or Docker container features. Only Mesos 0.20.0 and later supports Docker containerization.

This cookbook supports installation in both ways—that is, building Mesos from source and from the Mesosphere package. By default, this cookbook builds Mesos from source. One can switch between the source and Mesosphere by setting the following type variable:

```
node[:mesos][:type]
```

Recipes

The following are the recipes used by this cookbook to install and configure Mesos:

- `mesos::default`: This installs Mesos using the source or Mesosphere recipe, depending on the type variable discussed before.

- `mesos::build_from_source`: This installs Mesos in the usual way — that is, download zip from GitHub, configure, make, and install.

- `mesos::mesosphere`: This variable installs Mesos using Mesosphere's `mesos` package. Along with it, we can use the following variable to install the ZooKeeper package.

  ○ `node[:mesos][:mesosphere][:with_zookeeper]`

- `mesos::master`: This configures the Mesos master and cluster deployment configuration files and uses `mesos-master` to start the service. The following are the variables associated with the configurations:

  ○ `node[:mesos][:prefix]/var/mesos/deploy/masters`

  ○ `node[:mesos][:prefix]/var/mesos/deploy/slaves`

  ○ `node[:mesos][:prefix]/var/mesos/deploy/mesos-deploy-env.sh`

  ○ `node[:mesos][:prefix]/var/mesos/deploy/mesos-master-env.sh`

If we select `mesosphere` as the type to build, then the default ":" prefix attribute location will be `/usr/local` as the package from Mesosphere installs Mesos in this directory. This recipe also configures the upstart files at the following locations:

- `/etc/mesos/zk`
- `/etc/defaults/mesos`
- `/etc/defaults/mesos-master`

Configuring mesos-master

The `mesos-master` command-line parameters can be used to configure the `node[:mesos][:master]` attribute. An example is given here:

```
node[:mesos][:master] = {
  :port    => "5050",
  :log_dir => "/var/log/mesos",
  :zk      => "zk://localhost:2181/mesos",
  :cluster => "MesosCluster",
  :quorum  => "1"
}
```

The `mesos-master` command will be invoked with the options given in the configuration as follows:

```
mesos-master --zk=zk://localhost:2181/mesos --port=5050 --log_dir=/
var/log/mesos --cluster=MesosCluster
```

The `mesos::slave` command provides configurations for the Mesos slave and starts the `mesos-slave` instance. We can use the following variable to point to the `mesos-slave-env.sh` file:

*   `node[:mesos][:prefix]/var/mesos/deploy/mesos-slave-env.sh`

The upstart configuration files for `mesos-slave` are as follows:

*   `/etc/mesos/zk`
*   `/etc/defaults/mesos`
*   `/etc/defaults/mesos-slave`

Configuring mesos-slave

The `mesos-slave` command-line options can be configured using the `node[:mesos][:slave]` hash. An example configuration is given here:

```
node[:mesos][:slave] = {
  :master      => "zk://localhost:2181/mesos",
  :log_dir     => "/var/log/mesos",
  :containerizers => "docker,mesos",
  :isolation  => "cgroups/cpu,cgroups/mem",
  :work_dir   => "/var/run/work"
}
```

The `mesos-slave` command is invoked as follows:

```
mesos-slave --master=zk://localhost:2181/mesos
  --log_dir=/var/log/mesos --containerizers=docker,mesos
  --isolation=cgroups/cpu,cgroups/mem --work_dir=/var/run/work
```

Now, let's take a look at how we can put all this together in a vagrant file and launch a standalone Mesos cluster. Create a `Vagrantfile` with the following contents:

```
# -*- mode: ruby -*-
# vi: set ft=ruby:
# vagrant plugins required:
# vagrant-berkshelf, vagrant-omnibus, vagrant-hosts
```

```
Vagrant.configure("2") do |config|
  config.vm.box = "Official Ubuntu 14.04 daily Cloud Image amd64
    (Development release,  No Guest Additions)"
  config.vm.box_url =
    "https://cloud-images.ubuntu.com/vagrant/trusty/current/
    trusty-server-cloudimg-amd64-vagrant-disk1.box"

# config.vm.box = "chef/centos-6.5"

  # enable plugins
  config.berkshelf.enabled = true
  config.omnibus.chef_version = :latest
  # if you want to use vagrant-cachier,
  # please activate below.
  config.cache.auto_detect = true

  # please customize hostname and private ip configuration
    if you need it.
  config.vm.hostname = "mesos"
  private_ip = "192.168.1.10"
  config.vm.network :private_network, ip: private_ip
  config.vm.provision :hosts do |provisioner|
    provisioner.add_host private_ip , [ config.vm.hostname ]
  end
  # for mesos web UI.
  config.vm.network :forwarded_port, guest: 5050, host: 5050
  config.vm.provider :virtualbox do |vb|
    vb.name = 'cookbook-mesos-sample-source'
    # Use VBoxManage to customize the VM.
      For example, to change memory:
    vb.customize ["modifyvm", :id, "--memory", "#{1024*4}"]
    vb.customize ["modifyvm", :id,  "--cpus",  "2"]
  end

  config.vm.provision :shell do |s|
      s.path = "scripts/populate_sshkey.sh"
      s.args = "/home/vagrant vagrant"
  end

  # mesos-master doesn't create its work_dir.
  config.vm.provision :shell, :inline => "mkdir -p /tmp/mesos"

  # Mesos master depends on zookeeper emsamble since 0.19.0
  # for Ubuntu
```

```
config.vm.provision :shell,
  :inline => "apt-get update &&
  apt-get install -y zookeeper zookeeperd zookeeper-bin"
# For CentOS
# config.vm.provision :shell, :inline => <<-EOH
#   rpm -Uvh
  http://archive.cloudera.com/cdh4/
  one-click-install/redhat/6/x86_64/cloudera-cdh-4-0.x86_64.rpm
#   yum install -y -q curl
#   curl -sSfL http://archive.cloudera.com/cdh4/
  redhat/6/x86_64/cdh/RPM-GPG-KEY-cloudera --output /tmp/cdh.key
#   rpm --import /tmp/cdh.key
#   yum install -y -q
  java-1.7.0-openjdk zookeeper zookeeper-server
#   service zookeeper-server init
#   service zookeeper-server start
# EOH

config.vm.provision :chef_solo do |chef|
#   chef.log_level = :debug
  chef.add_recipe "mesos"
  chef.add_recipe "mesos::master"
  chef.add_recipe "mesos::slave"

  # You may also specify custom JSON attributes:
  chef.json = {
    :java => {
      'install_flavor' => "openjdk",
      'jdk_version' => "7",
    },
    :maven => {
      :version => "3",
      "3" => {
        :version => "3.0.5"
      },
      :mavenrc => {
        :opts => "-Dmaven.repo.local=$HOME/.m2/repository
          -Xmx384m -XX:MaxPermSize=192m"
      }
    },
    :mesos => {
      :home         => "/home/vagrant",
      # command line options for mesos-master
      :master => {
        :zk => "zk://localhost:2181/mesos",
```

```
          :log_dir => "/var/log/mesos",
          :cluster => "MesosCluster",
          :quorum  => "1"
        },
        # command line options for mesos-slave
        :slave =>{
          :master => "zk://localhost:2181/mesos",
          :isolation => "posix/cpu,posix/mem",
          :log_dir => "/var/log/mesos",
          :work_dir => "/var/run/work"
        },
        # below ip lists are for mesos-[start|stop]-cluster.sh
        :master_ips => ["localhost"],
        :slave_ips  => ["localhost"]
      }
    }
  end
end
```

Now, type in the following command to have a fully functional standalone Mesos cluster:

```
$ vagrant up
```

Deploying and configuring a Mesos cluster using Terraform

Terraform is an infrastructure building, changing, and versioning tool to handle the existing popular services as well as custom in-house solutions safely and efficiently that is owned by HashiCorp and written in Go language. In this module, we will first discuss how we can install Terraform, and then, we will consider how we can use Terraform to spin up a Mesos cluster.

Installing Terraform

Head to `https://www.terraform.io/downloads.html`, download the appropriate version for your platform, and unzip it, as follows:

```
$ wget
  https://releases.hashicorp.com/
  terraform/0.6.9/terraform_0.6.9_linux_amd64.zip

$ unzip terraform_0.6.9_linux_amd64.zip
```

You will note that the `terraform` archive is a bunch of binaries once you unzip them, which looks similar to the following:

```
terraform                        terraform-provider-mysql
terraform-provider-atlas         terraform-provider-null
terraform-provider-aws           terraform-provider-openstack
terraform-provider-azure         terraform-provider-packet
terraform-provider-azurerm       terraform-provider-postgresql
terraform-provider-chef          terraform-provider-rundeck
terraform-provider-cloudflare    terraform-provider-statuscake
terraform-provider-cloudstack    terraform-provider-template
terraform-provider-consul        terraform-provider-terraform
terraform-provider-digitalocean  terraform-provider-tls
terraform-provider-dme           terraform-provider-vcd
terraform-provider-dnsimple      terraform-provider-vsphere
terraform-provider-docker        terraform-provisioner-chef
terraform-provider-dyn           terraform-provisioner-file
terraform-provider-google        terraform-provisioner-local-exec
terraform-provider-heroku        terraform-provisioner-remote-exec
terraform-provider-mailgun
```

Now, add the path to the directory in the PATH variable so that you can access the `terraform` command from any directory.

If everything goes well, then you can see the usage of `terraform` once you execute the `terraform` command in the Terminal:

```
usage: terraform [--version] [--help] <command> [<args>]

Available commands are:
    apply      Builds or changes infrastructure
    destroy    Destroy Terraform-managed infrastructure
    get        Download and install modules for the configuration
    graph      Create a visual graph of Terraform resources
    init       Initializes Terraform configuration from a module
    output     Read an output from a state file
    plan       Generate and show an execution plan
    push       Upload this Terraform module to Atlas to run
    refresh    Update local state file against real resources
    remote     Configure remote state storage
    show       Inspect Terraform state or plan
    taint      Manually mark a resource for recreation
    version    Prints the Terraform version
```

Spinning up a Mesos cluster using Terraform on Google Cloud

To spin up a Mesos cluster in Google Cloud Engine (GCE) with Terraform, you are required to have a JSON key file to authenticate. Head to https://console.developers.google.com and then generate a new JSON key by navigating to the **Credentials | Service** account. A file will then be downloaded, which will be needed later to launch machines.

We can now create a `terraform` configuration file for our Mesos cluster. Create a `mesos.tf` file with the following contents:

```
module "mesos" {
  source = "github.com/ContainerSolutions/terraform-mesos"
  account_file = "/path/to/your/downloaded/key.json"
  project = "your google project"
  region = "europe-west1"
  zone = "europe-west1-d"
  gce_ssh_user = "user"
  gce_ssh_private_key_file = "/path/to/private.key"
  name = "mymesoscluster"
  masters = "3"
  slaves = "5"
  network = "10.20.30.0/24"
  domain = "example.com"
  image = "ubuntu-1404-trusty-v20150316"
  mesos_version = "0.22.1"
}
```

As we can note, a few of these configurations can be used to control versions, such as:

- `mesos_version`: This specifies the version of Mesos
- `image`: This is the Linux system image

Now, execute the following commands to start the deployment:

```
# Download the modules
$ terraform get


# Create a terraform plan and save it to a file
$ terraform plan -out my.plan -module-depth=1


# Create the cluster
$ terraform apply my.plan
```

Destroying the cluster

We can execute the following command to destroy the cluster:

```
$ terraform destroy
```

Deploying and configuring a Mesos cluster using Cloudformation

In this module, we will discuss how we can use Cloudformation scripts to launch a Mesos cluster on Amazon AWS. Before jumping into it, first make sure you install and configure aws-cli on the machines where you want to launch the cluster. Take a look at the instructions from the following repository to set up aws-cli:

```
https://github.com/aws/aws-cli.
```

The next thing that we need after setting up aws-cli is the cloudformation-zookeeper template for an exhibitor-managed ZooKeeper cluster.

Setting up cloudformation-zookeeper

We first need to clone the following repository as it contains the JSON file that has the parameters, descriptors, and configuration values:

```
$ git clone https://github.com/mbabineau/cloudformation-zookeeper
```

Log in to the AWS console and open up the following ports for security group:

- SSH Port: 22
- ZooKeeper Client Port: 2181
- Exhibitor HTTP Port: 8181

We can now use aws-cli to launch the cluster using the following command:

```
aws cloudformation create-stack \
  --template-body file://cloudformation-zookeeper/zookeeper.json \
  --stack-name <stack> \
  --capabilities CAPABILITY_IAM \
  --parameters \
    ParameterKey=KeyName,ParameterValue=<key> \
    ParameterKey=ExhibitorS3Bucket,ParameterValue=<bucket> \
    ParameterKey=ExhibitorS3Region,ParameterValue=<region> \
    ParameterKey=ExhibitorS3Prefix,ParameterValue=<cluster_name> \
    ParameterKey=VpcId,ParameterValue=<vpc_id> \
    ParameterKey=Subnets,ParameterValue='<subnet_id_1>\,
      <subnet_id_2>' \
    ParameterKey=AdminSecurityGroup,ParameterValue=<sg_id>
```

Using cloudformation-mesos

You can clone the project repository from the following URL:

```
$ git clone https://github.com/mbabineau/cloudformation-mesos
```

The project primarily includes three templates in the JSON format, which defines the parameters, configurations, and descriptors, as follows:

- `mesos-master.json`: This is used to launch a set of Mesos masters, which run Marathon in an autoscaling group.

- `mesos-slave.json`: Similar to the preceding one, this launches a set of Mesos slaves in an autoscaling group.

- `mesos.json`: This creates both the `mesos-master` and `mesos-slave` stacks from the corresponding templates, which were listed previously. This is the general template used to launch a Mesos cluster.

A few configurable properties from `master.json` are listed as follows:

```
"MasterInstanceCount" : {
    "Description" : "Number of master nodes to launch",
    "Type" : "Number",
    "Default" : "1"
},
"MasterQuorumCount" : {
    "Description" : "Number of masters needed for Mesos replicated
log registry quorum (should be ceiling(<MasterInstanceCount>/2))",
    "Type" : "Number",
    "Default" : "1"
},
```

`MasterInstanceCount` and `MasterQuorumCount` control the number of master machines that are required in the cluster. Take a look at the following code:

```
"SlaveInstanceCount" : {
    "Description" : "Number of slave nodes to launch",
    "Type" : "Number",
    "Default" : "1"
},
```

Similarly, `SlaveInstanceCount` is used to control the number of slave instances in the cluster.

Cloudformation updates the autoscaling groups, and Mesos then transparently handles the scaling up by adding more nodes and scaling down by removing nodes. Take a look:

```
"SlaveInstanceType" : {
  "Description" : "EC2 instance type",
  "Type" : "String",
  "Default" : "t2.micro",
  "AllowedValues" : [
    "t2.micro", "t2.small", "t2.medium",
    "m3.medium", "m3.large", "m3.xlarge",
    "m3.2xlarge",
    "c3.large", "c3.xlarge", "c3.2xlarge", "c3.4xlarge",
    "c3.8xlarge", "c4.large", "c4.xlarge", "c4.2xlarge",
    "c4.4xlarge", "c4.8xlarge",
    "r3.large", "r3.xlarge", "r3.2xlarge",
    "r3.4xlarge", "r3.8xlarge",
    "i2.xlarge", "i2.2xlarge", "i2.4xlarge", "i2.8xlarge",
    "hs1.8xlarge", "g2.2xlarge"],
  "ConstraintDescription" :
    "must be a valid, HVM-compatible EC2 instance type."
},
```

We can also use the `InstanceType` configuration property for both the master (`MasterInstanceType`) and slave (`SlaveInstanceType`) to control the size of the machine in the AWS cloud.

Again, in the security group that we created earlier, open up the following ports for Mesos communication:

- Mesos master port: 5050
- Marathon port : 8080

Once we configure the values in the `mesos-master.json`, `mesos-slave.json` files, we can upload these files into S3 using the following command:

```
$ aws s3 cp mesos-master.json s3://cloudformationbucket/
$ aws s3 cp mesos-slave.json s3://cloudformationbucket/
```

We can now use aws-cli to launch our Mesos cluster with the following command:

```
aws cloudformation create-stack \
  --template-body file://mesos.json \
  --stack-name <stack> \
  --capabilities CAPABILITY_IAM \
```

```
--parameters \
  ParameterKey=KeyName,ParameterValue=<key> \
  ParameterKey=ExhibitorDiscoveryUrl,ParameterValue=<url> \
  ParameterKey=ZkClientSecurityGroup,ParameterValue=<sg_id> \
  ParameterKey=VpcId,ParameterValue=<vpc_id> \
  ParameterKey=Subnets,ParameterValue='
    <subnet_id_1>\,<subnet_id_2>' \
  ParameterKey=AdminSecurityGroup,ParameterValue=<sg_id> \
  ParameterKey=MesosMasterTemplateUrl,
    ParameterValue=https://s3.amazonaws.com/
    cloudformationbucket/mesos-master.json \
  ParameterKey=MesosSlaveTemplateUrl,
    ParameterValue=
    https://s3.amazonaws.com/
    cloudformationbucket/mesos-slave.json
```

Creating test environments using Playa Mesos

Apache Mesos test environments can be quickly created using Playa Mesos. You can take a look at the official repository from the following URL:

`https://github.com/mesosphere/playa-mesos.`

Before using this project, make sure in your environment that you install and configure VirtualBox, Vagrant, and an Ubuntu machine image that contains Mesos and Marathon preinstalled.

Installations

Follow the below instructions to get started with Playa Mesos

- **Install VirtualBox**: You can navigate to `https://www.virtualbox.org/wiki/Downloads` and download and install the appropriate version for your environment

- **Install Vagrant**: You can use the methods described in the *Installing Aurora* section of *Chapter 4, Service Scheduling and Management Frameworks*, to get started with Vagrant

- **Playa**: You can clone the repository with the following command:

```
$ git clone https://github.com/mesosphere/playa-mesos
# Make sure the tests are passed
$ cd playa-mesos
$ bin/test
# Start the environment
$ vagrant up
```

If everything goes well, we will be able to see the Mesos master Web UI by pointing the browser to `10.141.141.10:5050` and the Marathon Web UI from `10.141.141.10:8080`.

Once the machine is started, then we can use `ssh` to log in to the machine with the following command:

```
$ vagrant ssh
```

We can also use the following command to halt and terminate the test environment:

```
# Halting the machine
$ vagrant halt


#Destroying the VM
$ vagrant destroy
```

Apart from this, if you wish to tweak the configurations a bit, then you can do this by editing the `config.json` file located at the root of the `playa-mesos` repository.

We can use the following configuration properties in the `config.json` file:

- `platform`: This is the virtualization platform. We will use VirtualBox, although VMware Fusion and VMware workstation can also be used.
- `box_name`: This is the name of the vagrant instance.
- `base_url`: This is the base URL where Vagrant images are stored.
- `ip_address`: This is the private network IP address of the VM.
- `mesos_release`: This parameter is optional, which specifies the version of Mesos. This should be the full string returned by `apt-cache policy mesos`. An example would be `0.22.1-1.0.ubuntu1404`.
- `vm_ram`: This is the memory allocated to the Vagrant VM.
- `vm_cpus`: This is the number of cores allocated to the Vagrant VM.

We can create a sample `config.json` file by putting up all these configuration parameters, and it would look similar to the following:

```
{

    "platform": "virtualbox",

    "box_name": "playa_mesos_ubuntu_14.04_201601041324",

    "base_url": "http://downloads.mesosphere.io/playa-mesos",

    "ip_address": "10.141.141.10",

    "vm_ram": "2048",

    "vm_cpus": "2"

}
```

As you can note here, we allocated 2,040 MB memory and two cores, and the machine will run on the `10.141.141.10` IP address.

Monitoring the Mesos cluster using Nagios

Monitoring is a vital part of keeping the infrastructure up and running. Mesos integrates well with the existing monitoring solutions and has plugins for most monitoring solutions, such as **Nagios**. This module will give you a walkthrough of how to install Nagios on your cluster and enable monitoring to send you e-mail alerts whenever something goes wrong in your cluster.

Installing Nagios 4

The first thing we need to do before installing Nagios is to add an Nagios user to the system from which the Nagios process can run and send out alerts. We can create a new user and a new usergroup for Nagios by executing the following commands:

```
$ sudo useradd nagios
$ sudo groupadd nagcmd
$ sudo usermod -a -G nagcmd nagios
```

Here, we created a user, Nagios, and a user group, `nagcmd`, which is assigned to the user Nagios in the third command listed before.

Now, install the dependency packages with the following command:

```
$ sudo apt-get install build-essential
  libgd2-xpm-dev openssl libssl-dev xinetd apache2-utils unzip
```

Once the dependencies are installed and the user is added, we can start downloading and installing `nagios` by executing the following commands:

```
#Download the nagios archive.
$ wget https://assets.nagios.com/downloads/
  nagioscore/releases/nagios-4.1.1.tar.gz
# Extract the archive.
$ tar xvf nagios-*.tar.gz
# Change the working directory to nagios
$ cd nagios*


# Configure and build nagios
$ ./configure --with-nagios-group=nagios
  --with-command-group=nagcmd
  --with-mail=/usr/sbin/sendmail
$ make all


# Install nagios, init scripts and sample configuration file
$ sudo make install
$ sudo make install-commandmode
$ sudo make install-init
$ sudo make install-config
$ sudo /usr/bin/install -c -m 644 sample
  -config/httpd.conf /etc/apache2/sites-available/nagios.conf
```

Once `nagios` is installed, we can install the `nagios` plugin by downloading and building it by issuing the following commands:

```
$ wget http://nagios-plugins.org/download/
  nagios-plugins-2.1.1.tar.gz

$ tar xvf nagios-plugins-*.tar.gz

$ cd nagios-plugins-*

$ ./configure --with-nagios-user=nagios
  --with-nagios-group=nagios --with-openssl

$ make

$ sudo make install
```

Once the plugins are installed, we can install **NRPE (Nagios Remote Plugin Executor)** to take status updates from remote machines. It can be installed by executing the following commands:

```
$ wget http://downloads.sourceforge.net/
  project/nagios/nrpe-2.x/nrpe-2.15/nrpe-2.15.tar.gz


$ tar xf nrpe*.tar.gz
$ cd nrpe*


$ ./configure --enable-command-args
  --with-nagios-user=nagios
  --with-nagios-group=nagios
  --with-ssl=/usr/bin/openssl
  --with-ssl-lib=/usr/lib/x86_64-linux-gnu


$ make all
$ sudo make install
$ sudo make install-xinetd
$ sudo make install-daemon-config
```

For security reasons, edit the file located at `/etc/xinetd.d/nrpe` with the following content:

```
only_from = 127.0.0.1 10.132.224.168
```

Replace the IP address with our `nagios` server IP address so that only our `nagios` server is able to make remote calls. Once this is done, save the file and exit and then restart the `xintend` service by executing the following command:

```
$ sudo service xinetd restart
```

Now that `nagios` is installed, we can configure the contact e-mail addresses to which the notifications will be sent by editing the following file:

```
$ sudo vi /usr/local/nagios/etc/objects/contacts.cfg
```

Find and replace the following line with your own e-mail address:

```
email nagios@localhost ; << ** Change this to your email address **
```

Add a user to `nagios` so that we can log in from the browser and see the activities by executing the following command. Here, we used `nagiosadmin` as the username and password, as follows:

```
$ sudo htpasswd -c /usr/local/nagios/etc/htpasswd.users nagiosadmin
```

Now, restart the `nagios` service by issuing the following command:

```
$ sudo service nagios restart
```

We can now log in to the `nagios` admin panel by accessing the following URL from the browser:

```
http://MachineIP/nagios
```

`MachineIP` is the IP address of the machine on which we installed `nagios`, and it will prompt you with an authentication form in which you can give the username and password as `nagiosadmin`.

Upon authentication, you will reach the Nagios home page. To view which hosts are being monitored by Nagios, click on the **Hosts** link present on the left-hand side, as shown in the following screenshot (source: `https://www.digitalocean.com/community/tutorials/how-to-install-nagios-4-and-monitor-your-servers-on-ubuntu-14-04`):

Now, we will discuss how we can use NRPE to monitor the nodes in our Mesos cluster.

The following section will add a machine to Nagios to monitor, and we can repeat the same steps to add as many machines as required. For the time being, we will choose the Mesos master node to be monitored, and it will trigger an e-mail if the disk usage for a particular drive exceeds the given amount.

Now, on the master machine, install the Nagios plugins and `nrpe-server` with the following command:

```
$ sudo apt-get install nagios-plugins nagios-nrpe-server
```

As mentioned earlier, for security reasons, edit the `/etc/nagios/nrpe.cfg` file and put the `nagios` server IP address for communication under the `allowed_hosts` property.

Now, edit the `nrpe` configuration file with the properties to monitor the disk usage via the following command:

```
$ sudo vi /etc/nagios/nrpe.cfg
```

Then, add the following content:

```
server_address=client_private_IP
allowed_hosts=nagios_server_private_IP
command[check_hda1]=
   /usr/lib/nagios/plugins/check_disk -w 20% -c 10% -p /dev/vda
```

Here, `server_address` is the IP address of the machine, `allowed_hosts` is the `nagios` server address, and the command is the actual command to pull the disk usage. We used the `check_disk` plugin that comes with `nagios` and passes the arguments to the command as `-w 20% -c 10%`. Whenever the server exceeds 20% disk usage, Nagios will trigger an e-mail alert.

Once we edit the file, restart the `nrpe` server with the following command:

```
$ sudo service nagios-nrpe-server restart
```

Now that we have configured the Mesos master to check the disk usage, we also need to add this Mesos master to the `nagios` server so that it can keep on checking the disk usage and alert the administrators when it exceeds the quota.

Add a new configuration file on the `nagios` server to monitor, and we can add the file in `/usr/local/nagios/etc/servers/`, as follows:

```
$ sudo vi /usr/local/nagios/etc/servers/mesos-master.cfg
```

Then, add the following content:

```
define host {
        use                          linux-server
        host_name                    mesos-master
        alias                        Mesos master server
        address                      10.132.234.52
        max_check_attempts           5
        check_period                 24x7
        notification_interval        30
        notification_period          24x7
}
```

This configuration will keep monitoring the Mesos master machine to check whether it is still running. The administrator (or others, as specified in the e-mail list) will get an e-mail notification if the Mesos master machine goes down.

We can also enable the network usage checking by adding the following service:

```
define service {
        use                          generic-service
        host_name                    mesos-master
        service_description          PING
        check_command                check_
ping!100.0,20%!500.0,60%

}
```

Once we set the configurations for the new host, we need to restart `nagios` by executing the following command:

```
$ sudo service nagios reload
```

We can create new configuration files for slave nodes, as well, by following the steps listed previously.

Monitoring the Mesos cluster using Satellite

Satellite is another tool for monitoring Mesos, and the Satellite project is maintained by Two Sigma Investments, which is written in Clojure. The Satellite master instance monitors the Mesos masters and receives the monitoring information from Mesos slaves through the Satellite slaves. For each Mesos master and Mesos slave, there exists a Satellite master and slave process, with the `satellite-slave` processes sending one type of message to all `satellite-masters` in the cluster.

Aggregate statistics of the cluster, such as the utilization of resources, the number of lost tasks and events specific to the master, such as how many leaders are currently active and so on, are usually pulled. Satellite also provides a **Representational State Transfer (REST)** interface to interact with the Mesos master whitelist. Whitelists are text files that contain the list of hosts to which the master will consider sending tasks. It also provides a REST interface to access the cached Mesos tasks metadata. Satellite itself never caches any of this information and only provides an interface to retrieve it if it is cached. This is an optional feature, but it is useful if we have persisted tasks metadata within Mesos itself.

Satellite adds two additional conceptual whitelists to the mix:

- **Managed whitelist**: These are the hosts that are are entered automatically
- **Manual whitelist**: If a host is present in this whitelist, then its status overrides that in the managed whitelist discussed previously. These are the REST endpoints taking the PUT and DELETE requests.

At intervals, a merge operation actually merges these two into the whitelist file.

Satellite installation

Satellite needs to be installed on all the machines that are present in the Mesos cluster. We will need to install satellite-master on the Mesos master machines and the satellite-slave on the Mesos slave machines. Run the following code:

```
# Install lein on all the machines
$ wget https://raw.githubusercontent.com/technomancy/leiningen/stable/bin/lein
$ chmod +x lein
$ export PATH=$PATH:/path/to/lein


# Clone the satellite repository
$ git clone https://github.com/twosigma/satellite


# Compile the satellite-master jar
$ cd satellite/satellite-master
$ lein release-jar
```

The preceding command will create a jar in the target directory, which we can copy to all the Mesos master machines.

Executing the following command by passing the configuration will run the satellite process on the machines:

```
$ java -jar ./target/satellite.jar ./config/satellite-config.clj
```

Common deployment issues and solutions

This module contains a few common issues that are faced while installing or setting up the tools and modules described in this chapter:

1. For the Ansible python-setup tools, take a look at the following screenshot:

```
Ansible now needs setuptools in order to build. Install it using your package manager (usually python-setuptools) or via pip (pip install setuptools).

Setting up Ansible to run out of checkout...

PATH=/home/akhld/mobi/book/mesos/ansible/bin:/home/akhld/google-cloud-sdk/bin:/usr/local/sbin:/usr/local/bin:/usr/sbin:/usr/bin:/sbin:/bin:/usr/games:/usr/local/games:/ho
me/akhld/mobi/localcluster/hadoop/bin/:/home/akhld/mobi/localcluster/codes/sbt/bin/:/home/akhld/mobi/localcluster/codes/pig/bin/:/home/akhld/gdbc-seattle/hadoop/bin:/home
/akhld/gdbc-seattle/hadoop/sbin:/home/akhld/mobi/localcluster/mongodb/bin
PYTHONPATH=/home/akhld/mobi/book/mesos/ansible/lib:
MANPATH=/home/akhld/mobi/book/mesos/ansible/docs/man:

Remember, you may wish to specify your host file with -i

Done!
```

   If your Ansible installation shows the preceding message, then execute the following command to resolve it:

   ```
   $ sudo pip install setuptools
   ```

2. SSH runs on a different port, and `nagios` shows a `connection refused` error.

   You will get the following exception if you run your `ssh` server on a different port:

   ```
   SERVICE ALERT: localhost;SSH;CRITICAL;HARD;4;Connection refused
   ```

   This can be fixed by editing the following line from `/etc/nagios/conf.d/services_nagios.cfg`:

   ```
   # check that ssh services are running
   define service {
       hostgroup_name          ssh-servers
       service_description     SSH
       check_command           check_ssh_port!6666!server
       use                     generic-service
       notification_interval   0 ;
         set > 0 if you want to be renotified
   ```

Here, we used `6666` as the `ssh` port, rather than `22`, to get rid of the error message.

3. Chef fails to unzip packages.

Sometimes, the Chef setup fails to retrieve the packages and gives the following error stack:

```
==> master1: [2015-12-25T22:28:39+00:00]
  INFO: Running queued delayed notifications
  before re-raising exception
==> master1: [2015-12-25T22:28:39+00:00]
  ERROR: Running exception handlers
==> master1: [2015-12-25T22:28:39+00:00]
  ERROR: Exception handlers complete
==> master1: [2015-12-25T22:28:39+00:00]
  FATAL: Stacktrace dumped to
  /var/chef/cache/chef-stacktrace.out
==> master1: [2015-12-25T22:28:39+00:00]
  ERROR: packageunzip had an error:
  Mixlib::ShellOut::ShellCommandFailed:
  Expected process to exit with [0],
  but received '100'
==> master1: ----
  Begin output of apt-get -q -y install
  unzip=6.0-8ubuntu2 ----
==> master1: STDOUT: Reading package lists...
==> master1: Building dependency tree...
==> master1: Reading state information...
==> master1:
  The following packages were
  automatically installed and
  are no longer required:
==> master1: erubis ohai
  ruby-bunny ruby-erubis ruby-highline
  ruby-i18n ruby-ipaddress
==> master1: ruby-mime-types
  ruby-mixlib-authentication ruby-mixlib-cli
==> master1: ruby-mixlib-config ruby-mixlib-log
  ruby-mixlib-shellout ruby-moneta
==> master1: ruby-net-ssh ruby-net-ssh-gateway
  ruby-net-ssh-multi ruby-polyglot
==> master1: ruby-rest-client ruby-sigar
  ruby-systemu ruby-treetop ruby-uuidtools
==> master1: ruby-yajl
==> master1:
  Use 'apt-get autoremove' to remove them.
```

```
==> master1: Suggested packages:
==> master1: zip
==> master1:
   The following NEW packages will be installed:
==> master1: unzip
==> master1: 0 upgraded, 1 newly installed,
   0 to remove and 0 not upgraded.
==> master1: Need to get 192 kB of archives.
==> master1: After this operation,
   394 kB of additional disk space will be used.
==> master1: WARNING:
   The following packages cannot be authenticated!
==> master1: unzip
==> master1: STDERR: E: There are problems and
   -y was used without --force-yes
==> master1: ---- End output of apt-get -q
   -y install unzip=6.0-8ubuntu2 ----
==> master1: Ran apt-get -q
   -y install unzip=6.0-8ubuntu2 returned 100
==> master1: [2015-12-25T22:28:40+00:00]
   FATAL: Chef::Exceptions::ChildConvergeError:
   Chef run process exited unsuccessfully
   (exit code 1)
Chef never successfully completed!
   Any errors should be visible in the
output above. Please fix your recipes so that
   they properly complete.
```

This error shows up when your apt's key is old. To resolve this issue, you need to update the keys by executing the following command:

```
$ sudo apt-key update
```

4. ZooKeeper throws an error "no masters are currently leading".

    This is a known ZooKeeper error due to the incorrect configuration of the ZooKeeper properties. We can resolve this error by editing the ZooKeeper configuration file located at /etc/zookeeper/conf/zoo.cfg properly. Add the following properties beside the server IP listed in the file:

```
tickTime=2000
dataDir=/var/zookeeper
clientPort=2181
```

Summary

After reading this chapter, you should now be able to use any standard deployment tool to launch and configure a Mesos cluster on a distributed infrastructure. You would also be able to understand various security, multitenancy, and maintenance features supported by Mesos and learn how to implement them for production-grade setups.

In the next chapter, we will explore Mesos frameworks in greater detail. We will discuss the various features of frameworks and the process of porting an existing framework on Mesos and understand how to develop custom frameworks on top of Mesos to address specific applications.

6
Mesos Frameworks

This chapter walks the reader through the concept and features of Mesos frameworks in detail. It also provides a detailed overview of the Mesos API, including the new HTTP Scheduler API, and provides the recipe for building custom frameworks on Mesos. The following topics will be covered in this chapter:

- Introduction to Mesos frameworks
- Framework authentication
- Framework authorization
- Access Control Lists (ACLs)
- The scheduler HTTP API
- Building custom distributed frameworks on Mesos

Introduction to Mesos frameworks

A Mesos framework sits between Mesos and the application and acts as a layer for managing task scheduling and execution. As its implementation is application-specific, the term is often used to refer to the application itself. Earlier, a Mesos framework could interact with the Mesos API using only the libmesos C++ library, due to which other language bindings were developed for Java, Scala, Python, and Go among others, which leveraged libmesos heavily. Since v0.19.0, changes made to the HTTP-based protocol enabled developers to develop frameworks using the language they wanted without having to rely on the C++ code. A framework consists of two components:

- A scheduler
- An executor

The **scheduler** is responsible for taking decisions on the resource offers made to it and tracking the current state of the cluster. Communication with the Mesos master is handled by the `SchedulerDriver` module, which registers the framework with the master, launches tasks, and passes messages to other components.

The second component, **Executor**, as its name suggests, is responsible for the execution of tasks on the slave nodes. Communication with the slaves is handled by the `ExecutorDriver` module, which is also responsible for sending status updates to the scheduler.

Frameworks – Authentication, authorization, and access control

From the user's perspective, authentication, authorization, and access control often appear to be the same thing because they are typically implemented together. However, there are some important distinctions between them. Some of these are listed below to provide better clarity on what each of these concepts means:

- **Authentication:** Authentication is a process by which you verify that someone or something is who or what they claim to be, respectively. It typically involves implementing one or more methods of demonstrating identity. The result of an authentication procedure is normally a yes/no answer.

- **Authorization:** Authorization is used to establish whether the application or user (already authenticated) is allowed to perform the requested task. It is used to define and determine what an authenticated application/user can and cannot do. An authorization module typically includes a mechanism for defining rules (such as roles, privileges, and so on).

- **Access Control:** Access Control is the process of ensuring that nonauthenticated or unauthorized applications/users cannot bypass the system and perform restricted actions. It typically involves implementing a variety of security features to ensure that no loopholes are present in the system.

Framework authentication

Framework authentication support for Mesos was added v0.15 onward, and slave authentication support was introduced in v0.19. This is a very useful feature to prevent unauthorized applications from running on Mesos.

For a framework to register with the Mesos master, it needs to be authenticated. Similarly, the authentication of slaves is necessary for them to be able to register with the master as otherwise, unauthorized processes could launch **Distributed Denial of Service (DDoS)** attacks, obtain task information, and so on. It also prohibits rogue access to the /teardown HTTP endpoint so that the frameworks can't be illegally terminated.

The **Cyrus Simple Authentication and Security Layer (SASL)** library, a flexible framework with support for various mechanisms, such as CRAM-MD5, Plain, GSSAPI, and so on, is leveraged by Mesos to enable authentication. The **CRAM-MD5** mechanism is currently supported by Mesos though users have the ability to implement their own modules as well. CRAM-MD5 implements a shared secret authentication mechanism in which a principal (in this case, the framework) and authenticator (Mesos) share a mutually known "secret" key with each other to encrypt and decrypt information. Whenever the framework communicates with Mesos, it is asked to decrypt or encrypt information successfully using this "secret" key so that Mesos can understand that it is really the authorized framework that wishes to communicate with it. It should be noted that this is not the same as the framework user, which is what an executor uses to run tasks.

Configuration options

The authentication module uses the following configuration options:

- Masters:
    - --[no-]authenticate: If true, then the registration of authenticated frameworks is permitted. If false, then other frameworks can register as well.
    - --[no-]authenticate_slaves: If true, then the registration of authenticated slaves is permitted. If false, then other slaves can register as well.
    - --authenticators: This is used to specify which authentication mechanism needs to be used to authenticate the master, with CRAM-MD5 being the default. The –modules option may be used to add other mechanisms as well.
    - --credentials: This is used to specify the location of the file containing a valid credentials list and can be optional based on which mechanism is employed for authentication.

- Slaves:

    ○ `--authenticate`: This is used to specify which authentication mechanism needs to be used to authenticate the slave, with CRAM-MD5 being the default.

    ○ `--credential`: This is used to specify the location of the file containing the credentials, which needs to be used to determine the slave.

Framework authorization

Authorization refers to the process of determining whether an already authenticated user has the required permissions to execute the requested task or access specific resources. Since Mesos 0.24, the authorization API has been modularized so that system administrators can implement authorization backend/protocols of their choice (Lightweight directory access protocol or LDAP, for example).

When starting the master, authorization can be configured by specifying the `--acls` flag.

The following authorizations are currently supported:

- The registration of frameworks with specified roles
- Task launching by frameworks as authorized users
- The shutting down of frameworks by authorized principals
- Quota setting by authorized principals
- Reservation and freeing up of resources by authorized principals
- Creation and destruction of persistent volumes by authorized principals

Access Control Lists (ACLs)

Access Control Lists or **ACLs** are used to implement *authorization* capabilities in Mesos. An ACL needs to be defined in the JSON format for each of the six supported authorizations mentioned before. In every ACL, a list of Subjects need to be defined that can carry out Actions on a group of Objects. The Mesos master then checks these to confirm whether a request received by it is an authorized one or not.

The supported Actions list is as follows:

- `register_frameworks`: This is used for framework registration
- `run_tasks`: This is used to run tasks

- `shutdown_frameworks`: This is used to terminate frameworks
- `set_quotas`: This is used for quota setting
- `reserve_resources`: This is used for resource reservation
- `unreserve_resources` : This is used to free up resources
- `create_volumes`: This is used to create persistent volumes
- `destroy_volumes`: This is used to destroy persistent volumes

The supported `Subjects` list is as follows:

- `principals`: These can be of two types:
    - Framework principals
    - Usernames

The supported `Objects` list is as follows:

- `roles`
- `users`
- `framework_principals`
- `resources`
- `reserver_principals`
- `volume_types`
- `creator_principals`

For example, when a framework attempts to register with the master, it checks the `register_frameworks` ACLs to verify that the framework attempting to register with it is authorized to receive resources offers for the specified role. The scheduler is terminated, and an error message is sent if the framework is an unauthorized one.

Another example is that of a framework trying to launch a set of tasks. In this case, the `run_tasks` ACLs are checked to verify that the framework is permitted to run the required tasks and as the specified user. A `TASK_LOST` message is sent back if the framework is unauthorized and the tasks do not get launched.

For more information, visit `http://mesos.apache.org/documentation/latest/authorization/`.

> ACLs are checked in setup order; that is, the first relevant ACL is used to determine the request authorization status.
>
> The ACLs.permissive field determines how a nonmatching request should be treated. The default is true, which means that if no matching ACL exists, then the request is authorized.

Examples

A few examples of how to implement ACLs are as follows:

- The A and B frameworks can run tasks as user U. Take a look at the following code:

```
{
"run_tasks": [
{
"principals": { "values": ["A", "B"] },
"users": { "values": ["U"] }
}
]
}
```

Any framework can run tasks as user guest, as shown by the following code:

```
{
"run_tasks": [
{
"principals": { "type": "ANY" },
"users": { "values": ["guest"] }
}
]
}
```

No framework can run tasks as root, as follows:

```
{
"run_tasks": [
{
"principals": { "type": "NONE" },
"users": { "values": ["root"] }
}
]
}
```

- The framework A can run tasks only as user guest and no other user, as demonstrated by the following code:

```
    {
"run_tasks": [
{
"principals": { "values": [ "A" ] },
"users": { "values": ["guest"] }
},
{
"principals": { "values": [ "A" ] },
"users": { "type": "NONE" }
}
]
    }
```

The framework A can register with X and Y roles, as follows:

```
{
"register_frameworks": [
{
"principals": { "values": ["A"] },
"roles": { "values": ["X", "Y"] }
}
]
}
```

Only the framework A and no one else can register with X role, as follows:

```
    {
"register_frameworks": [
{
"principals": { "values": ["A"] },
"roles": { "values": ["X"] }
},
{
"principals": { "type": "NONE" },
"roles": { "values": ["X"] }
}
]
    }
```

- The framework A can only register with the X role but no other roles. Also, no other framework can register with any roles, as in the following code:

```
 {
"permissive" : false,
"register_frameworks": [
{
"principals": { "values": ["A"] },
"roles": { "values": ["X"] }
}
]
}
```

Only the P principal can shut down any frameworks through the / teardown HTTP endpoint. Take a look at the following code:

```
 {
"permissive" : false,
"shutdown_frameworks":[
{
"principals": { "values": ["P"] },
"framework_principals":{"type":"ANY"}
}
]
 }
```

The Mesos API

Mesos provides an API to allow developers to build custom frameworks that can run on top of the underlying distributed infrastructure. Refer to the *API details* section in *Chapter 1, Introducing Mesos* for a detailed explanation of the Mesos API. The detailed steps involved in developing bespoke frameworks leveraging this API will be described in the subsequent section with the help of an example.

Mesos also implements an **actor style message-passing programming model** to enable nonblocking communication between different Mesos components and leverages protocol buffers for the same.

In addition, there is also a new scheduler HTTP API that was recently introduced, and it will be briefly discussed in the next section.

The scheduler HTTP API

Since Mesos version 0.24.0, experimental support has been introduced for a new HTTP API (only scheduler for the time being). The Mesos master hosts the api/v1/ scheduler endpoint with which the scheduler communicates.

Request Calls

The master currently accepts the following request calls:

Subscribe

The scheduler sends a Subscribe message, including the relevant framework information such as name and so on, via an HTTP POST request to enable communication with the master. The response includes a subscription confirmation and details such as the framework ID, which will be used in all subsequent communications.

The SUBSCRIBE request (JSON) is as follows:

```
POST /api/v1/scheduler  HTTP/1.1

{
"type"      : "SUBSCRIBE",

"subscribe"  : {
"framework_info"  : {
"user" :  "U",
"name" :  "N"
},

"force" : true
  }
}
```

The SUBSCRIBE response (JSON) is as follows:

```
HTTP/1.1 200 OK
```

TEARDOWN

The scheduler sends this request when it wants to shut itself. When it receives this request, Mesos will terminate all executors, killing all the running tasks in the process. It will then proceed to remove the framework and end all communication between the Mesos master and scheduler.

The TEARDOWN request (JSON) is as follows:

```
POST /api/v1/scheduler  HTTP/1.1

{
"framework_id"    : {"value" : "<some_value>"},
```

```
"type"              : "TEARDOWN",
}
```

The TEARDOWN response is as follows:

```
HTTP/1.1 202 Accepted
```

ACCEPT

When the scheduler wants to accept the resource offers made by the Mesos master, it sends this request. The operations that the scheduler intends to carry out are included as parameters in the request (for example, launch task, create volumes, and reserve resources).

The ACCEPT request (JSON) is as follows:

```
POST /api/v1/scheduler  HTTP/1.1

{
"framework_id"      : {"value" : "<some_Value>"},
"type"              : "ACCEPT",
"accept"            : {
"offer_ids"       : [
{"value" : "<some_Value>"},
{"value" : "<some_value>"}
],
"operations"      : [ {"type" : "LAUNCH", "launch" : {...}} ],
"filters"         : {...}
  }
}
```

The ACCEPT response is as follows:

```
HTTP/1.1 202 Accepted
```

DECLINE

When the scheduler wants to decline the resource offers made by the Mesos master, it sends this request.

The DECLINE request (JSON) is as follows:

```
POST /api/v1/scheduler  HTTP/1.1

{
"framework_id"      : {"value" : "<some_Value>"},
```

```
"type"               :  "DECLINE",
"decline"            :  {
"offer_ids"          :  [
                            {"value" : "<some_value>"},
                            {"value" : "<some_Value>"}
                         ],
"filters"            :  {...}
    }
}
```

The DECLINE response is as follows:

```
HTTP/1.1 202 Accepted
```

REVIVE

If any filters are set by prior accept or decline requests, then the scheduler can send a revive call to remove them.

The REVIVE request (JSON) is as follows:

```
POST /api/v1/scheduler  HTTP/1.1

{
"framework_id"       :  {"value" : "<some_value>"},
"type"               :  "REVIVE",
}
```

The REVIVE response is as follows:

```
HTTP/1.1 202 Accepted
```

KILL

If a specific task needs to be killed, then the scheduler can send a KILL request. If a custom executor is present, then the request is passed on to this executor, in which it can be processed. If the master is unaware of the task that is requested to be killed, it will generate a Task_Lost message.

The KILL request (JSON) is as follows:

```
POST /api/v1/scheduler  HTTP/1.1

{
"framework_id"       :  {"value" : "<some_value>"},
"type"               :  "KILL",
```

```
"kill"              : {
"task_id"    :  {"value" : "<some_Value>"},
"agent_id"   :  {"value" : "<some_value>"}
   }
}
```

The KILL response is as follows:

```
HTTP/1.1 202 Accepted
```

SHUTDOWN

This newly introduced call is sent by the scheduler when it wants to end specific custom executors.

The SHUTDOWN request (JSON) is as follows:

```
POST /api/v1/scheduler  HTTP/1.1

{
"framework_id"      : {"value" : "<some_value>"},
"type"              : "SHUTDOWN",
"shutdown"          : {
"executor_id":  {"value" : "<some_value>"},
"agent_id":  {"value" : "<some_value>"}
   }
}
```

The SHUTDOWN response is as follows:

```
HTTP/1.1 202 Accepted
```

ACKNOWLEDGE

When a status update needs to be acknowledged, the scheduler sends this request.

The ACKNOWLEDGE request (JSON) is as follows:

```
POST /api/v1/scheduler  HTTP/1.1

{
"framework_id"      : {"value" : "<some_value>"},
"type"              : "ACKNOWLEDGE",
"acknowledge"       : {
"agent_id"   :  {"value" : "<some_Value>"},
"task_id"    :  {"value" : "<some_value>"},
```

```
"uuid"          :   "<some_value>"
    }
}
```

The ACKNOWLEDGE response is as follows:

```
HTTP/1.1 202 Accepted
```

RECONCILE

When the status nonterminal tasks needs to be queried, the scheduler sends this request. For every task in the list, an Update event is sent back by the master.

The RECONCILE request (JSON) is as follows:

```
POST /api/v1/scheduler  HTTP/1.1

{
"framework_id"     : {"value" : "<some_value>"},
"type"             : "RECONCILE",
"reconcile"        : {
"tasks"      : [
                    { "task_id"   : { "<some_value>" },
"agent_id" : { "<some_value>" }
                    }
                ]
    }
}
```

The RECONCILE response is as follows:

```
HTTP/1.1 202 Accepted
```

MESSAGE

If arbitrary binary data needs to be sent to the executor, the scheduler makes use of this request.

The MESSAGE request (JSON) is as follows:

```
POST /api/v1/scheduler  HTTP/1.1

{
"framework_id"     : {"value" : "<some_value>"},
"type"             : "MESSAGE",
"message"          : {
```

```
"agent_id"         : {"value" : "<some_value>"},
"executor_id"      : {"value" : "<some_value>"},
"data"             : "<some_Value>"
    }
  }
```

The MESSAGE response is as follows:

```
HTTP/1.1 202 Accepted
```

REQUEST

This is used by the scheduler to request resources from the master.

The REQUEST request (JSON) is as follows:

```
POST /api/v1/scheduler  HTTP/1.1

{
"framework_id"     : {"value" : "<some_value>"},
"type"             : "REQUEST",
"requests"         : [
        {
"agent_id"         : {"value" : "<some_value>"},
"resources"        : {}
        },
    ]
}
```

The REQUEST response is as follows:

```
HTTP/1.1 202 Accepted
```

Response events

The master currently sends the following events as responses.

SUBSCRIBED

When a Subscribe request is made by the scheduler, the first event sent by the master is the Subscribed event. The format is given as follows:

The SUBSCRIBED event (JSON) is as follows:

```
<event-length>
{
"type"          : "SUBSCRIBED",
"subscribed"    : {
"framework_id"                : {"value":"<some_value>"},
"heartbeat_interval_seconds" : 10
    }
}
```

OFFERS

The master sends this event whenever it can offer frameworks a new set of resources. Every offer corresponds to a group of resources on a slave. The resources are assumed to be allocated till the scheduler makes an Accept or Decline call to the master. The offer is rescinded if a slave is lost or times out.

The OFFERS event (JSON) is as follows:

```
<event-length>
{
"type"    : "OFFERS",
"offers"  : [
    {
"offer_id":{"value": "<some_value>"},
"framework_id":{"value": "<some_Value>"},
"agent_id":{"value": "<some_value>"},
"hostname":"agent.host",
"resources":[...],
"attributes":[...],
"executor_ids":[]
    }
  ]
}
```

RESCIND

When an offer's validity expires (for example, when the slave mentioned in the offer is lost) the master sends this event to rescind the offer. If the scheduler makes any calls in the future, these are considered invalid.

The `RESCIND` event (JSON) is as follows:

```
<event-length>
{
"type":"RESCIND",
"rescind":{
"offer_id":{"value":"<some_value>"}
}
}
```

UPDATE

The master sends this event if the executor creates a status update regarding the running tasks. For example, if the `Task_Finished` update is generated, then the master can release the resources given to the task for use elsewhere.

The `UPDATE` event (JSON) is as follows:

```
<event-length>
{
"type"      : "UPDATE",
"update"   : {
"status"    : {
"task_id"   : { "value" : "<some_value>"},
"state"     : "TASK_FINISHED",
"source"    : "SOURCE_EXECUTOR",
"uuid"      : "<some_value>",
"bytes"     : "<some_Value"

        }
    }
}
```

MESSAGE

The Mesos master forwards executor-generated messages to the scheduler without interpretation or delivery guarantee by passing the `Message` event. If the message delivery fails for any reason, the executor needs to resend the request.

The `MESSAGE` event (JSON) is as follows:

```
<event-length>
{
"type":"MESSAGE",
"message":{
```

```
"agent_id":{"value":"<some_value>"},
"executor_id":{"value":"<some_value>"},
"data":"<some_value>"
}
}
```

FAILURE

The master sends this event upon slave removal or executor termination.

The FAILURE event (JSON) is as follows:

```
<event-length>
{
"type":"FAILURE",
"failure":{
"agent_id":{"value":"<some_Value>"},
"executor_id":{"value":"<some_Value>"},
"status": 1
}
}
```

ERROR

The master sends this event upon the occurrence of an error (for example, a framework with the given role unauthorized to subscribe to the requested resources). The recommendation is that the framework should abort upon the receipt of this event and the resubscribe.

The ERROR event (JSON) is as follows:

```
<event-length>
{
"type":"ERROR",
"message":"Framework is not authorized"
}
```

HEARTBEAT

The master sends this event at periodic intervals to communicate to the scheduler that an established subscribed connection is alive. This helps make sure that a live connection is not terminated due to insufficient data movement.

The HEARTBEAT event (JSON) is as follows:

```
<event-length>
{
"type":"HEARTBEAT",
}
```

For more information regarding the scheduler HTTP API, visit http://mesos. apache.org/documentation/latest/scheduler-http-api/.

Building a custom framework on Mesos

As we already know, a Mesos framework is an application running on Mesos. In this module, we will see how we can create our own Mesos framework. For the sake of simplicity, we will create a simple Java application to calculate the value of *pi*. A Mesos framework consists of the following three components:

- **Driver**: This is the piece of code that submits tasks to the framework
- **Executor:** This is the piece of code that is launched on the Mesos slave nodes to run the framework's tasks
- **Scheduler**: This is the piece of code that registers with the master, asks for resources from it, and runs tasks on the executor

Now, let's take a look at how we can develop each of these components to build a custom Mesos framework in the following sections.

Driver implementation

The driver program is the one that creates the **executor information**. The executor information consists of an executorID being a String value and a command that is executed through the Linux /bin/sh-c command. This can be implemented in our Java code as follows:

```
Protos.ExecutorInfopiExecutorInfo =
Protos.ExecutorInfo.newBuilder()
.setExecutorId(Protos.ExecutorID.newBuilder()
.setValue("CalculatePi"))
.setCommand(piCommandInfo)
.setName("PiExecutor")
.setSource("java")
.build();
```

Here, we used Google Protocol Buffers to communicate with Mesos and craft the executor information with the Builder pattern.

Now that we have the executor information ready, next in line is information about the framework. This contains information such as under which Unix user the tasks should be launched (which can be set to the default if we leave the field empty) and the failover time, which makes the master wait before removing the framework in case of scheduler failure. These two properties are set using the `.setUser` and `.setFailOverTimeout` calls, which would look as follows:

```
Protos.FrameworkInfo.BuilderframeworkBuilder = Protos.FrameworkInfo.
newBuilder()
.setFailoverTimeout(120000)
.setUser("")
.setName("PiFramework");
```

We can now initialize the `Scheduler` with the number of tasks that are submitted to the executor to run our program. This is done with the following code:

```
Scheduler scheduler = new PiScheduler(piExecutorInfo, 1);
```

`PiScheduler` is instantiated with one task as we only require one task to compute it.

`MesosSchedulerDriver` is used to launch and kill tasks on Mesos. It also manages the life cycle of our scheduler with the `start`, `stop`, and `wait for tasks to finish` calls. This is done with the following piece of code:

```
MesosSchedulerDriverschedulerDriver =
new MesosSchedulerDriver(scheduler,frameworkBuilder.build(), MESOS-
MASTER);
int status = schedulerDriver.run() == Protos.Status.DRIVER_STOPPED ? 0
: 1;
schedulerDriver.stop();
System.exit(status);
```

Now that we have discussed all the parts of the driver program, let's assemble them all together and take a look at how the real code looks. This is shown as follows:

```
/* Create the PiDriver class with the following contents: */

import com.google.protobuf.ByteString;
import org.apache.log4j.Logger;
import org.apache.mesos.MesosSchedulerDriver;
import org.apache.mesos.Protos;
import org.apache.mesos.Scheduler;


public class PiDriver {
```

```
private final static Logger LOGGER =
Logger.getLogger(PiDriver.class);

public static void main(String[] args) {

String path = System.getProperty("user.dir") +
"/target/scala-2.10/mesos-pi-assembly-1.0.jar";

/* Defining the executor */

Protos.CommandInfo.URIuri
Protos.CommandInfo.URI.newBuilder()
.setValue(path)
.setExtract(false)
.build();
String commandPi =
"java -cpmesos-pi-assembly-1.0.jarPiExecutor";
Protos.CommandInfopiCommandInfo =
Protos.CommandInfo.newBuilder()
.setValue(commandPi).addUris(uri).build();


/* Setting the executor information */

Protos.ExecutorInfopiExecutorInfo =
Protos.ExecutorInfo.newBuilder()
.setExecutorId(Protos.ExecutorID.newBuilder()
.setValue("CalculatePi")).setCommand(piCommandInfo)
.setName("PiExecutor").setSource("java").build();

/* Defining framework & specifying related information*/

Protos.FrameworkInfo.BuilderframeworkBuilder =
Protos.FrameworkInfo.newBuilder()
.setFailoverTimeout(120000).setUser("")
.setName("PiFramework")
.setPrincipal("test-framework-java");

/* Enabling checkpointing */

if (System.getenv("MESOS_CHECKPOINT") != null) {
System.out.println
("Enabling checkpoint for the framework");
frameworkBuilder.setCheckpoint(true);
}
```

```
/* Initializing the scheduler */

Scheduler scheduler = new PiScheduler(piExecutorInfo, 1);

/* Defining the scheduler driver */

MesosSchedulerDriverschedulerDriver =
new MesosSchedulerDriver
(scheduler, frameworkBuilder.build(), args[0]);;


int status = schedulerDriver.run() ==
Protos.Status.DRIVER_STOPPED ? 0 : 1;
schedulerDriver.stop();
System.exit(status);
}


}
```

Executor implementation

PiExecutor is our executor component. We will need to implement the *Executor*
interface and override a few methods. Here, we will focus on the core method, that
is, the launchTask() call—which is the call to actually compute the value of pi in
our case. We will also need to set a few properties of our task within this function,
which are explained as follows:

```
@Override
public void launchTask(final ExecutorDriver
executorDriver, final Protos.TaskInfotaskInfo)
{

/* Set the task status as running for the task ID
with a builder pattern. */

Protos.TaskStatustaskStatus = Protos.TaskStatus.newBuilder()
.setTaskId(taskInfo.getTaskId())
.setState(Protos.TaskState.TASK_RUNNING).build();

/* Send the status update to the framework scheduler
retrying as necessary until an acknowledgement has been received
 or the executor is terminated, in which case,
 a TASK_LOST status update will be sent.+*/
```

```
executorDriver.sendStatusUpdate(taskStatus);

/* Actual Pi computation */

try {
message = computePi().getBytes();
}
catch (IOException e) {
LOGGER.error("Error computing Pi :" + e.getMessage());
}

/* Return the value of Pi to framework */

executorDriver.sendFrameworkMessage(message);


/* Mark state of task as finished and
send status update to framework scheduler. */

taskStatus = Protos.TaskStatus.newBuilder()
.setTaskId(taskInfo.getTaskId())
.setState(Protos.TaskState.TASK_FINISHED)
.build();

executorDriver.sendStatusUpdate(taskStatus);

}
```

We can now create a PiExecutor class by implementing the Executor class and overriding the default methods. The complete code is given as follows:

```
/* Create the PiExecutor class with the following contents: */

import org.apache.log4j.Logger;
import org.apache.mesos.Executor;
import org.apache.mesos.ExecutorDriver;
import org.apache.mesos.MesosExecutorDriver;
import org.apache.mesos.Protos;

import java.io.IOException;

public class PiExecutor implements Executor {
private final static Logger LOGGER =
Logger.getLogger(PiExecutor.class);
```

```
/**
*Invoked once the executor driver has been able to
*successfully connect with Mesos.
*In particular, a scheduler can pass some
*data to it's executors through the
*{@linkorg.apache.mesos.Protos.ExecutorInfo#getData()}field.
*@param driver - The executor driver that was registered
and connectedto the Mesos cluster.
*@paramexecutorInfo - Describes information about the
registered executor.
*@paramframeworkInfo - Describes the framework that was
registered.
*@paramslaveInfo - Describes the slave that will be used to
launchthe tasks for this executor.
*For more details, seeorg.apache.mesos.ExecutorDriver and
org.apache.mesos.MesosSchedulerDriver

*/

@Override
public void registered
(ExecutorDriver driver, Protos.ExecutorInfoexecutorInfo,
Protos.FrameworkInfoframeworkInfo,
Protos.SlaveInfoslaveInfo) {
LOGGER.info("Registered PinUserBoardExecutor on " +
slaveInfo.getHostname());
}

/*
* Invoked when executor re-registers with a restarted slave.
    * @param driver - The executor driver that
was re-registered with Mesos master.
    * @paramslaveInfo - Describes the slave that will be
used to launch the tasks for this executor.
    * For more details, see org.apache.mesos.ExecutorDriver
*/

@Override
public void reregistered
(ExecutorDriver driver, Protos.SlaveInfoslaveInfo) {

}

/*
    * Invoked when executor becomes 'disconnected' from  slave.
```

```
        * (e.g. when the slave is being restarted due to an upgrade)
        * @param driver - The executor driver that was disconnected.

    */

    @Override
    public void disconnected(ExecutorDriver driver) {

    }

    /*
        * Invoked when a task has been launched on this executor
        * (initiated via
        * {@linkorg.apache.mesos.SchedulerDriver#launchTasks}.
        * Note that this task can be realized with a
        * thread, a process, or some simple computation,
        * however, no other callbacks will be invoked on this executor
        * until this callback has returned.
        *
    * @param driver - The executor driver that launched the task.
        * @param task - Describes the task that was launched.
        * For more details, see
        * org.apache.mesos.ExecutorDriver and
        * org.apache.mesos.Protos.TaskInfo
    */

    @Override
    public void launchTask
    (ExecutorDriver driver, Protos.TaskInfo task) {
    LOGGER.info("Launching task in PinUserBoardExecutor..");
    Protos.TaskStatustaskStatus =
    Protos.TaskStatus.newBuilder().setTaskId(task.getTaskId())
    .setState(Protos.TaskState.TASK_RUNNING).build();
    driver.sendStatusUpdate(taskStatus);
    String url = task.getData().toStringUtf8();

    byte[] message = new byte[0];

    try {
    message = computePi().getBytes();
    }
    catch (IOException e) {
    LOGGER.error("Error computing Pi :" + e.getMessage());
    }
```

```
LOGGER.info
("Sending framework message and marking task finished."
+ getClass().getName());
driver.sendFrameworkMessage(message);

taskStatus = Protos.TaskStatus.newBuilder()
.setTaskId(task.getTaskId())
.setState(Protos.TaskState.TASK_FINISHED)
.build();

driver.sendStatusUpdate(taskStatus);
}

/* Code to compute Pi */

private String computePi() throws IOException {

double pi = 0;
double y = 1;

intlps = 90000000*2;
intcnt = 0;
for(int x=1; x <lps; x+=2) {
pi = pi + (y/x);
y = -y;
cnt++;
}

return "Value of PI=" + 4*pi + " after " + cnt;
/* PI=3.141592642478473 after 90000000 */

}

    /*
    * Invoked when a task running within this executor
    * has been killed
    * (via {@link org.apache.mesos.SchedulerDriver#killTask}).
    * Note that no status update will be sent
    * on behalf of the executor, the executor is responsible for
    * creating new TaskStatus (i.e., with TASK_KILLED) &invoking
    * {@link org.apache.mesos.ExecutorDriver#sendStatusUpdate}.

    * @param driver - The executor driver that
owned the task that was killed.
```

```
@param task - The ID of the task that was killed.

@For more details, see
org.apache.mesos.ExecutorDriver and
org.apache.mesos.Protos.TaskID

*/

@Override
public void killTask
(ExecutorDriver driver, Protos.TaskIDtaskId) {

}

/*
@Invoked when a framework message has arrived
*for this executor.
*These messages are best effort;
*do not expect a framework message to be
*retransmitted in any reliable fashion.
*@param driver - The executor driver
that received the message.
@param data - The message payload.
    * For more details, see
    * org.apache.mesos.ExecutorDriver
*/

@Override
public void frameworkMessage
(ExecutorDriver driver, byte[] data) {

}

/*
    * Invoked when the executor should terminate
    * all of it's currently running tasks.
    * Note that after Mesos has determined that
    * an executor has terminated any tasks that
    * the executor did not send terminal status updates
    * for (e.g. TASK_KILLED, TASK_FINISHED, TASK_FAILED and so on)
    * a TASK_LOST status update will be created.
    * @param driver - The executor driver that should terminate
    * For more details, see org.apache.mesos.ExecutorDriver
```

```
*/

@Override
public void shutdown(ExecutorDriver driver) {

}

/*
 * Invoked when a fatal error has occurred with
     * the executor and/or executor driver.
     * The driver will be aborted BEFORE invoking this callback
     * @param driver - The executor driver that was aborted
due to this error
     * @param message - The error message.
     * For more details, see org.apache.mesos.ExecutorDriver

*/

@Override
public void error(ExecutorDriver driver, String message) {

}


/* The main method in which we initiates and calls the run() method in
MesosExecutorDriver */

public static void main(String[] args) {
MesosExecutorDrivermesosExecutorDriver =
new MesosExecutorDriver(new PiExecutor());
System.exit(mesosExecutorDriver.run() ==
Protos.Status.DRIVER_STOPPED ? 0 : 1);
}

}
```

Scheduler implementation

We will now discuss the scheduler implementation, which is responsible for the framework's scheduling. We will create PiScheduler, which actually implements the Scheduler interface of Mesos. We will focus on overriding the resourceOffer(), statusUpdate(), and frameworkMessage() methods, which form a core part of PiScheduler.

The complete code is as follows:

```
import org.apache.log4j.Logger;
import org.apache.mesos.Protos;
import org.apache.mesos.Scheduler;
import org.apache.mesos.SchedulerDriver;

import java.util.ArrayList;
import java.util.List;

public class PiScheduler implements Scheduler {

private final static Logger LOGGER =
Logger.getLogger(PiScheduler.class);

private final Protos.ExecutorInfopiExecutor;
private final inttotalTasks;
private intlaunchedTasks = 0;
private intfinishedTasks = 0;


/**ThePiSchedulertakes information from the PiExecutor and
  * the total number of tasks through its constructor
  * which is implemented below
*/

public PiScheduler
(Protos.ExecutorInfo _piExecutor, int _totalTasks) {
this.totalTasks = _totalTasks;
this.piExecutor = _piExecutor;
}

@Override public void registered
(SchedulerDriverschedulerDriver, Protos.FrameworkID
  frameworkID, Protos.MasterInfomasterInfo) {
LOGGER.info("Registered! ID = " + frameworkID.getValue());
}

@Override public void reregistered
(SchedulerDriverschedulerDriver,
Protos.MasterInfomasterInfo) {


}
```

```
/**The resourceoffer() method is invoked when resources
  * have been offered to this framework.
* We will set the number of CPUs, and amount of memory that
  * our framework requires through the call described below
*/

@Override public void resourceOffers
(SchedulerDriverschedulerDriver, List<Protos.Offer> list) {

/* The amount of CPU cores and Memory required
for our tasks is specified */

double CPUS_PER_TASK = 1;
double MEM_PER_TASK = 128;

for (Protos.Offer offer : list) {
List<Protos.TaskInfo>taskInfoList =
new ArrayList<Protos.TaskInfo>();
double offerCpus = 0;
double offerMem = 0;

for (Protos.Resource resource : offer.getResourcesList()) {
if (resource.getName().equals("cpus")) {
offerCpus += resource.getScalar().getValue();
} else if (resource.getName().equals("mem")) {
offerMem += resource.getScalar().getValue();
}
}

LOGGER.info
("Received Offer : " + offer.getId().getValue() + "
with cpus = " + offerCpus + " and mem ="+ offerMem);

double remainingCpus = offerCpus;
double remainingMem = offerMem;

if (launchedTasks<totalTasks&&remainingCpus>=
CPUS_PER_TASK&&remainingMem>= MEM_PER_TASK) {

Protos.TaskIDtaskID = Protos.TaskID.newBuilder()
.setValue(Integer.toString(launchedTasks++)).build();
LOGGER.info("Launching task :" + taskID.getValue() +
" using the offer : " + offer.getId().getValue());
```

```
/* PiExecutor is created as a task and is launched*/

Protos.TaskInfopiTaskInfo = Protos.TaskInfo.newBuilder()
.setName("task " + taskID.getValue())
.setTaskId(taskID)
.setSlaveId(offer.getSlaveId())
.addResources(Protos.Resource.newBuilder()
.setName("cpus")
.setType(Protos.Value.Type.SCALAR)
.setScalar(Protos.Value.Scalar.newBuilder()
.setValue(CPUS_PER_TASK)))
.addResources(Protos.Resource.newBuilder()
.setName("mem")
.setType(Protos.Value.Type.SCALAR)
.setScalar(Protos.Value.Scalar.newBuilder()
.setValue(MEM_PER_TASK)))
.setExecutor(Protos.ExecutorInfo
.newBuilder(piExecutor))
.build();

taskID = Protos.TaskID.newBuilder()
.setValue(Integer.toString(launchedTasks++))
.build();

LOGGER.info
("Launching task :" + taskID.getValue() +
" using the offer : " + offer.getId().getValue());

taskInfoList.add(piTaskInfo);

}

schedulerDriver.launchTasks(offer.getId(), taskInfoList);

}

}

/** Invoked when an offer is no longer valid
 * (e.g., the slave was lost or another framework used
 * resources in the offer).
 * If for whatever reason an offer is never rescinded
 * (e.g., dropped message, failing over framework and so on),
 * a framework that attempts to launch tasks
 * using an invalid offer will receive TASK_LOST
 * status update for those tasks */
```

```
    */
@Override public void offerRescinded
(SchedulerDriverschedulerDriver, Protos.OfferIDofferID) {


}

/**The statusUpdate() call is invoked when
  * the status of a task has changed
  * (e.g., a slave is lost which means the task is lost,
  * a task finishes and executor sends a status update)
*/

@Override public void statusUpdate
(SchedulerDriverschedulerDriver,
Protos.TaskStatustaskStatus) {

LOGGER.info
("Status update : Task ID "+ taskStatus.getTaskId()
.getValue() + "in state : "+ taskStatus.getState()
.getValueDescriptor().getName());
if (taskStatus.getState() == Protos.TaskState.TASK_FINISHED) {
finishedTasks++;
LOGGER.info("Finished tasks : " + finishedTasks);

/* We can stop the scheduler once the tasks are completed */

if (finishedTasks == totalTasks) {
schedulerDriver.stop();
}
}

if (taskStatus.getState() == Protos.TaskState.TASK_FAILED
|| taskStatus.getState() == Protos.TaskState.TASK_KILLED
|| taskStatus.getState() == Protos.TaskState.TASK_LOST) {
LOGGER.error("Aborting because the task "
+ taskStatus.getTaskId().getValue()
+ " is in unexpected state : "
+ taskStatus.getState()
.getValueDescriptor().getName()
+ "with reason : "+ taskStatus.getReason()
.getValueDescriptor().getName()
+ " from source : "+ taskStatus.getSource()
.getValueDescriptor().getName()
+ " with message : "+ taskStatus.getMessage());
schedulerDriver.abort();
}
```

```
}


/**The frameworkMessage() is invoked when an executor
  * sends a message. In our case we will be sending
  * the value of Pi from our executor as the message.
*/

@Override public void frameworkMessage
(SchedulerDriverschedulerDriver, Protos.ExecutorID
executorID,Protos.SlaveIDslaveID, byte[] bytes) {
String data = new String(bytes);
System.out.println(data);
LOGGER.info("Output :\n=========\n " + data);
}

/* Invoked when scheduler becomes disconnected from master
  * (e.g. master fails and another is taking over)
*/

@Override public void disconnected
(SchedulerDriverschedulerDriver) {


}

/* Invoked when a slave has been determined unreachable
  * (e.g., machine failure, network partition).
  * Most frameworks will need to reschedule
  * any tasks launched on this slave on a new slave.
*/

@Override public void slaveLost
(SchedulerDriverschedulerDriver, Protos.SlaveIDslaveID) {


}

/* Invoked when an executor has exited/terminated.
  * Note that any tasks running will have
  * TASK_LOST status updates automatically generated.
*/

@Override public void executorLost
(SchedulerDriverschedulerDriver,
Protos.ExecutorIDexecutorID,Protos.SlaveIDslaveID, inti) {
```

```
}

/* Invoked when there is an unrecoverable error
 * in the scheduler or driver.
 * The driver will be aborted before invoking this callback.
 */

@Override public void error
(SchedulerDriverschedulerDriver, String s) {
LOGGER.error("Error : " + s);
}

}
```

Running the framework

We need to package the jar with all the dependencies in order to run the framework. For this, we can create a `build.sbt` file with Mesos and log4j as dependencies. This will look similar to the following:

```
import AssemblyKeys._

assemblySettings

name := "mesos-pi"

version := "1.0"

scalaVersion := "2.10.4"

libraryDependencies += "org.apache.mesos" % "mesos" % "0.26.0"

libraryDependencies += "log4j" % "log4j" % "1.2.17"
```

We can now create an uber jar with the following `sbt` command:

```
$ sbt assembly
```

Then, we will run the program with the following command:

```
$ sbt'run 127.0.0.1:5050'
Multiple main classes detected, select one to run:
 [1] PiDriver
 [2] PiExecutor

Enter number: 1
```

Note that we specified the Mesos master URI as an argument to our `PiDriver` program.

Once we run the program, you will see the following output in the Terminal:

```
Value of PI=3.141592642478473 after 90000000
```

We can also see the framework being registered in the Mesos master UI, which runs on port `5050`, as shown in the following screenshot:

We can also see the single task that calculated the value of Pi has finished in the same UI if we click on the framework ID:

Summary

After reading this chapter, you should have a fair idea of framework security features such as authorization, authentication, and access control in Mesos. You should also now be able to use the Mesos API to build your own custom application/framework on Mesos. In addition, the experimental scheduler HTTP API was also introduced in this chapter.

In the next chapter, we will explore some interesting projects, such as Myriad (YARN on Mesos) and Kubernetes on Mesos. We will also discuss how to deploy containerized apps using Docker and how a continuous integration process can be set up using Jenkins on Mesos.

7
Mesos Containerizers

This chapter briefly introduces the concepts of **containers,** and talks a bit about **Docker**, probably the most popular container technology available today. It also provides a detailed overview of the different *containerizer* options in Mesos besides introducing some other topics such as networking for Mesos-managed containers and fetcher cache. Finally, an example for deploying containerized apps in Mesos is provided for better understanding. The following topics will be covered in this chapter:

- Containers
- Docker
- Mesos Containerizer
  - ° Mesos Containerizer
  - ° Docker Containerizer
  - ° Composing Containerizer
- Networking for Mesos-managed containers
- Mesos Image Provisioning
- Fetcher Cache
- Deploying containerized apps using Docker and Mesos

Containers

A Linux Container, (referred to simply as container for the rest of this chapter) allows applications to run on an allocated share of resources within an isolated, individual environment. Since all containers share the **Operating system (OS)** of the host machine and do not require the OS to be loaded up, they can be created in a matter of seconds.

Container technology, based on operating system level virtualization, has been present for over a decade now. OS level virtualization is a method by which an OS kernel allows creation of many user namespace instances (also called containers) instead of only one.

We can look at containers as encapsulated, individually deployable components running as isolated instances on the same kernel. Containers have a big advantage over traditional technologies such as bare metal, meaning servers with an operating system or virtualized environments such as **Microsoft Hyper-V**. From a developer's point of view, we can just package our application and dependencies into a container, and deploy it to any environment that supports containers. By doing this, we also make our application easy to update, upgrade, and even easily portable from one environment to another, for example, from a development environment on the desktop to a test environment in the cloud.

Two popular models for containers are:

- **Hypervisor-based**: The hypervisor-based model includes redundant OS kernels and other libraries, which makes this an inefficient setup, as shown in the subsequent image (source: `http://aucouranton.com/2014/06/13/ linux-containers-parallels-lxc-openvz-docker-and-more/`):

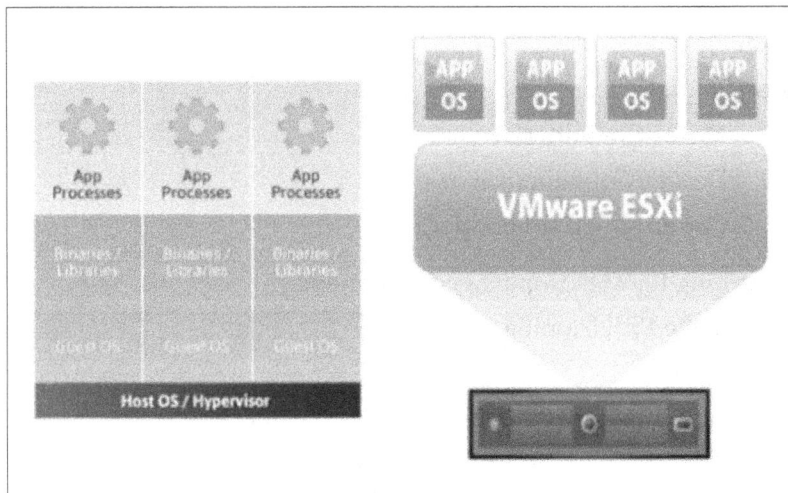

- **Container-based**: The container-based approach involves encapsulated, individually deployable components running as isolated instances on the same kernel, as shown in the following image (source: `http://aucouranton.com/2014/06/13/linux-containers-parallels-lxc-openvz-docker-and-more/`):

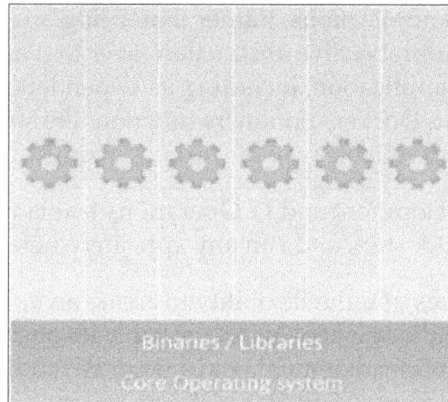

Why containers?

The following are some important benefits of using containers are:

- Application-centric management
- Separation of deployment and build
- Simplifies the application deployment process
- Supports Agile development through Continuous Integration and deployment
- Allows breakdown of large monolithic applications into manageable micro-services
- Infrastructure environment consistency
- High portability
- Resource isolation
- Resource utilization

Docker

Docker is an open-source platform that automates the process by which any application is deployed in the form of a container that is portable, lightweight, self-sufficient, and which can run virtually anywhere. Primarily based on the **LXC** or **Linux Container**, Docker is used by developers and system administrators while working with distributed applications. Rather than being an underlying technology, this platform acts as a comprehensive abstraction layer that enables developers to *package* or *containerize* an application, including its dependencies, and run it on any infrastructure. Simply put, Docker containers function like shipping containers which offer a standard and reliable way of shipping literally any application.

Docker provides the Development and IT Operations teams with much needed agility and control to 'build, ship, and run any app, anywhere.'

- **Build**: Docker gives you the flexibility to create an application from micro-services, and not worry about probable inconsistencies between the production and development environments. Additionally, there is no restriction on using any particular platform or language.

- **Ship**: Docker allows you to design the entire cycle comprising application development, testing, and distribution, and simplifies its management via a consistent user interface.

- **Run**: Docker offers you the ability to choose from a variety of platforms to deploy scalable services in a secure and reliable fashion.

However, the chief advantage of Docker is that it presents an 'application first' architecture, which also allows developers and IT Ops / System Admins to focus on their core job functions.

- **Developers**: They are concerned only with what's *inside* the container, such as their code, data, apps, libraries, and the package manager.

- **IT Ops**: They have to focus on what's *outside* the container, namely logging, monitoring, remote access, and network configuration

What Docker essentially brings to the table can be effectively summarized in the following points:-

- **Agility**: Using Docker, a developer has the freedom to define an environment. Creation and deployment of apps can be carried out in a fast and easier manner with IT ops having the flexibility to rapidly respond to change.

- **Control**: Ensures that ownership of the code, all the way from infrastructure to the app, lies solely with the developer. The IT operations governs the manageability aspect in terms of standardizing, securing, and scaling the operating environment.

- **Portability**: Gives you the choice, minus the complexity, of working with a single developer or a team, and using private infrastructure or public cloud providers.

For a better understanding of the platform, let us look at some of the core terms associated with the Docker solution.

- **Image**: Basis of a Docker container when it is at rest. When instantiated through a Docker run command, they turn into a container.

- **Dockerfile**: Its main function is to inform the image builder as to what the image has to look like.

- **Docker Engine**: Can be installed on physical, virtual, or cloud hosts. This provides several core functions, which include the ability to pull Docker images, create and run new containers, scale existing containers, or stop and remove them.

- **Container**: These are built from Docker images. Their lightweight nature is attributed to the fact that they share image layer, and use union filesystems.

- **Registry**: This is where Docker images are managed, distributed, and also stored.

- **Docker Hub**: This is Docker's hosted registry service for managing images.

- **Docker Machine**: This automates container provisioning on the chosen network or in the cloud. It can be installed on machines on Linux, Windows or, Mac OS X.

- **Docker Compose**: This defines applications that require multiple containers.

- **Docker Toolbox**: This delivers all the Docker tools consisting of Engine, Machine, Compose, and Kitematic to a Mac OS X or Windows system.

- **Docker Trusted Registry (DTR)**: This provides a private, dedicated image registry.

- **Docker Swarm**: This is used to host clusters and schedule containers.

- **Kitematic**: Basically a Desktop GUI for Docker.

A basic Docker system is shown in the following image.

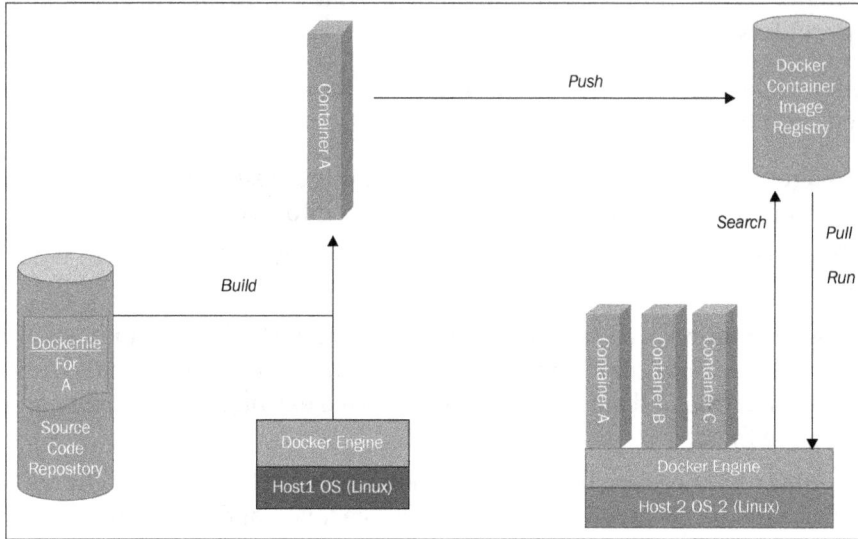

As can be seen in the preceding diagram, a Docker container encloses a piece of software with everything that it needs to run, such as code, runtime, system libraries/tools. This encapsulation and isolation provided by a container warrants that the container will run in the same manner, irrespective of the environment it is run in.

A virtual machine and a Docker container is shown in the following image (source: http://www.jayway.com/2015/03/21/a-not-very-short-introduction-to-docker/):

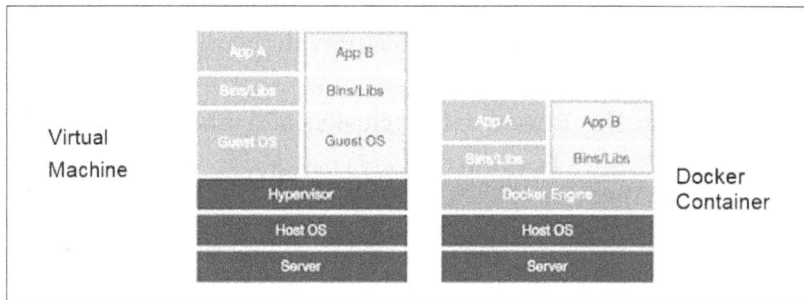

The figure that we just saw showcases the architectural difference between a virtual machine and a Docker container. The Docker container comprises only the application and its associated dependencies, and thus enjoys the benefits of both resource isolation and allocation like virtual machines, but is far more efficient and portable.

Docker's pluggable architecture is further leveraged by the presence of several open APIs (Swarm, Compose, Hub, and so on), which support the creation of an ecosystem with seamless application delivery. It is this combination that empowers Docker containers to make distributed applications composable, portable, dynamic, and ideal for agile teams.

Docker High-Level Architecture is shown in the subsequent image (source: `http://www.docker.com`):

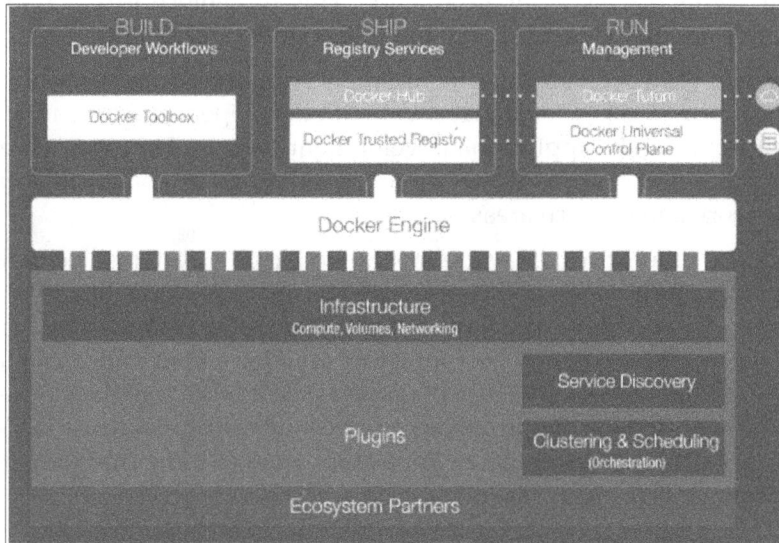

These advantages become increasingly apparent when we consider some enterprise use cases wherein organizations have used the Docker platform to tackle certain technical or business challenges:

- **Continuous Integration**: Powered by integration with tools like GitHub and Jenkins, Docker provides developers the ability to develop and test applications faster and within an environment of their choice. The entire process is perfectly streamlined with developers being able to submit code in GitHub, test it, and automatically trigger a build via Jenkins. The moment the image is complete, it can be easily added to the Docker registries. This functionality not only saves time on build and setup processes, but allows developers to automate the running of tests while they simultaneously work on other projects. Add to this the absence of inconsistencies while dealing with different types of environments, and you get a substantial improvement in efficiency levels on using Docker for continuous integration jobs.

- **Continuous Delivery**: In addition to being language agnostic, Docker works in any environment and effectively eliminates problems arising out of irregularities between environments. Docker guarantees continuous delivery of code to quality assurance teams and customers in a manner that is quick, easy to consume, and supportive of a speedy resolution of issues. Combined with Docker registries, the integration with other production platforms such as Docker Universal Control Plane and Tutum, facilitates code to be distributed to teams that can fully test it within the staging environment itself, before placing it into production. This aids enterprises by reducing the time and money required to build and ship applications.

- **DevOps**: With organizations increasingly adopting the DevOps philosophy, Docker provides key tools that assist both developers and operations teams in improvising the application development process. These tools break down the traditional barrier between the aforesaid teams by compartmentalizing their work and concern areas.

- **Big Data**: Enterprises today are moving to big data systems/technologies in a bid to derive deep and comprehensive analysis of the data they collect. However, data sources are variant and multiple (images, videos, metadata and so on). Herein lies the advantage of utilizing a system that can uniformly transport data across analytics platforms. The adoption of the Docker platform provides a significant competitive advantage, because it facilitates the unobstructed movement of applications across different types of environments to ensure seamless data analysis.

- **Infrastructure Optimization**: Unlike virtual machines that require a guest OS or hypervisor, Docker containers consist of only what is necessary to build, ship, and run applications. Add to this the ability to spin up or down containers based on requirements, and Docker proves to be a great value-add to enterprises.

Docker goes a step further and provides cloud portability that frees IT ops teams from being tied down to specific environment tools. Effectively, Docker reduces the amount of storage and infrastructure costs for enterprises, and also increases efficiency.

Containerizer

Containers, as described in the previous section, are used for the following:

- Isolating a task from other tasks
- Ensuring that tasks run in finite or restricted resource environments
- Programmatically controlling the individual resources of a task

- Running applications in different environments through a packaged image
- Breaking applications into smaller, manageable micro-services

Tasks can be run in containers through **containerizers**. Mesos provides support for popular container technologies such as Docker while also having its own container technology. Recently, support has also been added for combining and allowing different container technologies to work together (for example, Mesos and Docker).

Motivation

One of the key requirements of a cluster manager is to ensure that the allocation of resources to a particular framework does not have any impact on any active running jobs of some other framework. Provision for isolation mechanisms on slaves for compartmentalizing different tasks is, thus, a key feature of Mesos. Mesos leverages containers for resource isolation, which has a pluggable architecture as well. The Mesos slave uses Containerizer API to provide an isolated environment to run a framework's executor and its corresponding tasks. The Containerizer API's objective is to support a wide range of implementations, which implies that custom containerizers and isolators can be developed. When a slave process starts, the containerizer to be used to launch containers and the set of isolators to enforce the resource constraints can be specified.

Containerizer types

The following containerizer options are available in Mesos version 0.27:

- Composing
- Docker
- Mesos (default)

The containerizer type can be specified by the user through the agent flag, `--containerizers`.

For example:

```
--containerizers=mesos
```

Containerizer creation

A containerizer is created by the slave based on the flag configuration (using agent flag `--containerizers`). The composing containerizer is used to create the containerizer in cases where multiple containerizers (for example, Mesos and Docker) are listed through the `--containerizers` flag.

The Mesos agent utilizes the task default executor in cases where an executor is not specifically mentioned in `TaskInfo`.

Containerization in Mesos is shown in the ensuing figure (source: Apache Mesos Essentials: `https://www.packtpub.com/big-data-and-business-intelligence/apache-mesos-essentials`):

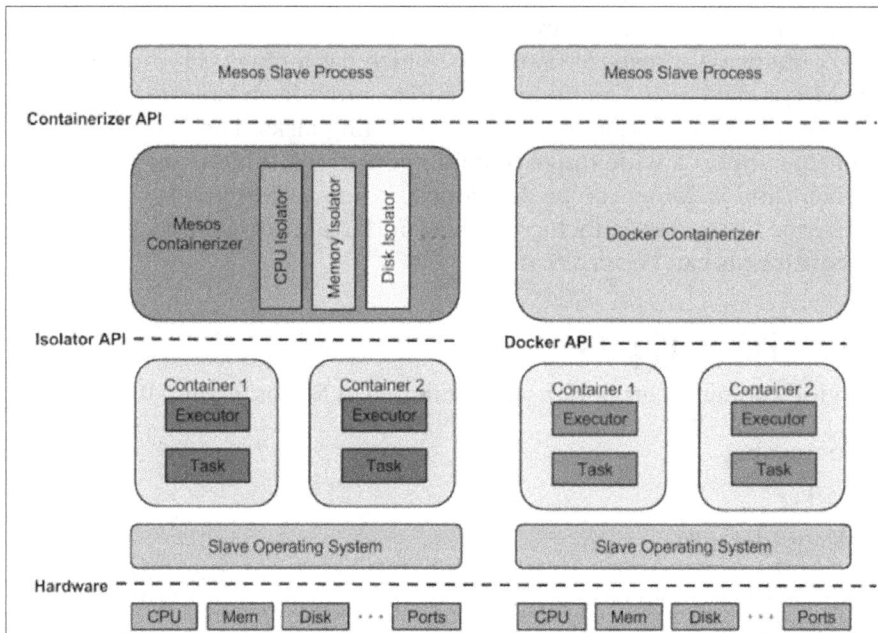

Mesos containerizer

This is the default containerizer type provided by Mesos. In this type, tasks can be run through an array of pluggable isolators provided by Mesos. It can be enabled by configuring the agent flag as

```
--containerizers=mesos
```

This type is typically used when:

- User needs to control the task environment through Mesos without having to rely on other container solutions.
- Fine-grained OS controls are desired.
- Custom resource isolation needs to be added for tasks.
- User needs to control certain resource parameters (for example, disk usage limits) which are not exposed by other container solutions.

Any task which doesn't specify `ContainerInfo::DockerInfo` will be handled by the Mesos containerizer.

The launching process

The container launching process includes the following steps:

- Preparation of calls is done on every **isolator**.
- The launcher, responsible for forking/destroying containers, is used to fork the executor. The forked 'child' cannot execute until the isolation step is completed.
- The **executor** is isolated by calling the isolators. Isolators are responsible for creating an environment for the containers, where resources like CPU, network, storage, and memory can be isolated from other containers.
- The executor is fetched and the forked child notified to execute. Isolator preparation commands are run first, followed by the execution.

Mesos containerizer states

The different Mesos containerizer states are as follows:

- PREPARING
- ISOLATING
- FETCHING
- RUNNING
- DESTROYING

Internals

By leveraging Linux features such as namespaces and **control groups** (**cgroups**), the Mesos Containerizer provides resource isolation and lightweight containerization. It provides the capability for different isolators to be selectively enabled. In addition, support for **POSIX** (**Portable Operating system Interface**) systems is also present, though it only includes usage reporting and not actual isolation.

There are three isolator options present and they are described as follows:

Shared Filesystem

Modifications to every container's shared filesystem view can be enabled using the Shared Filesystem isolator on Linux hosts.

The modifications can be specified either through the `-default_container_info` agent flag or by the framework in the `ContainerInfo`.

Volumes, used to map sections of the shared filesystem (such as host path with the container's view of the shared filesystem, that is, container path), can be specified through `ContainerInfo` as read-only or read-and-write. The path of the host can be absolute or relative. If absolute, it also results in the filesystem subtree being made accessible for every container under the container path. If relative, then it is taken to be a directory which is relative to the work directory of the executor. The directory is created, and permissions from the corresponding existing directory in the shared filesystem are copied over.

The main reason why this isolator is used is to make certain shared filesystem sections private to every container selectively. As an example, a private directory `/dir_name` can be set by making `host_path="dir_name"` and `container_path="/dir_name"`. This creates a directory `dir_name` inside the executor's work directory while also mounting it as `/dir_name` within the container. The container won't be able to see the host's `/dir_name` or any other container's `/dir_name`, and this action is transparent to the processes running within it.

Pid namespace

This isolator is used to isolate every container in a different pid namespace, which gives the following two advantages:

1. **Visibility**: The executor and descendant processes running within the container cannot view or interact with external processes running outside the namespace.

2. **Clean Termination**: If the leading process in a pid namespace is terminated, the kernel terminates all other processes running within the namespace.

Posix Disk isolator

This isolator, which can be used on both OS X as well as Linux, is used for providing basic disk isolation. The disk utilization for every sandbox can be reported using this, and any set disk quotas can be enforced as well.

When starting the slave, `posix/disk` must be added to the `--isolation` flag to enable this isolator.

The disk quota enforcement is disabled by default. When starting the slave, specify `--enforce_container_disk_quota` to enable it.

Disk utilization for every sandbox is reported by periodically running the `du` command. The resource statistics endpoint (`/monitor/statistics.json`) provides a way to retrieve the disk utilization statistics.

The time interval between two `du` commands can be configured through the agent flag `--container_disk_watch_interval`. For example, `--container_disk_watch_interval = 1 mins` specifies the time interval as 1 minute. 15 seconds is the default time interval.

Docker containerizer

This containerizer type permits running of tasks inside a Docker container. A Docker image can either be launched as an executor or as a task. It can be enabled by configuring the agent flag as

```
--containerizers=docker
```

It is normally used when:

- The Docker package needs to be leveraged for running tasks.
- A Mesos slave is running within a Docker container.

Setup

In order to enable the Docker Containerizer on a slave, the slave must be launched with "Docker" as one of the containerizer options.

```
mesos-slave --containerizers=docker
```

Every slave where the Docker containerizer is specified must also have the Docker Command Line Interface client (version 1.0.0 or above) installed.

If `iptables` are enabled on the slave, ensure that the `iptables` permit all traffic from the bridge interface by making the following change:

```
iptables -A INPUT -s 172.17.0.0/16 -i docker0 -p tcp -j ACCEPT
```

Launching process

The container launching process is as follows:

- Task launching in Docker is attempted only if `ContainerInfo::type` is set to `DOCKER`
- The image is pulled first from the specified repository
- The pre-launch hook is then called

The executor is then launched in one of the following two ways:

1. Mesos agent runs in a Docker container in the following cases:
    - If the flag `--docker_mesos_image` is present, it indicates that the Mesos agent is running within a Docker container
    - The flag `--docker_mesos_image` value is considered to be the Docker image that will be used for launching the Mesos agent
    - If an executor different from the default command executor is used by the task to run, it gets launched within a Docker container
    - If `TaskInfo` is used by the task, then the default `mesos-docker-executor` gets launched within a Docker container to execute commands through the Docker Command Line Interface.

2. Mesos agent does not run in a Docker container in the following cases :
    - If `TaskInfo` is used by a task, a sub-process to run default `mesos-docker-executor` is forked. Shells are spawned by this executor to run Docker commands through the Docker Command Line Interface.
    - If a custom executor is used by the task to run, it gets launched within a Docker container.

Docker containerizer states

Following are the different Docker containerizer states:

- FETCHING
- PULLING
- RUNNING
- DESTROYING

Composing containerizer

This type allows for combining and allowing different container technologies to work together (for example, Mesos and Docker). It can be enabled by configuring the --containerizers agent flag with a comma-separated list of required containerizer names

```
--containerizers=mesos,docker
```

The first containerizer specified in the list, which provides support for the task's container configuration, is used for task launching.

* This option is generally used when tasks having different resource isolation types need to be tested. A framework can leverage the composer containerizer to test a task using the controlled environment provided by the Mesos containerizer, while simultaneously ensuring that the task works with Docker containers.

Networking for Mesos-managed containers

One of the major goals to provide networking-related support in Mesos was to develop a pluggable architecture leveraging which custom networking mechanisms could be implemented by users as per their requirements. Since networking requirements vary across different deployment scenarios (cloud, on-premise, private cloud, or other hybrid models), it is not practical to create a monolithic networking mechanism that caters to all needs. Mesos' pluggable architecture proves to be very useful in tackling this.

To provide networking support, many opt-in extensions were introduced in Mesos components from version 0.25.0 onwards. The opt-in structure allows existing frameworks without networking support to continue operating seamlessly on newer Mesos versions. Mesos enables integration with other networking mechanisms, and provides features like service discovery, IP per container, and isolation of tasks.

Networking support is provided through a Mesos module, which implies that it is abstracted away from the Mesos master and slaves. All the required support needs to be enabled from the networking module itself. Since IP requests are handled on a best-effort basis, frameworks also need to be able to take care of cases where a request is ignored due to networking modules not being implemented, or where a request is denied due to inability of the module to assign an IP.

Framework Schedulers need to opt in for network isolation through use of additional data structures in `TaskInfo`. This structure ensures that backward compatibility is maintained with older frameworks.

Architecture

The solution architecture with a description of the different components is provided as shown in the following diagram (source: `http://mesos.apache.org/documentation/latest/networking-for-mesos-managed-containers/`):

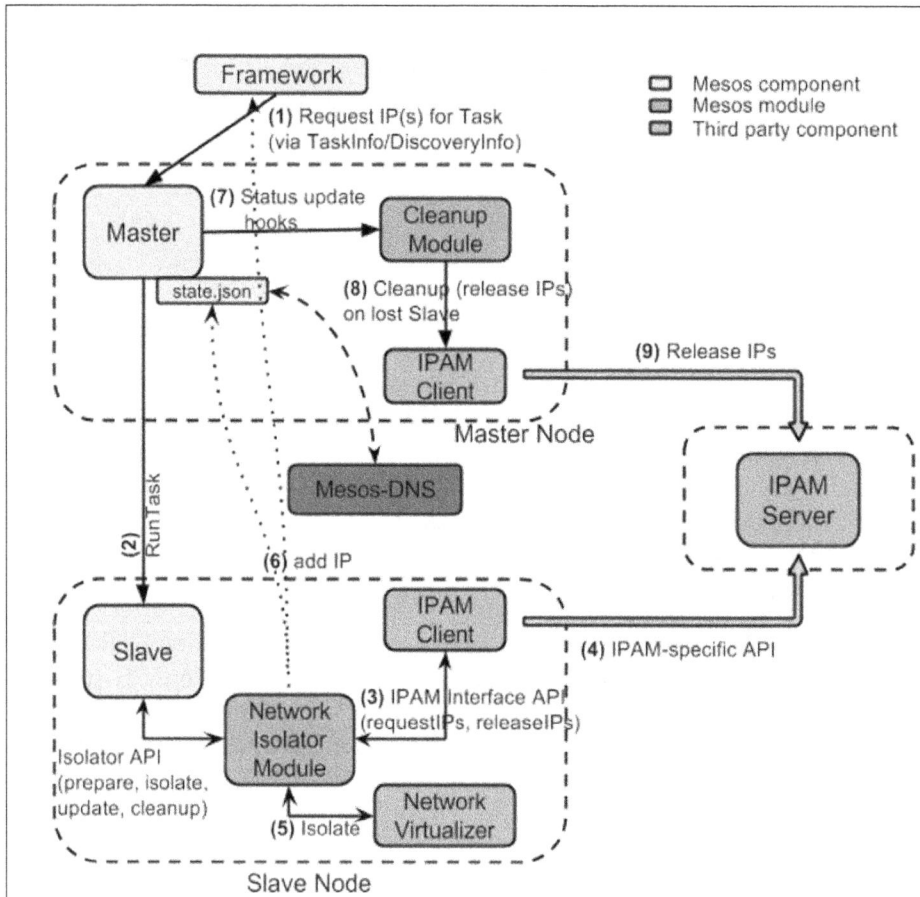

Key terms

Some key terms regarding networking are as follows:

- **IP Address Management (IPAM) Server**
    - ◦ IPs are assigned on demand
    - ◦ IPs are recycled upon being released
    - ◦ IPs can be optionally tagged with the provided ID

- **IPAM client**
    - ◦ Coupled tightly with the corresponding IPAM server
    - ◦ Serves as a bridge between the IPAM server and Network Isolator Module
    - ◦ Handles IP-related communications with the server (release, request, and so on)

- **Network Isolator Module (NIM)**
    - ◦ Mesos module for the slave where the isolator interface is implemented
    - ◦ Task IP requirements are determined by looking at `TaskInfo`
    - ◦ Handles IP-related communications with the IPAM client (release, request, and so on)
    - ◦ Enables network isolation by communicating with the external network virtualizer

- **Cleanup Module**:
    - ◦ Handles cleanup tasks (such as IP release) when the slave is lost

The process

1. A Mesos framework requests IPs for every container being launched, using the `TaskInfo` message.
2. The Mesos master forwards these messages to the slave after processing them for launching and running tasks.
3. The Mesos slave figures out the container requirements by analyzing these messages, and prepares the different isolators for them.
4. The **Network Isolator Module** analyzes the messages, and decides whether the network isolators should be enabled or not.

5. The Network Isolator Module then communicates with the IPAM client to request the IP addresses, provided it decides that the network isolator needs to be enabled, and gives a status update to the slave.

6. Upon receiving this update, a container is launched by the slave within a different namespace. This is done by the Network Isolator Module which informs the network virtualizer to perform container isolation upon getting instructions from the slave to do so.

7. The IP information is added to `TaskStatus` by the Network Isolator Module.

8. The Network Isolator Module then makes the IP addresses from `TaskStatus` available at the master's state endpoint, while also making the frameworks aware of the IP addresses by forwarding the `TaskStatus` to them.

9. If a task is lost, the Network Isolator Module informs the IPAM client of the same, and gets the IP addresses released.

10. The cleanup module then gets notified, and then recycles all the IP addresses released by the IPAM client.

A sample implementation of a Networking Isolator Module can be seen at `https://github.com/mesosphere/net-modules`.

IP-per-container capability in frameworks

Frameworks that seek to implement IP per container, need to pass the message `NetworkInfo` within `TaskInfo`. The `NetworkInfo` message details are given in the following section.

NetworkInfo message

A new `NetworkInfo` message can be introduced as:

```
message NetworkInfo {
  enum Protocol {
    IPv4 = 1;
    IPv6 = 2;
  }

  message IPAddress {
    optional Protocol protocol = 1;

    optional string ip_address = 2;
  }
```

```
      repeated IPAddress ip_addresses = 5;

      repeated string groups = 3;

      optional Labels labels = 4;
    };
```

The protocol field needs to be set to IPv4 or IPv6 while an IP address from the IP Address Management is requested. If supported by the Network Isolator Module, a framework can set a static IP address for each container. This can be done by providing a valid IP as the ip_address string. This is typically required when tasks that get killed or lost need to be relaunched on another node with the same IP address.

Examples for specifying network requirements

The frameworks which want to enable an IP per container need to provide NetworkInfo message in TaskInfo. Here are a few examples:

1. Request for single IP address without a protocol version being specified using the default command executor:

```
TaskInfo {
    ...
    command: ...,
    container: ContainerInfo {
      network_infos: [
        NetworkInfo {
          ip_addresses: [
            IPAddress {
              protocol: None;
              ip_address: None;
            }
          ]
          groups: [];
          labels: None;
        }
      ]
    }
}
```

2. Request for two IP addresses, one of IPv4 protocol and another of IPv6 protocol, in two sets using the default command executor:

```
TaskInfo {
    ...
    command: ...,
    container: ContainerInfo {
      network_infos: [
        NetworkInfo {
          ip_addresses: [
            IPAddress {
              protocol: IPv4;
              ip_address: None;
            },
            IPAddress {
              protocol: IPv6;
              ip_address: None;
            }
          ]
          groups: ["A", "B"];
          labels: None;
        }
      ]
    }
}
```

3. Request for two network interfaces, each with one IP address and each in a different network group using the default command executor:

```
TaskInfo {
    ...
    command: ...,
    container: ContainerInfo {
      network_infos: [
        NetworkInfo {
          ip_addresses: [
            IPAddress {
              protocol: None;
              ip_address: None;
            }
          ]
          groups: ["A"];
          labels: None;
        },
        NetworkInfo {
```

```
                  ip_addresses: [
                    IPAddress {
                      protocol: None;
                      ip_address: None;
                    }
                  ]
                  groups: ["B"];
                  labels: None;
                },
              ]
            }
          }
        }
```

4. Request for a specific IP address using a custom executor:

```
TaskInfo {
    ...
    executor: ExecutorInfo {
        ...,
        container: ContainerInfo {
          network_infos: [
            NetworkInfo {
              ip_addresses: [
                IPAddress {
                  protocol: None;
                  ip_address: "xx.xx.x.x";
                }
              ]
              groups: [];
              labels: None;
            }
          ]
        }
      }
    }
```

Address discovery

As seen earlier, frameworks can request IP addresses for assignment during launching of tasks on the Mesos slaves by passing the `NetworkInfo` message within the `TaskInfo` message. The frameworks, after opting for network isolation, also need a mechanism for knowing the IP addresses finally assigned so that monitoring and other communication activities can be undertaken. This can be done by introducing an additional field in the `TaskStatus` message as follows:

```
message ContainerStatus {
  repeated NetworkInfo network_infos;
}

message TaskStatus {
  ...
  optional ContainerStatus container;
  ...
};
```

Implementing a Custom Network Isolator Module

Mesos provides an Isolator API to enable custom Network Isolator Module implementations on top of it. The implemented module gets manifested as a dynamic shared library within the Mesos slave, and seamlessly integrates with the container launch. A network isolator often communicates with network virtualizers and IPAM clients to meet the framework needs.

The three key functions that a Network Isolator Module must implement are described as follows:

1. `Isolator::prepare()`: This gives the module an option to determine whether or not network isolation needs to be enabled for the specified container. The `Isolator::prepare` function instructs the slave to create a different network namespace if network isolation is to be enabled. This interface is also responsible for creating an IP address for the container.

2. `Isolator::isolate()`: This gives the module the chance to isolate the task container after its creation but before launching of an executor within it. It involves a virtual Ethernet adapter creation for the container and the assignment of an IP address to it. It can also leverage an external virtualizer for network setup.

3. `Isolator::cleanup()`: This function is called upon container termination. Its main job is to recover and recycle released IP addresses, and undertake any other cleanups as necessary.

Monitoring container network statistics

Statistics for every container network are provided via the `/monitor/statistics.json` slave endpoint by Mesos.

The following counters are reported:

Metric	Description	Type
net_rx_bytes	Bytes received	Counter
net_rx_dropped	Dropped packets (receive)	Counter
net_rx_errors	Reported errors (receive)	Counter
net_rx_packets	Received packets	Counter
net_tx_bytes	Bytes sent	Counter
net_tx_dropped	Dropped packets (send)	Counter
net_tx_errors	Reported errors (send)	Counter
net_tx_packets	Sent Packets	Counter

Additionally, the following counters and gauges can be reported for the elements which implement bloat reduction or bandwidth limiting under the `statistics/net_traffic_control_statistics` key:

Metric	Description	Type
backlog	Queued bytes (only on bloat reduction interface)	Gauge
bytes	Bytes sent	Counter
drops	Dropped packets (send)	Counter
overlimits	Number of times interface was over its transmit limit	Counter
packets	Sent packets	Counter
qlen	Queued packets	Gauge
ratebps	Rate of transmission (currently, always 0 bytes/second)	Gauge
ratepps	Rate of transmission (currently, always 0 packets/second)	Gauge
requeues	Failed packets	Counter

Example statistics

An example of the statistics obtained is given as follows:

```
$ curl -s http://localhost:5051/monitor/statistics | python2.6
  -mjson.tool

[
  {
    "executor_id": "job.<job_id>",
    "executor_name": "Command Executor
      (Task: job.<job_id>) (Command: sh -c 'iperf ....')",
    "framework_id": "<some_id>",
    "source": "job.<job_id>",
    "statistics": {
      "cpus_limit": <some_value>,
      "cpus_nr_periods": <some_value>,
      "cpus_nr_throttled": <some_value>,
      "cpus_system_time_secs": <some_value>,
      "cpus_throttled_time_secs": <some_value>,
      "cpus_user_time_secs": <some_value>,
      "mem_anon_bytes": <some_value>,
      "mem_cache_bytes": <some_value>,
      "mem_critical_pressure_counter": <some_value>,
      "mem_file_bytes": <some_value>,
      "mem_limit_bytes": <some_value>,
      "mem_low_pressure_counter": <some_value>,
      "mem_mapped_file_bytes": <some_value>,
      "mem_medium_pressure_counter": <some_value>,
      "mem_rss_bytes": <some_value>,
      "mem_total_bytes": <some_value>,
      "net_rx_bytes": <some_value>,
      "net_rx_dropped": <some_value>,
      "net_rx_errors": <some_value>,
      "net_rx_packets": <some_value>,
      "net_traffic_control_statistics": [
        {
          "backlog": <some_value>,
          "bytes": <some_value>,
          "drops": <some_value>,
          "id": "bw_limit",
          "overlimits": <some_value>,
          "packets": <some_value>,
          "qlen": <some_value>,
          "ratebps": 0,
          "ratepps": 0,
          "requeues": 0
```

```
      },
      {
        "backlog": <some_value>,
        "bytes": <some_value>,
        "drops": <some_value>,
        "id": "bloat_reduction",
        "overlimits": <some_value>,
        "packets": <some_value>,
        "qlen": <some_value>,
        "ratebps": 0,
        "ratepps": 0,
        "requeues": 0
      }
    ],
    "net_tx_bytes": <some_value>,
    "net_tx_dropped": <some_value>,
    "net_tx_errors": <some_value>,
    "net_tx_packets": <some_value>,
    "perf": {
      "duration": <some_value>,
    "timestamp": <some_value>,
    },
    "timestamp": <some_value>,
  }
 }
]
```

Mesos Image Provisioner

An **Image** is an ordered collection of root filesystem changes and the corresponding execution parameters for use within a container runtime.

Most of the container specifications, such as Docker, **App Container (AppC)**, or **Open Container Project (OCP)**, combine implementation and specification of the image format with other container components such as resource isolation and task execution to a large extent. The Mesos **Image Provisioner** seeks to enhance the capabilities of Mesos Containerizer by providing support for container filesystem provisioning from multiple image formats, while also providing features such as resource isolation by combining with other components such as Isolators.

Mesos containers created using the Mesos Containerizer are provided with a root filesystem already provisioned with Docker or AppC images using the Mesos Image Provisioner.

The container filesystem image is described by a new message `Image`, which is given in the following code:

```
message Image {
  enum Type {
    DOCKER = 1;
    APPC = 2;
    // More Image types.
  }

  message Docker {
    // Docker configurations
  }

  message Appc {
    // Appc configurations.
  }


  required Type type = 1;

  // Only one of the following image messages should be
    set to match
  // the type.
optional Docker docker = xx;
optional Appc appc = yy;


}
```

This message contains both the image specification type as well as the corresponding type configurations. This message can be passed through either 'Volume' or `ContainerInfo`. A root filesystem is provided to the task when an image is configured in `ContainerInfo`, while volumes are mounted with the image filesystem in cases where the 'Image' message is specified within 'Volume'.

The request for container image is forwarded to the respective provider for provisioning the layers. Layers are generally filesystem changesets, which are nothing but an archive of the added, modified, or deleted files. The Provisioner further asks the configured setup to provision a root filesystem from these layers.

Setup and configuration options

To enable Mesos containerizer on the slave, it must be launched with the `mesos containerizer` (default) option, as shown earlier in this chapter. The slave also needs to be running on Linux with root permissions.

Next, filesystem/Linux must be set as the isolator option via the `--isolation` flag. The image providers can be configured by passing them as a comma-separated list in the agent flag `--image_providers`, and the supported backend can be specified though the flag `--image_provisioner_backend`. Additional configurations for every image provider can also be provided if required.

The following is an example:

```
mesos-slave --containerizers=mesos --image_providers=appc,docker
  --image_provisioner_backend=copy --isolation=filesystem/linux
```

For more information, visit `http://mesos.apache.org/documentation/latest/mesos-provisioner/`.

Mesos fetcher

The Mesos fetcher is a way by which resources can be downloaded in the `task sandbox` directory while preparing the task execution. The framework requesting the execution of the task sends a list of `CommandInfo::URI` values as part of the `TaskInfo` message, which in turn serves as the Mesos fetcher input.

The Mesos fetcher natively supports the FTP and HTTP protocols, and is also able to copy over files from a filesystem. It also supports all Hadoop client protocols such as **Amazon Simple Storage Service (S3)**, **Hadoop distributed Filesystem (HDFS)**, and so on.

Every Uniform Resource Identifier (URI) that is requested gets downloaded, by default, directly into the `sandbox` directory. Multiple requests for the same URI results in copies of that resource being downloaded again and again. The downloaded URIs can also alternatively be cached in a specified directory for reuse.

Mechanism

The mechanism comprises the following:

1. Each slave consists of one internal fetcher instance which is leveraged by all containerizer types. The fetcher process, included in the slave program, is responsible for performing book-keeping around what is present in the cache.

2. There is also an external `mesos-fetcher` program that gets called by the internal program mentioned in Step 1 whenever resources need to be downloaded from specified URIs into the cache or directories. It is also called when resources from cache need to be moved over to the `sandbox` directory. All disk and network operations, barring deletions and querying file size, are performed by it. It acts more like a simple helper program while all the intelligence is located in the internal program.

No persistent state is maintained in the entire system except for the cache files. This helps manage the complexity involved in simultaneous fetching and caching, and generally simplifies the overall architecture.

The following diagram depicts the interactions between the internal fetcher process and the external `mesos-fetcher` program. Subsequent diagrams dive into the internal workflow in more detail. Source: `http://mesos.apache.org/documentation/latest/fetcher-cache-internals/`.

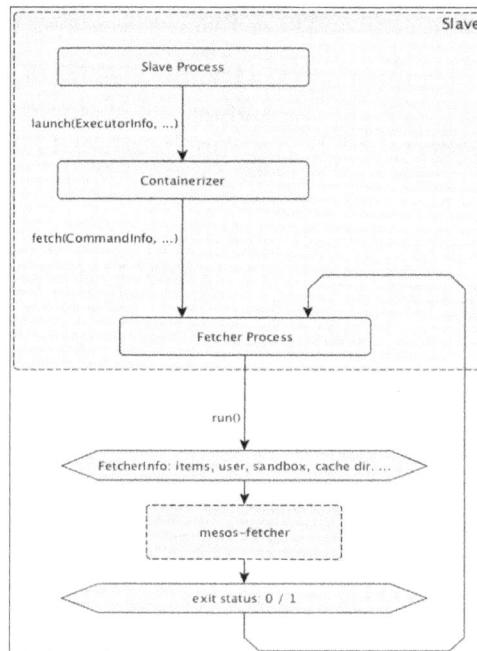

Cache entry

The fetcher process can provide details around the cached URIs besides giving information regarding the location of the cache files, the processing stage, and so on.

A **HashMap** is used to store all the information mentioned previously. Each of the `Cache::Entry` objects contain the details of one cache file. These objects can be referenced by numerous callbacks corresponding to the multiple fetches while being stored in the HashMap.

Each cache entry has a one-to-one correspondence with a disk cache file during the entire duration of the file, which also includes the period before and after its creation. The entry includes all relevant state information regarding the stage as well as the corresponding URI fetching results.

A cache entry cannot be removed by any fetch attempt seeking to free up space for a newly downloaded cache file while it is being referenced.

The next diagram shows the various states of a cache entry. It illustrates the sequence of events that take place during a single fetch run. The colors in the diagram represent the following:

- **Blue**: No cache exists
- **Green**: Cache entry unreferenced by this run
- **Orange**: Cache entry referenced

A cache entry should not be removed as long as any event is referencing it. This is enforced by something called **reference counting**. The value of a field called reference count within each cache entry is increased whenever it is being used by a fetch attempt, and decreased when the run is over, regardless of whether the run was successful or not. The value is incremented in the following cases:

- Creation of a new cache entry
- Waiting for file download of an existing entry
- Fetching of the cache file corresponding to an entry

Each value increase is noted within a list. At the end of the activity causing the increment, the value is decreased.

The figure given illustrates the different states which a cache entry can be in.

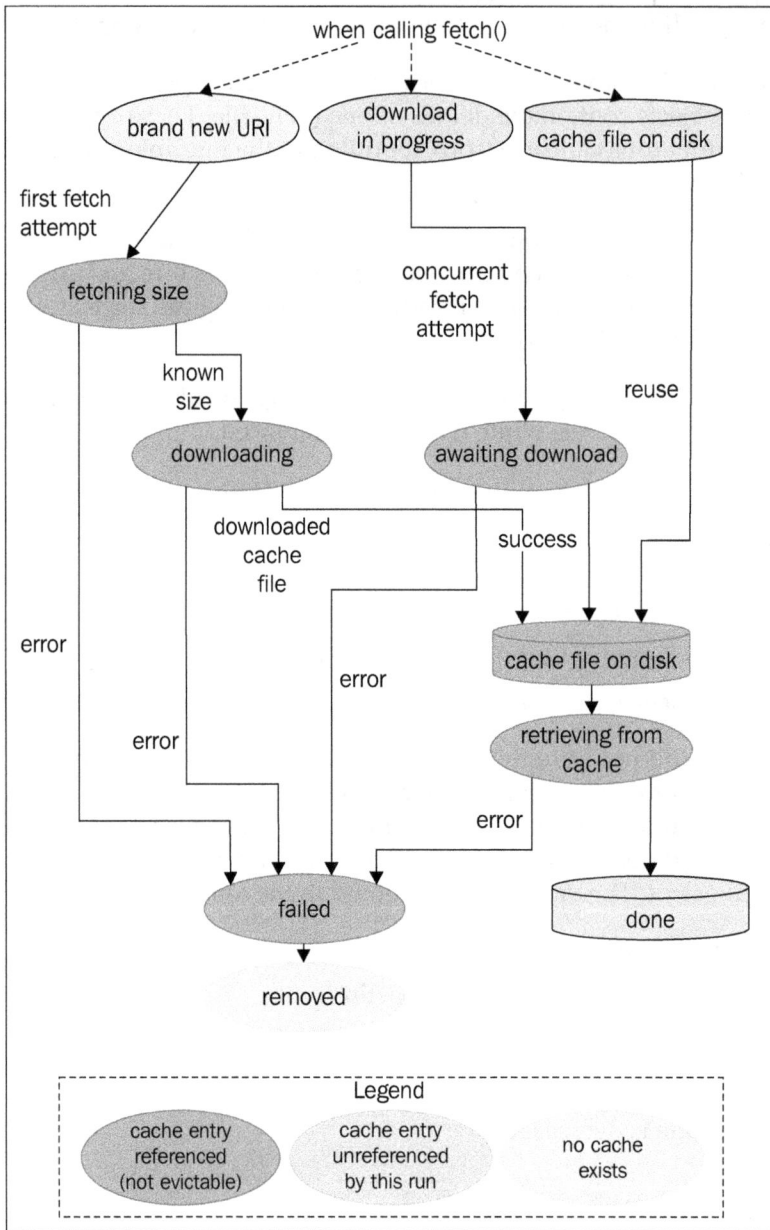

URI flow diagram

The fetcher process determines the control logic for handling every URI being fetched. The following is a diagram illustrating the flowchart for this:

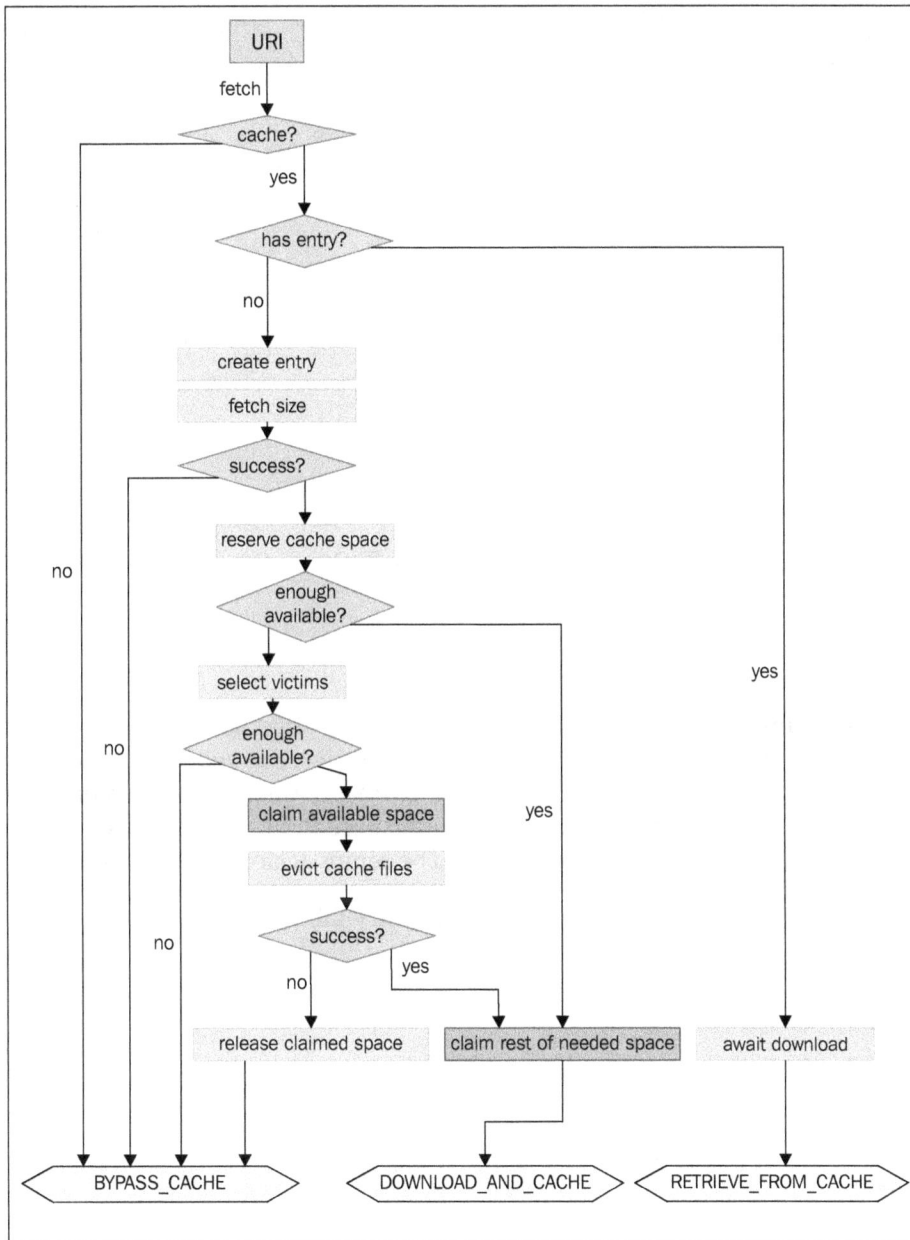

Cache eviction

Consider the case where a couple of resources, *A* and *B*, have been fetched and cached into two sandboxes respectively, as shown in the following diagram. In this process, one cache file for each resource is created along with the cache entries mapping the resources with the corresponding cache files. Source: `http://mesos.apache.org/documentation/latest/fetcher-cache-internals/`.

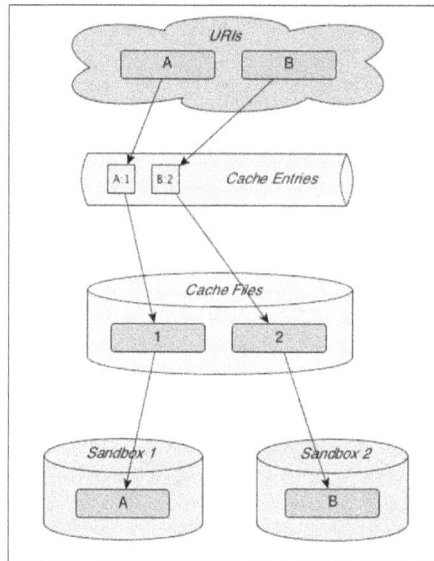

Now let us assume a third resource *C*, which is downloaded and cached into a new sandbox. Assuming there is no space for all three entries, this requires removal or eviction of an existing cache file along with its corresponding entry to accommodate the new one. Assuming resource *A* was fetched before *B*, the cache eviction process would remove *A*, since it is the oldest entry. The removal steps are as follows:

1. Cache entry for *A* is removed from the entry table.

2. *C* is fetched, which creates a new cache file of a different name along with the associated cache entry.

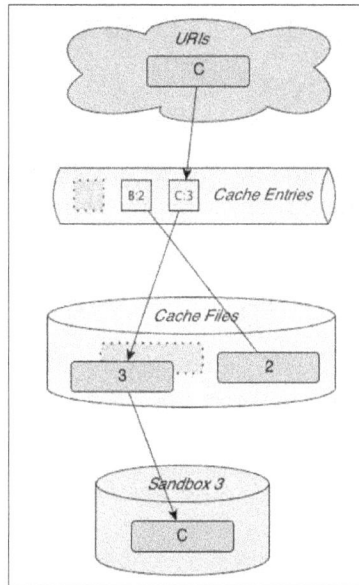

If the first resource *A* is fetched again, then *B* would now get evicted, since it is the oldest present entry; the assumption, of course, being that there is no space to accommodate three cache files.

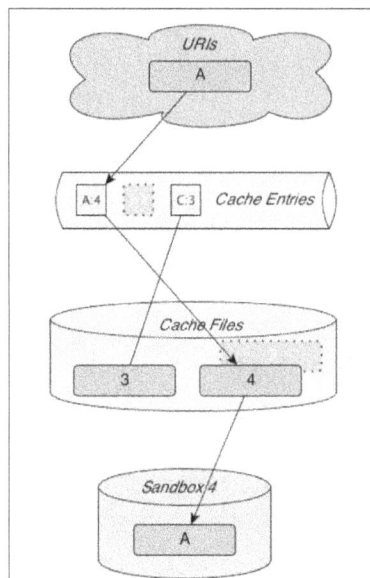

Deploying containerized apps using Docker and Mesos

This section gives a brief overview of deploying a Docker containerized Node.js application on Mesos using Marathon. This requires you to have Docker and fig already installed on the machine. Let's follow the steps listed next to carry out the deployment:

1. Since we are deploying a simple Node.js application, we can start off by creating a simple App.js to print Hello World, a simple hello world Node.js program.

```
var http = require('http');
// Configure our HTTP server to respond with
  Hello World to all requests.
var server = http.createServer
  (function (request, response) {
  response.writeHead(200, {"Content-Type": "text/plain"});
  response.end("Hello World      ");
});
// Listen on port 8000, IP defaults to "0.0.0.0"
server.listen(8000);
// Put a friendly message on the terminal
console.log("Server running at http://127.0.0.1:8000/");
```

2. Next we create the package.json file with the following contents:

```
{
  "name": "hello-world",
  "description": "hello world",
  "version": "0.0.1",
  "private": true,
  "dependencies": {
    "express": "3.x"
  },
  "scripts": {"start": "node app.js"}
}
```

3. The next step is to dockerize our application. For that, we can create a Dockerfile with the following contents:

```
FROM google/nodejs
WORKDIR /app
ADD package.json /app/
RUN npm install
ADD . /app
```

```
EXPOSE 8000
CMD []
ENTRYPOINT ["/nodejs/bin/npm", "start"]
```

4. We can now build the container with the following commands:

    ```
    $ docker build -t my_nodejs_image .
    ```

    ```
    $ docker run -p 8000:8000 my_nodejs_image
    ```

We can make sure everything is working correctly by opening the `localhost:8000` from the browser, which should display our **Hello World** text.

1. The next step is to build our `fig.yml` file. Here we will be using fig as an orchestration engine to deploy all central services from a single command. The `fig.yml` file will look like the following:

```
# Zookeeper: -p 2181:2181 -p 2888:2888 -p 3888:3888

zookeeper:
  image: jplock/zookeeper:3.4.5
  ports:
    - "2181"
master:
  image: redjack/mesos-master:0.21.0
  hostname: master
  links:
    - zookeeper:zookeeper
  environment:
    - MESOS_ZK=zk://zookeeper:2181/mesos
    - MESOS_QUORUM=1
    - MESOS_WORK_DIR=/var/lib/mesos
    - MESOS_LOG_DIR=/var/log
  ports:
    - "5050:5050"
marathon:
  #image: garland/mesosphere-docker-marathon
  image: mesosphere/marathon
```

```
  links:
    - zookeeper:zookeeper
  ports:
    - "8080:8080"
  # Adding the params via command
  command: --master zk://zookeeper:2181/mesos --zk zk://
zookeeper:2181/marathon
slave:
  image: redjack/mesos-slave:0.21.0
  links:
    - zookeeper:zookeeper
    - master:master
  environment:
    - MESOS_MASTER=zk://zookeeper:2181/mesos
    - MESOS_EXECUTOR_REGISTRATION_TIMEOUT=5mins
    - MESOS_CONTAINERIZERS=docker,mesos
    - MESOS_ISOLATOR=cgroups/cpu,cgroups/mem
    - MESOS_LOG_DIR=/var/log
  volumes:
    - /var/run/docker.sock:/run/docker.sock
    - /usr/bin/docker:/usr/bin/docker
    - /sys:/sys:ro
    - mesosslace-stuff:/var/log
  expose:
    - "5051"
registry:
  image: registry
  environment:
    - STORAGE_PATH=/registry
  volumes:
    - registry-stuff:/registry
  ports:
    - "5000:5000"
```

2. In the preceding configuration, we have configured the Docker registry to run on port `5000` along with a single Mesos slave, Mesos master, Marathon, and ZooKeeper for internal communication.

3. We can now start the Docker registry service with the following command:

```
$ fig up
```

This command will start all the services listed in the preceding configuration file such as Mesos master, Mesos slave, Marathon, ZooKeeper, and Docker registry.

4. We can now build the Docker image, and push it to the registry with the following commands:

```
# Build an image
$ docker build -t localhost:5000/containersol/nodejs_app


# Push it to the registry
$ docker push localhost:5000/containersol/nodejs_app
```

5. Now that we have the cluster ready, we can deploy our Node.js application through Marathon. For that we need to create an application configuration file (app_marathon.json) with the following contents:

```
{
  "id": "app",
  "container": {
    "docker": {
      "image":
        "localhost:5000/containersol/nodejs_app:latest",
      "network": "BRIDGE",
      "portMappings": [
        {"containerPort": 8000, "servicePort": 8000}
      ]
    }
  },
  "cpus": 0.2,
  "mem": 512.0,
  "instances": 1
}
```

6. This is then deployed on Marathon with the following command:

```
$ curl -X POST -H "Content-Type: application/json"
  http://localhost:8080/v2/apps -d@app_marathon.json
```

7. We can now open the Marathon Web UI running on port `8080`, and see our Node.js application up and running:

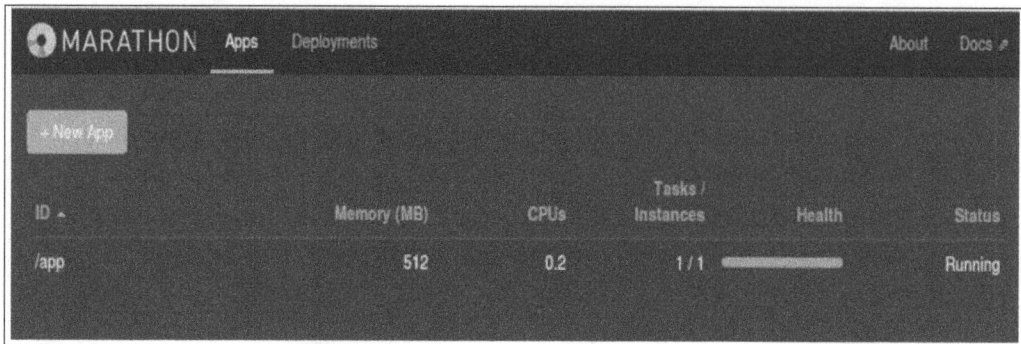

And we can see our Node.js hello world application by pointing the browser to `localhost:31000` port:

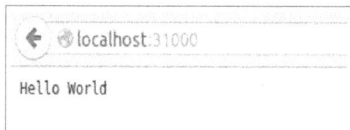

(Reference: `http://container-solutions.com/continuous-delivery-with-docker-on-mesos-in-less-than-a-minute/`

`http://container-solutions.com/continuous-delivery-with-docker-on-mesos-in-less-than-a-minute-part-2/`)

Summary

This chapter touched upon several important topics related to containerization in Mesos. Resource isolation is one of the most touted features of Mesos, and the topics explained in this chapter have hopefully helped you understand this feature.

In the next chapter, we will see some of the important Big Data frameworks which are currently supported by Mesos such as Hadoop, Spark, and Storm and understand how these can be set up and configured on Mesos.

8
Mesos Big Data Frameworks

This chapter is a guide to deploy important big data processing frameworks, such as Hadoop, Spark, Storm, and Samza, on top of Mesos.

Hadoop on Mesos

This section will introduce Hadoop, explain how to set up the Hadoop stack on Mesos, and discuss the problems commonly encountered while setting up the stack.

Introduction to Hadoop

Hadoop was developed by Mike Cafarella and Doug Cutting in 2006 to manage the distribution for the Nutch project. The project was named after Doug's son's toy elephant.

The following modules make up the Apache Hadoop framework:

- **Hadoop Common**: This has the common libraries and utilities required by other modules

- **Hadoop Distributed File System** (**HDFS**): This is a distributed, scalable filesystem capable of storing petabytes of data on commodity hardware

- **Hadoop YARN**: This is a resource manager to manage cluster resources (similar to Mesos)

- **Hadoop MapReduce**: This is a processing model for parallel data processing at scale

MapReduce

MapReduce is a processing model using which large amounts of data can be processed in parallel on a distributed, commodity hardware-based infrastructure reliably and in a fault-tolerant way.

The word MapReduce is a combination of the Map and Reduce tasks, which are described here:

- **The Map Task**: In this step, an operation is performed on all the elements of the input dataset to transform it as needed (for example applying a filter condition)

- **The Reduce Task**: The next step uses the output generated by the map task as its input and applies an aggregate operation on it to generate the final output (for example, summing all values)

The scheduling, execution, and monitoring of the tasks is reliably handled by the framework without the application programmer having to worry about it.

Hadoop Distributed File System

Based on **Google Filesystem** or **GFS**, Hadoop Distributed File System (HDFS) provides a scalable, distributed filesystem to store large amounts of data in a reliable, fault-tolerant way.

HDFS is based on a master/slave architecture, with the master consisting of a solitary **NameNode**, which handles the metadata of the filesystem, and single or multiple slave nodes, which store the data and are also called **DataNode**.

Each file in HDFS is divided into multiple blocks, with each of these blocks being stored in DataNode. NameNode is responsible for maintaining information regarding which block is present in which DataNode. Operations such as read/write are handled by DataNode along with block management tasks such as the creation, removal, and replication of instructions from NameNode.

Interaction is through a shell, where a set of commands can be used to communicate with the filesystem.

HDFS Architecture

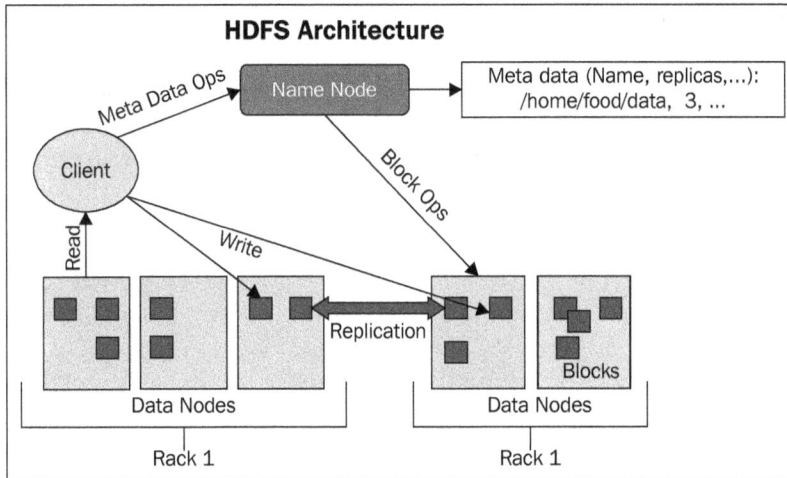

Setting up Hadoop on Mesos

This section will explain how to set up Hadoop on Mesos. An existing Hadoop distribution can also be set up on top of Mesos. To run Hadoop on Mesos, our Hadoop distribution must contain Hadoop-Mesos-0.1.0.jar (the version at the time of writing this book). This is required for any Hadoop distribution that uses a protobuf version higher than 2.5.0. We will also set a few configuration properties in order to complete the setup, as will be explained subsequently. Note that at the time of writing this chapter, YARN and MRv2 are not supported.

Let's follow the steps mentioned here:

1. Open up the Terminal on your cluster and fire up the following commands to set up Hadoop on Mesos:

```
# Install snappy-java package if not already installed.
$ sudo apt-get install libsnappy-dev


# Clone the repository
$ git clone https://github.com/Mesos/Hadoop


$ cd Hadoop


# Build the Hadoop-Mesos-0.1.0.jar
$ mvn package
```

2. Once the previous command is executed, it will create the `target/Hadoop-Mesos-0.1.0.jar` JAR.

    One thing to note here is that if you have an older version of Mesos and need to build the jar against this version, then you will have to edit the `pom.xml` file with the appropriate version. We can change the following versions in the `pom.xml` file:

    ```
    <!-- runtime deps versions -->
    <commons-logging.version>1.1.3</commons-logging.version>
    <commons-httpclient.version>3.1
      </commons-httpclient.version>
    <Hadoop-client.version>2.5.0-mr1-cdh5.2.0
      </Hadoop-client.version>
    <Mesos.version>0.23.1</Mesos.version>
    <protobuf.version>2.5.0</protobuf.version>
    <metrics.version>3.1.0</metrics.version>
    <snappy-java.version>1.0.5</snappy-java.version>
    ```

3. Now, we can download a Hadoop distribution. As you can see here, we have compiled `Hadoop-Mesos jar` with the `hadoop-2.5.0-mr1-cdh5.2.0` version. It can be downloaded with the following command:

    ```
    $ wget http://archive.cloudera.com/cdh5/cdh/5/
      hadoop-2.5.0-cdh5.2.0.tar.gz

    # Extract the contents

    $ tar zxf hadoop-2.5.0-cdh5.2.0.tar.gz
    ```

4. Now, we need to copy `Hadoop-Mesos-0.1.0.jar` into the Hadoop `share/Hadoop/common/lib` directory. This is done as shown here:

    ```
    $ cp hadoop-Mesos-0.1.0.jar
      hadoop-2.5.0-cdh5.2.0/share/hadoop/common/lib/
    ```

5. We now need to update the symlinks of the CHD5 distribution to point to the correct version (as it includes both MRv1 and MRv2 (YARN)) using the following set of commands:

    ```
    $ cd hadoop-2.5.0-cdh5.2.0

    $ mv bin bin-mapreduce2

    $ mv examples examples-mapreduce2

    $ ln -s bin-mapreduce1 bin

    $ ln -s examples-mapreduce1 examples


    $ pushd etc

    $ mv hadoop hadoop-mapreduce2
    ```

```
$ ln -s hadoop-mapreduce1 Hadoop
$ popd
$ pushd share/hadoop
$ rm mapreduce
$ ln -s mapreduce1 mapreduce
$ popd
```

6. All the configurations are now ready. We can archive and upload the Hadoop distribution to our existing Hadoop Distributed File System (HDFS) system, where it can be accessed by Mesos. Take a look at the following commands:

```
$ tar czf hadoop-2.5.0-cdh5.2.0.tar.gz
  hadoop-2.5.0-cdh5.2.0
$ hadoop fs -put hadoop-2.5.0-cdh5.2.0.tar.gz
  /hadoop-2.5.0-cdh5.2.0.tar.gz
```

7. Once done, we can configure `JobTracker` to launch each `TaskTracker` node on Mesos by editing the `mapred-site.xml` file, as follows:

```
<property>
  <name>mapred.job.tracker</name>
  <value>localhost:9001</value>
</property>

<property>
  <name>mapred.jobtracker.taskScheduler</name>
  <value>org.apache.Hadoop.mapred.MesosScheduler</value>
</property>

<property>
  <name>mapred.Mesos.taskScheduler</name>
  <value>
    org.apache.Hadoop.mapred.JobQueueTaskScheduler</value>
</property>

<property>
  <name>mapred.Mesos.master</name>
  <value>localhost:5050</value>
</property>

<property>
  <name>mapred.Mesos.executor.uri</name>
  <value>hdfs://localhost:9000
    /Hadoop-2.5.0-cdh5.2.0.tar.gz</value>
</property>
```

8. A few properties in the `mapred-site.xml` file are Mesos-specific, such as `mapred.Mesos.master` or `mapred.Mesos.executor.uri`.

9. We can now start the `JobTracker` service by including the Mesos native library using the following command:

```
$ MESOS_NATIVE_LIBRARY=/path/to/libMesos.so Hadoop jobtracker
```

An advanced configuration guide

More details regarding the configuration settings in Mesos can be found at `https://github.com/mesos/hadoop/blob/master/configuration.md`.

Common problems and solutions

The two most common problems encountered while setting up Hadoop on Mesos are:

- Inability to set the Mesos library in the environment
- Build failures

A solution for both these problems is described here:

- **Missing the Mesos library in the environment:** We will get an exception stack when we forget to set the Mesos library in the environment at the following URL: `https://github.com/mesos/hadoop/issues/25`.

  This can be resolved by setting the following environment variables:

  ```
  $ export MESOS_NATIVE_LIBRARY=/usr/local/lib/libMesos.so
  $ export MESOS_NATIVE_JAVA_LIBRARY=/usr/local/lib/libMesos.so
  ```

- **The Maven build failure:** We won't be able to build the package on some occasions due to build failures. One example of a build failure can be found here: `https://github.com/mesos/hadoop/issues/64`.

  This can be avoided by removing the older Maven dependencies from the environment and rebuilding it.

  Here's an example:

  ```
  $ mv ~/.m2 ~/.mv_back
  $ mvn package
  ```

Spark on Mesos

Apache **Spark** is a powerful open source processing engine built around speed, ease of use, and sophisticated analytics. It is currently one of the fastest growing big data technologies and is used by several leading companies in production.

Interestingly, Apache Spark was first started as a research project in 2009 at AmpLab, UC Berkeley, to prove that a distributed processing framework leveraging memory resources can run atop Apache Mesos. It was open sourced in 2010, entered the Apache incubator in 2013, and became an Apache top-level project in 2014. In its short existence, Apache Spark has managed to capture the attention of the developer community and is slowly finding its way into the lexicon of business decision makers as well. This, along with the fact that it is now in production in over 5000 organizations, speaks volumes about its versatility and utility.

Why Spark

With earlier distributed parallel computation frameworks such as **Map Reduce**, each computation step had to be read from and written to disk. For instance, consider the standard word count example of counting the number of occurrences of each word that appears in a set of text files. The first step here would be a map task that reads the text files from disk (breaking it up into smaller chunks if necessary), takes one line from it, splits it into individual words, and then outputs a key value pair of `<<word>,1>` (note that an intermediate combiner step can add the occurrences for each word from each mapper while it is still in memory for more efficiency). A number of mappers are spawned across the entire cluster to efficiently perform the preceding task in parallel over all the lines from each text file. The final output of all these map tasks is written to disk. In the next step, the reduce task needs to collect the same words in a single machine in order to add them all up and produce the final count. For this, there is a shuffle operation that reads the intermediate output generated from the map step and ensures that all the output for one word is sent to one and only one reducer. After the reduce step, the final output is collected and written to disk.

For iterative workloads, which involve multiple repetitions of the various preceding steps, this would lead to a lot of disk I/O. The mappers would read the first set of inputs and write out the intermediate output to disk. Then the reducers would read the intermediate output from disk and write out their outputs to disk, which would then be read by the mappers of stage 2, and so on. Disk reads are very slow, and for long, iterative computations, they would often be the bottleneck instead of the CPUs. This was one of the basic problems that Spark intended to resolve. Many iterative or latency-sensitive applications (interactive querying or stream processing, for example) weren't being adequately solved by batch processing frameworks such as Map Reduce due to fundamental design constraints. Spark set out to solve this problem by coming up with a novel architecture.

To minimize disk I/O, the creators of Spark decided to look at memory as a potential alternative. Trends demonstrated that memory cost was falling exponentially with each passing year. Affordable memory meant that more memory could be packed into commodity servers without bloating up the costs. In order to effectively handle the emerging class of business applications, such as iterative machine learning, interactive data mining, or stream processing, a memory-based framework also had to develop elegant solutions to the common problems of fault tolerance and partition control. For example, fault tolerance (or more accurately, high availability) can be achieved by replicating data across different machines or by updating the state at regular intervals in a database. However, this is a very time-consuming approach that utilizes a lot of network bandwidth and would have resulted in much slower job execution, something that the framework sought to solve in the first place. Partition control and having the flexibility to keep all the data required by a task as close to it as possible was also very important as without it, a high execution speed could not be achieved.

To tackle all these problems, a new higher-level abstraction called **Resilient Distributed Datasets** (**RDDs**) was developed. These new data structures allowed programmers to explicitly cache them in memory, place them in the desired partitions for optimal performance, and rebuild it based on a blueprint of how it was constructed if it is lost. Programmers need to simply write a driver program that encapsulates the logical workflow of their application and initiates the execution of the various comprising operations in parallel across the cluster.

The two main abstractions that Spark provides are:

1. Resilient distributed datasets (or RDDs), as mentioned before
2. The processing operations (map, filter, join, for each, collect, and so on) have to be applied on these datasets to generate the required output.

RDDs also permit the application of the same operation/function to multiple data points in parallel. By logging the process used to build a dataset (lineage), it can effectively reconstruct the dataset at even partition-level granularity in case there is a failure by leveraging this stored blueprint.

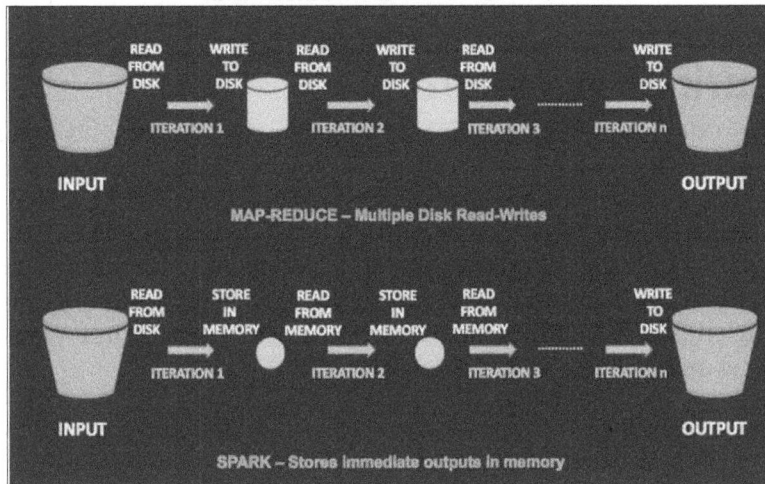

Spark has been shown to be 10 times faster on disk and 100 times faster in-memory than MapReduce for certain kinds of applications. It has also brought about a drastic reduction in writing the logical workflow itself, with even complex application programs now no longer extending beyond a few 100 lines of code instead of 1,000 and 10,000 lines earlier.

Logistic regression in Hadoop and Spark

Spark proves to be particularly useful in iterative machine learning, stream processing, and interactive querying use cases, in which the enhanced processing speeds and ease of programming brought by it is harnessed to drive more and more business or organizational value. Source: http://spark.apache.org.

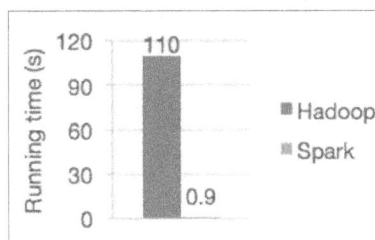

Spark's generality not only makes it a great fit for the use cases mentioned earlier but also for the traditional batch applications. Spark's versatility also extends to the fact that it offers rich, expressive APIs in Python, Java, Scala, and SQL among others, along with other inbuilt libraries. It is also highly interoperable and can work off all standard data storage tools, such as HDFS and Cassandra.

The Spark ecosystem

The Spark ecosystem comprises multiple complementary components that are designed to work with each other seamlessly. The versatile and general structure of Spark allows for specialized libraries geared towards specific workloads to be built on top of it, such as **Spark SQL** to query structured data through a SQL interface, **MLib** for machine learning, **Spark Streaming** to process data streams in motion, and **GraphX** for graph computations. Underpinning each of these components is the Spark core engine that defines the basic structure of Spark including its core abstraction, the resilient distributed dataset (or RDD).

Spark's design principle of high interoperability and several tightly coupled components feeding off a common core has multiple advantages. All the higher-level libraries in the ecosystem are directly able to leverage any feature additions or improvements made to the base framework. The total cost of ownership reduces as only one software stack needs to be set up and maintained instead of having multiple disparate systems. It also acts as a unified data analysis stack for varied use cases, reducing the overall learning curve and deployment, testing, and running cycle. Applications that involve a combination of processing streaming data, applying machine learning algorithms, and querying the final output through a SQL interface can be easily built using all the different libraries of Spark. Moreover, the enhanced speed and lower infrastructure costs provided by Spark has unlocked newer use cases as well, ranging from processing streaming data in real time to developing applications involving complex machine learning algorithms. Source: `http://spark.apache.org`.

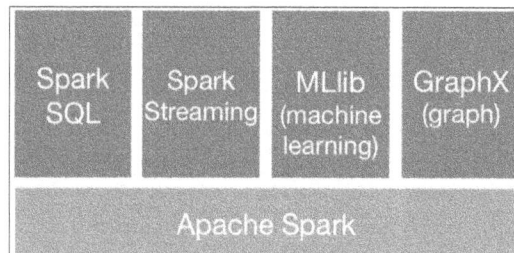

The components of the Spark ecosystem are described in the following sections.

Spark Core

Spark Core is the fundamental component that comprises the general execution engine and covers the core Spark functionalities. It includes features such as memory management, failure recovery, connectivity, or interoperability with different storage systems, job scheduling, and rich, expressive APIs (including the one that contains the definition for RDDs) to construct application workflows.

Spark SQL

Spark SQL is the component that allows analysts to use SQL to analyze and query structured datasets. It supports multiple data formats, including CSV, Parquet, JSON, and AVRO. As mentioned before, the integrated design of Spark also permits data engineers to intermingle complex analytics with Spark SQL queries, thus feeding the output of one component to others within a unified application through the common RDD abstraction.

Another important development in this area was the introduction of the DataFrame API (inspired by R and Python DataFrame), which was introduced in Spark 1.3. DataFrames are optimized, table-like, column-organized distributed datasets that allow a vast subsection of analysts and data scientists familiar with this concept to have the ability to leverage them using Spark. They can be generated from a lot of sources, such as structured files, Hive tables, or other RDDs, and can be operated upon using a provided DSL or domain-specific language.

Spark Streaming

Spark Streaming is a component that allows the processing of streaming data or data in motion, such as machine logs, server logs, social media feeds, and so on in real time. Its model for processing live streams of data is a logical extension of how the core API processes batch data. It operates on data in a minibatch mode; that is, it collects data for a window of time, applies the processing logic on this *minibatch*, then collects the next minibatch, and so on. This makes it extremely easy to reuse code written for batch workflows and apply them to a streaming data scenario.

MLlib

Spark comes with a scalable machine learning library containing a rich set of distributed algorithms for a wide range of use cases, such as classification, clustering, collaborative filtering, decomposition, and regression. It also includes a few deeper primitives, such as **gradient descent optimization**.

GraphX

The GraphX component is useful for operating on and processing graphs (for example, social network graphs) through a rich set of operators, such as mapVertices and subgraph, as well as standard algorithms for graph analytics (PageRank), community detection (triangle counting), and structured prediction (Gibbs sampling). The Spark API is extended (similarly to Spark SQL and Spark Streaming) to develop directed graphs in which customized properties can be assigned to each edge and vertex.

Spark's extendibility has also fostered the development of a multitude of third-party packages, connectors, and other libraries that further enhance its utility. Among some of the more popular ones are SparkR, launch scripts for different cloud infrastructure providers such as GCE developed by Sigmoid, connectors for Redshift and Elasticsearch, and a job execution server.

Setting up Spark on Mesos

This section explains how we can run Spark on top of Mesos in detail. Similar to the Hadoop setup, we will need the Spark binary package uploaded to a place accessible by Mesos and the Spark driver program configured to connect to Mesos.

Another alternative is to install Spark at the same location in all the Mesos slaves and set `Spark.Mesos.executor.home` to point to this location.

The following steps can be performed to upload the Spark binary to a location accessible by Mesos.

Whenever Mesos runs a task on the Mesos slave for the first time, the slave must have a Spark binary package to run the Spark Mesos executor backend (which comes with Spark). A location that is accessible by Mesos can be HDFS, HTTP, S3, and so on. We can download the latest version of Spark Binary from the official website by navigating to the following website:

`http://spark.apache.org/downloads.html.`

For example, at the time of writing this book, Spark's latest version is 1.6.0, and we can download and upload it to HDFS with the following commands:

```
$ wget http://d3kbcqa49mib13.cloudfront.net/
  spark-1.6.0-bin-hadoop2.6.tgz
$ hadoop fs -put spark-1.6.0-bin-hadoop2.6.tgz /
```

In the driver program, we can now give the master URL as the Mesos master URL, which will be in the `Mesos://master-host:5050` form for a single master Mesos cluster. It could be similar to `Mesos://zk://host1:2181,host2:2181` for a multimaster Mesos cluster.

There are two modes of submitting a Spark job to Mesos, which are explained in the following sections.

Submitting jobs in client mode

The Spark Mesos framework is launched directly on the client machine, and it waits for the driver output in client mode. We need to set a few Mesos-specific configurations in the `Spark-env.sh` file to interact with Mesos, which are listed here:

```
export MESOS_NATIVE_JAVA_LIBRARY=<path to libMesos.so>

export SPARK_EXECUTOR_URI=<URL of Spark-1.6.0.tar.gz uploaded above>
```

Now, when starting a Spark application on the cluster, pass the `Mesos://` URL as the master while creating `SparkContext`. Here's an example:

```
val conf = new SparkConf()
  .setMaster("Mesos://HOST:5050")
  .setAppName("My app")
  .set("Spark.executor.uri",
  "<path to Spark-1.6.0.tar.gz uploaded above>")
val sc = new SparkContext(conf)
```

Submitting jobs in cluster mode

In the cluster mode, the driver is launched in the cluster, and the client can find the results of the driver on the Mesos Web UI. We need to start `MesosClusterDispatcher` to use the cluster mode. The script to start `MesosClusterDispatcher` is located under the `sbin/start-Mesos-dispatcher.sh` script, which takes in the Mesos master URL. We can then submit the jobs to Mesos cluster by specifying the master URL to the URL of `MesosClusterDispatcher` (such as `Mesos://dispatcher:7077`). The driver status will be available on the Spark cluster Web UI.

Here's an example:

```
./bin/Spark-submit \
  --class org.apache.Spark.examples.SparkPi \
  --master Mesos://207.184.161.138:7077 \
  --deploy-mode cluster \
  --supervise
```

```
--executor-memory 20G \
--total-executor-cores 100 \
http://path/to/examples.jar \
1000
```

Note that the jars or Python files that are passed to Spark-submit should be URIs reachable by Mesos slaves, as the Spark driver doesn't automatically upload local jars.

An advanced configuration guide

Spark currently supports two modes to run on Mesos: **coarse-grained mode** and **fine-grained mode**:

- **Coarse-grained mode**: The coarse-grained mode is the default mode, and it will launch one long-running Spark task on each Mesos machine and dynamically schedule its own minitasks within it. This mode is usually used when we require a much lower startup overhead, but it comes with the cost of reserving the Mesos resources for the complete duration of the application. We can control the maximum number of resources that Spark acquires in the coarse-grained mode by setting the `Spark.cores.max` property in `SparkConf`. By default, it acquires all the resources available in the cluster.

- **Fine-grained mode**: In the fine-grained mode, each Spark task runs as a separate Mesos task. This allows better sharing of the cluster resources among other frameworks at a very fine granularity, where each application gets additional or fewer machines as it ramps up and down, depending on the workload. The drawback is that it comes with an additional overhead in launching each task. This mode is not preferred for low-latency requirements, such as interactive queries or serving web requests. To run in the fine-grained mode, we can turn the coarse-grained mode off by setting the following property:

```
conf.set("Spark.Mesos.coarse", "false")
```

Spark configuration properties

Mesos-specific Spark configuration properties can be found at `http://spark.apache.org/docs/latest/running-on-mesos.html#configuration`.

Storm on Mesos

Storm is a real-time **distributed data processing system** for processing data coming in at high velocities. It can process millions of records per second and is particularly useful for applications where millisecond-level latency is essential (for example, security threat detection, fraud detection, operational monitoring, and so on).

The Storm architecture

A typical Storm cluster has three types of nodes:

- **Nimbus or master node**: This is responsible for submitting and distributing the computations for execution apart from handling tasks such as launching slave nodes and monitoring the execution
- **ZooKeeper node**: This is responsible for coordinating the cluster
- **Supervisor node**: This is responsible for starting and stopping slave nodes based on the instructions sent by the Nimbus node

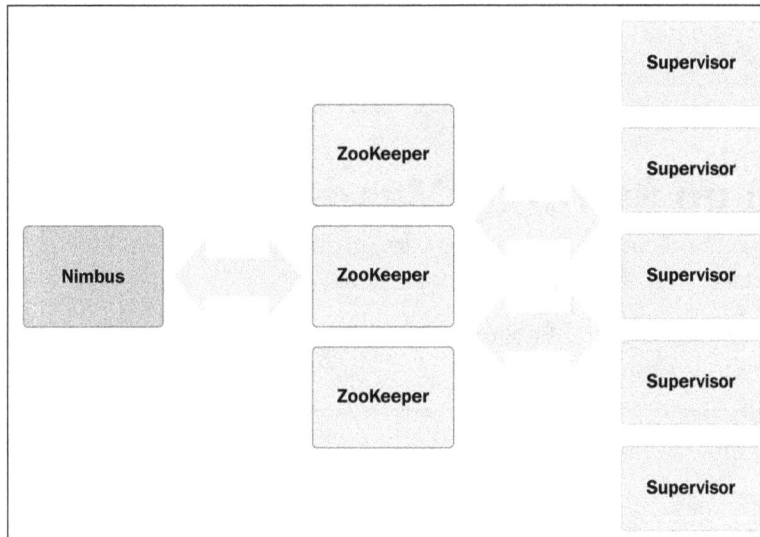

Some important terms used in Storm are:

- **Tuples**: This is an ordered list of elements
- **Streams**: This is a sequence of tuples
- **Spouts**: These are sources of streams in a computation (for example, the Twitter API)
- **Bolts**: These are process input streams and produce output streams

- **Topologies**: These are the overall calculation represented visually as a network of spouts and bolts, as follows:

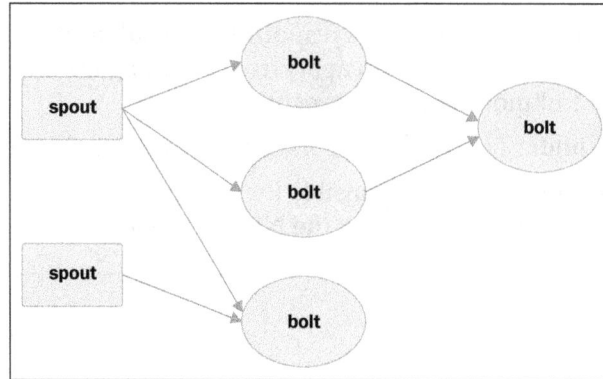

Setting up Storm on Mesos

This section explains how we can integrate Storm with the Mesos cluster resource manager. Let's follow the steps mentioned here:

1. We can first explore the Storm on Mesos repository by executing the following command:

    ```
    $ git clone https://github.com/Mesos/Storm
    $ cd Storm
    ```

2. We can now edit the configuration file listed in `conf/Storm.yaml`:

    ```
    # Please change these for your cluster
      to reflect your cluster settings
    # ---------------------------------------
      --------------------
    Mesos.master.url: "zk://localhost:2181/Mesos"
    Storm.zookeeper.servers:
    - "localhost"
    # ---------------------------------------
      -------------------

    # Worker resources
    topology.Mesos.worker.cpu: 1.0

    # Worker heap with 25% overhead
    topology.Mesos.worker.mem.mb: 512
    worker.childopts: "-Xmx384m"
    ```

```
# Supervisor resources
topology.Mesos.executor.cpu: 0.1
topology.Mesos.executor.mem.mb: 500
  # Supervisor memory, with 20% overhead
supervisor.childopts: "-Xmx400m"
```

```
# The default behavior is to launch the 'logviewer'
unless 'autostart' is false.
If you enable the logviewer, you'll need
to add memory overhead to the executor for the logviewer.
```

```
logviewer.port: 8000
logviewer.childopts: "-Xmx128m"
logviewer.cleanup.age.mins: 10080
logviewer.appender.name: "A1"
supervisor.autostart.logviewer: true
```

```
# Use the public Mesosphere Storm build.
Please note that it won't work with other distributions.
You may want to make this empty if you use
`Mesos.container.docker.image` instead.
# Mesos.executor.uri:
"file:///usr/local/Storm/Storm-Mesos-0.9.6.tgz"
```

```
# Alternatively, use a Docker image instead of URI.
If an image is specified, Docker will be used
instead of Mesos containers.
Mesos.container.docker.image: "Mesosphere/Storm"
```

```
# Use Netty to avoid ZMQ dependencies
Storm.messaging.transport:
  "backtype.Storm.messaging.netty.Context"
Storm.local.dir: "Storm-local"
```

```
# role must be one of the
  Mesos-master's roles defined in the --roles flag
Mesos.framework.role: "*"
Mesos.framework.checkpoint: true
Mesos.framework.name: "Storm"
```

```
# For setting up the necessary Mesos authentication
see Mesos authentication page and
set the Mesos-master flags --credentials,
--authenticate, --acls, and --roles.
```

```
Mesos.framework.principal: "Storm"

# The "secret" phrase cannot be followed by a NL

Mesos.framework.secret.file: "Storm-local/secret"

#Mesos.allowed.hosts:
  - host1
#Mesos.disallowed.hosts:
  - host1
```

3. Edit the properties according to the cluster that we have and execute the following command to start the nimbus:

    $ bin/Storm-Mesos nimbus

4. We need to start the UI on the same machine as the nimbus with the following command:

    $ bin/Storm ui

Topologies are submitted to a Storm/Mesos cluster in the exact same way that they are submitted to a regular Storm cluster. Storm/Mesos provides resource isolation between topologies. So, you don't need to worry about topologies interfering with one another.

Running a sample topology

Once nimbus is running, we can launch one of the Storm-starter topologies with the following command:

```
$ ./bin/Storm jar -c nimbus.host=10.0.0.1
  -c nimbus.thrift.port=32001 examples/Storm-starter/Storm-starter
  -topologies-0.9.6.jar Storm.starter.WordCountTopology word-count
```

Here, we specified the nimbus host and thrift port as parameters.

An advanced configuration guide

If we want to build the release against a different version of Mesos or Storm, then we can use the build-release.sh script to download the appropriate version by executing the following command:

```
STORM_RELEASE=x.x.x MESOS_RELEASE=y.y.y bin/build-release.sh
```

Here x.x.x and y.y.y are the appropriate versions of Storm and Mesos that we will build against. This command will build a Mesos executor package.

The `bin/build-release.sh` script takes in the following subcommands:

Subcommand	Usage
main	This is used to build a Storm package with the Mesos scheduler. The output of this command can be used as the package for `mesos.executor.uri`.
clean	This attempts to clean the working files and directories created when building.
downloadStormRelease	This is a utility function to download the Storm release tarball for the targeted Storm release. Set the MIRROR environment variable to configure the download mirror.
mvnPackage	This runs the Maven targets necessary to build the Storm Mesos framework.
prePackage	This prepares the working directories to be able to package the Storm Mesos framework and is an optional argument specifying the Storm release tarball to package against.
package	This packages the Storm Mesos framework.
dockerImage	This builds a Docker image from the current code.
help	This prints out usage information about the `build-release.sh` script.

Deploying Storm through Marathon

We can run Storm on Mesos with Marathon easily by setting the MESOS_MASTER_ZK environment variable to point to our ZooKeeper node of the cluster. The repository also includes a script, `bin/run-with-marathon.sh`, which sets the required parameters and starts the UI and nimbus. As Storm writes stateful data to the disk, we need to make sure that `storm.local.dir config` is set. We can run this from Marathon by submitting the following JSON data:

```
{
  "id": "storm-nimbus",
  "cmd": "./bin/run-with-marathon.sh",
  "cpus": 1.0,
  "mem": 1024,
  "ports": [0, 1],
  "instances": 1,
  "container": {
    "type": "DOCKER",
    "docker": {
      "image": "mesosphere/storm",
      "network": "HOST",
```

```
          "forcePullImage":true
      }
    },
    "healthChecks": [
      {
        "protocol": "HTTP",
        "portIndex": 0,
        "path": "/",
        "gracePeriodSeconds": 120,
        "intervalSeconds": 20,
        "maxConsecutiveFailures": 3
      }
    ]
}
```

We can save the preceding JSON code as `storm-mesos.json` and send a `curl` request to the Marathon API endpoint to deploy with the following command:

```
$ curl -X POST -H "Content-Type: application/json"
  -d storm-mesos.json http://marathon-machine:8080/v2/apps
```

Reference: `https://github.com/mesos/storm`.

Samza on Mesos

Samza is an open source distributed stream processing framework originally developed at LinkedIn. It has the following features:

- A simple API
- State management
- Fault tolerance
- Durability
- Scalability
- Pluggability
- Processor isolation

Important concepts of Samza

Some concepts in Samza are described in the following sections.

Streams

Samza processes streams of data—for example, website clickstreams, server logs, or any other event data. Messages can be added and read from a data stream. Multiple frameworks can access the same data stream and can partition the data based on the keys present in the message.

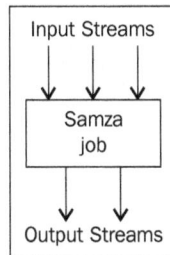

Jobs

A Samza job is the computation logic that reads data from input streams, applies some transformations to it, and outputs the resultant messages to a bunch of output streams.

Partitions

Every stream is split into single or multiple partitions. Every partition is an ordered sequence of messages.

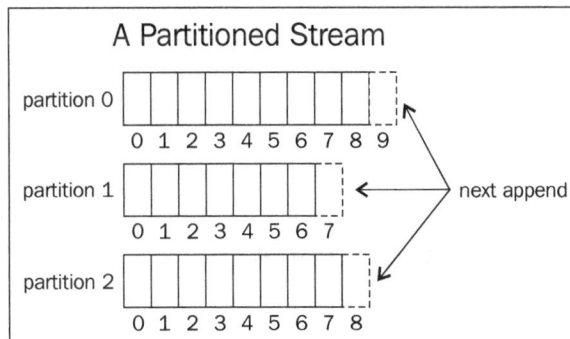

Tasks

A job is subdivided into multiple tasks for the parallelism of the computation. Every task reads data from a single partition for each input stream of the job.

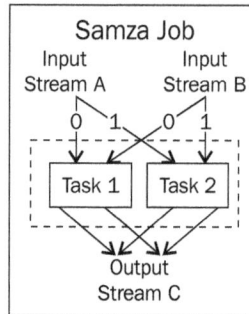

Dataflow graphs

Multiple jobs can be composed to develop a dataflow graph, in which the nodes are datastreams and the edges are the jobs.

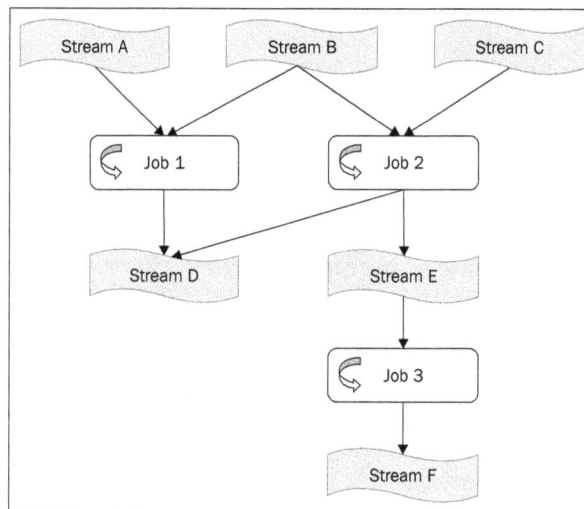

Setting up Samza on Mesos

This topic covers how we can run Samza jobs on a Mesos cluster. We will package the Samza jobs in a tarball for the sake of simplicity. Samza also supports packaging it in a Docker image.

At the time of writing this book, Samza on Mesos is in its early stages and hasn't been tested in a production environment to the best of our knowledge. Let's follow the steps mentioned here to set up Samza on Mesos:

1. We first need to deploy the `samza-mesos` jar in the environment. For this, we can clone the repository and build it with the following commands:

```
$ git clone https://github.com/Banno/samza-mesos
$ cd samza-mesos
$ mvn clean install
```

2. Once this is done, we can start importing the Maven dependency to our projects, as follows:

```
<dependency>
  <groupId>eu.inn</groupId>
  <artifactId>samza-mesos</artifactId>
  <version>0.1.0-SNAPSHOT</version>
</dependency>
```

The deployment of Samza through Marathon

Samza jobs can be deployed through Marathon. Each Samza job is a Mesos framework, which creates one Mesos task for each of the Samza containers. It is easier to deploy the Samza jobs on Mesos through Marathon, as described here.

Samza jobs are usually deployed in a tarball, which should contain the following as the top-level directories:

- `Bin`: This contains the standard Samza distributed shell scripts
- `Config`: This should be with your job `.properties` file(s)
- `Lib`: This contains all the `.jar` files

Now, let's take a look at how we can submit a Samza job to Marathon to deploy it on Mesos. The JSON request for the same will look similar to the following:

```
{
  "id": "samza-jobs.my-job", /Job ID/
  "uris": [
    "hdfs://master-machine/my-job.tgz" /Job Resource/
  ],
  "cmd": "bin/run-job.sh
    --config-path=file://$PWD/config/my-job.properties
    --config=job.factory.class=eu.inn.samza.mesos.MesosJobFactory
    --config=mesos.master.connect=
    zk://zookeeper-machine:2181/mesos
    --config=mesos.package.path=
```

```
      hdfs://master-machine/my-job.tgz
      --config=mesos.executor.count=1", /Job Properties/
  "cpus": 0.1,
  "mem": 64, /Resources/
  "instances": 1,
  "env": {
    "JAVA_HEAP_OPTS": "-Xms64M -Xmx64M"
  }
}
```

Note that here, `mesos.package.path` is the parameter pointing to the Samza tarball, which is kept in HDFS.

We can save the preceding JSON record to a file called `samza-job.json` and submit it to Marathon using the following `curl` command:

```
$ curl -X POST -H "Content-Type: application/json"
  -d samza-job.json http://marathon-machine:8080/v2/apps
```

An advanced configuration guide

The supported configuration properties are listed at `https://github.com/Banno/samza-mesos`.

Summary

This chapter introduced the reader to some important big data processing frameworks and covered topics such as the setup, configuration, and management of these frameworks on a distributed infrastructure using Mesos.

In the next chapter, we will discuss some of the important big data storage frameworks that are currently supported by Mesos (either in a beta or production-ready state), such as Cassandra, Elasticsearch, and Kafka, and understand how these can be set up and configured on Mesos.

9
Mesos Big Data
Frameworks 2

This chapter is a guide to deploying important big data storage frameworks, such as Cassandra, the Elasticsearch-Logstash-Kibana (ELK) stack, and Kafka, on Mesos.

Cassandra on Mesos

This section will introduce Cassandra and explain how to set up Cassandra on Mesos while also discussing the problems commonly encountered during the setup process.

Introduction to Cassandra

Cassandra is an open source, scalable NoSQL database that is fully distributed with no single point of failure and is highly performant for most standard use cases. It is both horizontally as well as vertically scalable. **Horizontal scalability** or **scale-out solution** involves adding more nodes with commodity hardware to the existing cluster while **vertical scalability** or **scale-up solution** means adding more CPU and memory resources to a node with specialized hardware.

Cassandra was developed by Facebook engineers to address the inbox search use case and was inspired by Google Bigtable, which served as the foundation for its storage model, and Amazon DynamoDB, which was the foundation of its distribution model. It was open sourced in 2008 and became an Apache top-level project in early 2010. It provides a query language called **Cassandra Query Language** or **CQL**, which has a SQL-like syntax, to communicate with the database.

Cassandra provides various capabilities, such as:

- High performance
- Continuous uptime (no single point of failure)
- Ease of use
- Data replication and distribution across datacenters

Instead of using a traditional master-slave or sharded design, Cassandra's architecture uses an elegant and simple **ring design** without any masters. This allows it to provide all the features and benefits listed earlier.

The Cassandra Ring Design diagram is shown as follows (source: www. planetcassandra.org):

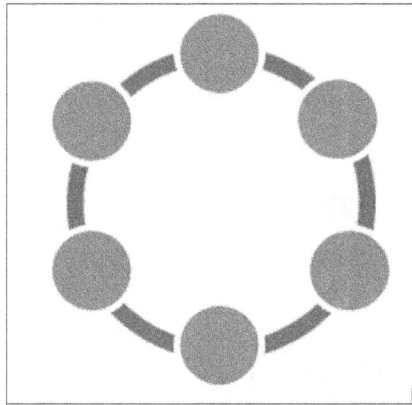

A large number of companies use Cassandra in production, including Apple, Instagram, eBay, Spotify, Comcast, and Netflix among others.

Cassandra is best used when you need:

- No single failure point
- Real-time writes
- Flexibility
- Horizontal scaling
- Reliability
- A clearly defined table schema in a NoSQL environment

Some of the common use cases are as follows:

- Storing, managing, and performing analysis on data generated by messaging applications (Instagram and Comcast, among others, use Cassandra for this purpose)
- Storing data patterns for the detection of fraudulent activity
- Storing user-selected and curated items (shopping cart, playlists, and so on)
- Recommendation and personalization

Performance benchmark

The following performance benchmark conducted by an independent database firm showed that for mixed operational and analytical workloads, Cassandra was far superior to other open source NoSQL technologies (source: www.datastax.com):

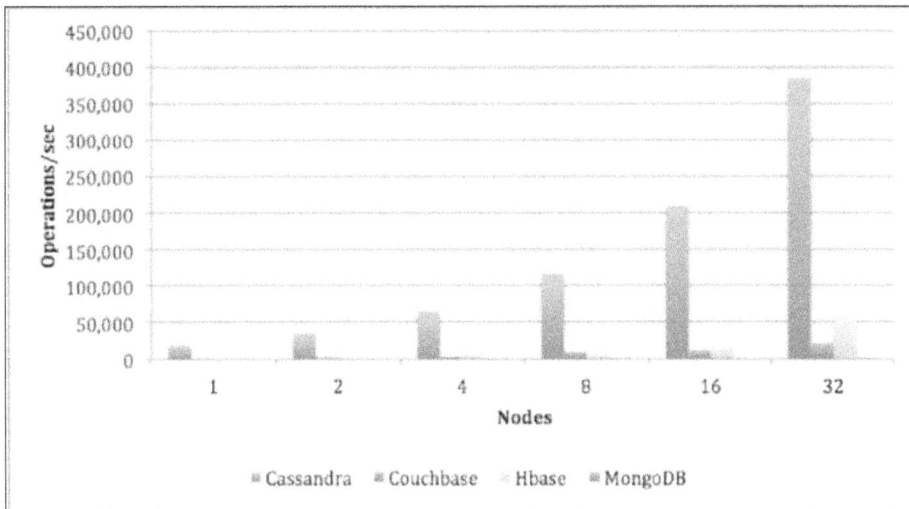

Setting up Cassandra on Mesos

This section covers the process of deploying Cassandra on top of Mesos. The recommended way of deploying Cassandra on Mesos is through Marathon. At the time of writing this book, Cassandra on Mesos is in an experimental stage, and the configuration described here might change in future releases.

The Mesosphere team has already packaged the necessary JAR files and the Cassandra executor in a tarball that can be directly submitted to Mesos through Marathon with the following JSON code:

```
{
  "healthChecks": [
    {
      "timeoutSeconds": 5,
      "protocol": "HTTP",
      "portIndex": 0,
      "path": "/health/cluster",
      "maxConsecutiveFailures": 0,
      "intervalSeconds": 30,
      "gracePeriodSeconds": 120
    },
    {
      "timeoutSeconds": 5,
      "protocol": "HTTP",
      "portIndex": 0,
      "path": "/health/process",
      "maxConsecutiveFailures": 3,
      "intervalSeconds": 30,
      "gracePeriodSeconds": 120
    }
  ],
  "id": "/cassandra/dev-test",
  "instances": 1,
  "cpus": 0.5,
  "mem": 512,
  "ports": [0],
  "uris": [
    "https://downloads.mesosphere.io/cassandra-mesos/artifacts/
      0.2.1-SNAPSHOT-608-master-d1c2cf30c8/cassandra-
      mesos-0.2.1-SNAPSHOT-608-master-d1c2cf30c8.tar.gz",
    "https://downloads.mesosphere.io/
      java/jre-7u76-linux-x64.tar.gz"
  ],
  "env": {
    "CASSANDRA_ZK_TIMEOUT_MS": "10000",
    "CASSANDRA_HEALTH_CHECK_INTERVAL_SECONDS": "60",
    "MESOS_ZK": "zk://localhost:2181/mesos",
    "JAVA_OPTS": "-Xms256m -Xmx256m",
    "CASSANDRA_CLUSTER_NAME": "dev-test",
    "CASSANDRA_ZK": "zk://localhost:2181/cassandra-mesos",
```

```
        "CASSANDRA_NODE_COUNT": "3",
        "CASSANDRA_RESOURCE_CPU_CORES": "2.0",
        "CASSANDRA_RESOURCE_MEM_MB": "2048",
        "CASSANDRA_RESOURCE_DISK_MB": "2048"
    },
    "cmd": "$(pwd)/jre*/bin/java
        $JAVA_OPTS -classpath
        cassandra-mesos-framework.jar
        io.mesosphere.mesos.frameworks.cassandra.framework.Main"
}
```

Edit the JSON code by pointing MESOS_ZK and any other parameters that you need to change accordingly, save this JSON code in cassandra-mesos.json, and then submit it to Marathon with the following command:

```
$ curl -X POST -H "Content-Type: application/json"
  -d cassandra-mesos.json http://marathon-machine:8080/v2/apps
```

Once submitted, the framework will bootstrap itself. We also need to expand the port ranges managed by each Mesos node to include the standard Cassandra ports. We can pass the port ranges as resources when starting the process.

Here's an example:

```
--resources='ports:
  [31000-32000,7000-7001,7199-7199,9042-9042,9160-9160]'
```

Cassandra on Mesos provides a REST endpoint to tune the setup. We can access this endpoint on port 18080 by default (unless changed).

An advanced configuration guide

As mentioned previously, Cassandra on Mesos takes in runtime configuration through environment variables. We can use the following environment variables to bootstrap the configuration of the framework. After the initial run, the configurations are read from the framework state stored in ZooKeeper:

```
# name of the cassandra cluster, this will
  be part of the framework name in Mesos
CASSANDRA_CLUSTER_NAME=dev-cluster

# Mesos ZooKeeper URL to locate leading master
MESOS_ZK=zk://localhost:2181/mesos

# ZooKeeper URL to be used to store framework state
CASSANDRA_ZK=zk://localhost:2181/cassandra-mesos
```

```
# The number of nodes in the cluster (default 3)
CASSANDRA_NODE_COUNT=3

# The number of seed nodes in the cluster (default 2)
# set this to 1, if you only want to spawn one node
CASSANDRA_SEED_COUNT=2

# The number of CPU Cores for each Cassandra Node (default 2.0)
CASSANDRA_RESOURCE_CPU_CORES=2.0

# The number of Megabytes of RAM
  for each Cassandra Node (default 2048)
CASSANDRA_RESOURCE_MEM_MB=2048

# The number of Megabytes of Disk
  for each Cassandra Node (default 2048)
CASSANDRA_RESOURCE_DISK_MB=2048

# The number of seconds
  between each health check of the Cassandra node (default 60)
CASSANDRA_HEALTH_CHECK_INTERVAL_SECONDS=60

# The default bootstrap grace time -
  the minimum interval between two node starts
# You may set this to a lower value
  in pure local development environments.
CASSANDRA_BOOTSTRAP_GRACE_TIME_SECONDS=120

# The number of seconds that should be used as the
  mesos framework timeout (default 604800 seconds / 7 days)
CASSANDRA_FAILOVER_TIMEOUT_SECONDS=604800

# The mesos role to used to reserve resources (default *).
  If this is set, the framework accepts offers
  that have resources for that role or the default role *
CASSANDRA_FRAMEWORK_MESOS_ROLE=*

# A pre-defined data directory specifying
  where Cassandra should write its data.
# Ensure that this directory can be created by the user
  the framework is running as (default. [mesos sandbox]).
# NOTE:
# This field is slated to be removed and
  the framework will be able to allocate the data volume itself.
CASSANDRA_DATA_DIRECTORY=.
```

Here are some references:

- `https://github.com/mesosphere/cassandra-mesos`
- `http://mesosphere.github.io/cassandra-mesos/`

The Elasticsearch-Logstash-Kibana (ELK) stack on Mesos

This section will introduce the **Elasticsearch-Logstash-Kibana** (ELK) stack and explain how to set it up on Mesos while also discussing the problems commonly encountered during the setup process.

Introduction to Elasticsearch, Logstash, and Kibana

The ELK stack, a combination of **Elasticsearch**, **Logstash**, and **Kibana**, is an end-to-end solution for **log analytics**. Elasticsearch provides search capabilities, Logstash is a log management software, while Kibana serves as the visualization layer. The stack is commercially backed by a company called **Elastic**.

Elasticsearch

Elasticsearch is a Lucene-based open source distributed search engine designed for high scalability and fast search query response time. It simplifies the usage of Lucene, a highly performant search engine library, by providing a powerful REST API on top. Some of the important concepts in Elasticsearch are highlighted as follows:

- **Document**: This is a JSON object stored in an index
- **Index**: This is a document collection
- **Type**: This is a logical partition of an index representing a category of documents
- **Field**: This is a key-value pair within a document
- **Mapping**: This is used to map every field with its datatype
- **Shard**: This is the physical location where an index's data is stored (the data is stored on one primary shard and copied on a set of replica shards)

Logstash

This is a tool to collect and process the log events generated by a wide variety of systems. It includes a rich set of input and output connectors to ingest the logs and make them available for analysis. Some of its important features are:

- The ability to convert logs to a common format for the ease of use
- The ability to process multiple log formats, including custom ones
- A rich set of input and output connectors

Kibana

This is an Elasticsearch-based data visualization tool with a wide variety of charting and dashboarding capabilities. It is powered by the data stored in the Elasticsearch indexes and is entirely developed using HTML and JavaScript. Some of its most important features are:

- A graphical user interface for dashboard construction
- A rich set of charts (map, pie charts, histograms, and so on)
- The ability to embed charts in user applications

The ELK stack data pipeline

Take a look at the following diagram (source: *Learning ELK Stack* by Packt Publishing):

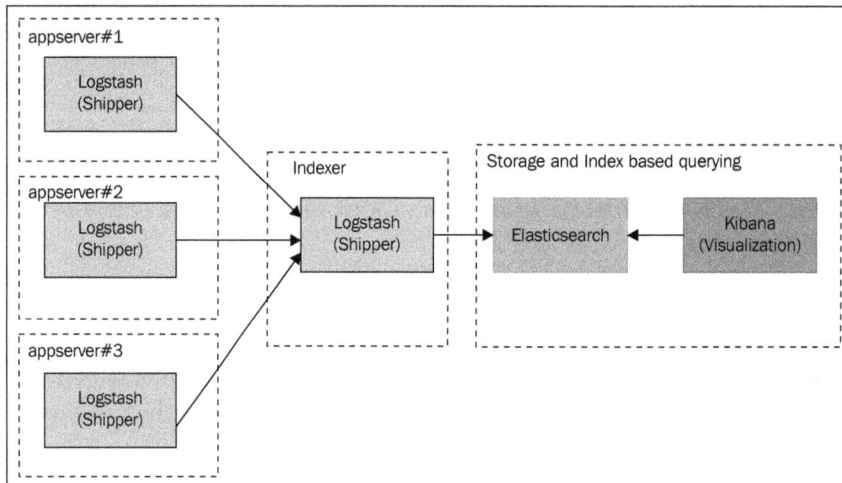

In a standard ELK stack pipeline, logs from various application servers are transported through Logstash to a central indexer module. This indexer then transmits the output to an Elasticsearch cluster, where it can be queried directly or visualized in a dashboard by leveraging Kibana.

Setting up Elasticsearch-Logstash-Kibana on Mesos

This section explains how to set up Elasticsearch, Logstash, and Kibana on top of Mesos. We will first take a look at how to set up Elasticsearch on top of Mesos followed by Logstash and Kibana.

Elasticsearch on Mesos

We will use Marathon to deploy Elasticsearch, and this can be done in two ways: through the Docker image, which is highly recommended, and through `elasticsearch-mesos jar`. Both are explained in the following section.

We can use the following Marathon file to deploy Elasticsearch on top of Mesos. It uses the Docker image:

```
{
  "id": "elasticsearch-mesos-scheduler",
  "container": {
    "docker": {
      "image": "mesos/elasticsearch-scheduler",
      "network": "HOST"
    }
  },
  "args": ["--zookeeperMesosUrl", "zk://zookeeper-node:2181/mesos"],
  "cpus": 0.2,
  "mem": 512.0,
  "env": {
    "JAVA_OPTS": "-Xms128m -Xmx256m"
  },
  "instances": 1
}
```

Ensure that `zookeeper-node` is changed to the address of the ZooKeeper node that you have on the cluster. We can save this to an `elasticsearch.json` file and then deploy it on Marathon with the following command:

```
$ curl -k -XPOST -d @elasticsearch.json
  -H "Content-Type: application/json"
  http://marathon-machine:8080/v2/apps
```

As mentioned before, we can also use the JAR file to deploy Elasticsearch on top of Mesos with the following Marathon file:

```
{
  "id": "elasticsearch",
  "cpus": 0.2,
  "mem": 512,
  "instances": 1,
  "cmd": "java -jar scheduler-0.7.0.jar
    --frameworkUseDocker false
    --zookeeperMesosUrl zk://10.0.0.254:2181
    --frameworkName elasticsearch
    --elasticsearchClusterName mesos-elasticsearch
    --elasticsearchCpu 1 --elasticsearchRam 1024
    --elasticsearchDisk 1024 --elasticsearchNodes 3
    --elasticsearchSettingsLocation
    /home/ubuntu/elasticsearch.yml",
  "uris":
    ["https://github.com/mesos/
    elasticsearch/releases/download/0.7.0/scheduler-0.7.0.jar"],
  "env": {
    "JAVA_OPTS": "-Xms256m -Xmx512m"
  },
  "ports": [31100],
  "requirePorts": true,
  "healthChecks": [
    {
      "gracePeriodSeconds": 120,
      "intervalSeconds": 10,
      "maxConsecutiveFailures": 6,
      "path": "/",
      "portIndex": 0,
      "protocol": "HTTP",
      "timeoutSeconds": 5
    }
  ]
}
```

In both cases, the JAVA_OPTS environment variable is required, and if it's not set, it will cause problems with the Java heap space. We can save this as elasticsearch.json and submit it to Marathon with the following command:

```
$ curl -k -XPOST -d @elasticsearch.json
  -H "Content-Type: application/json"
  http://MARATHON_IP_ADDRESS:8080/v2/apps
```

Both Docker image and the JAR file take in the following command-line arguments, similar to the `--zookeeperMesosUrl` argument:

```
--dataDir
      The host data directory used by Docker volumes
         in the executors. [DOCKER MODE ONLY]
      Default: /var/lib/mesos/slave/elasticsearch

--elasticsearchClusterName
      Name of the Elasticsearch cluster
      Default: mesos-ha

--elasticsearchCpu
      The amount of CPU resource to allocate
         to the Elasticsearch instance.
      Default: 1.0

--elasticsearchDisk
      The amount of Disk resource to allocate
         to the Elasticsearch instance
      (MB).
      Default: 1024.0

--elasticsearchExecutorCpu
      The amount of CPU resource to allocate
         to the Elasticsearch executor.
      Default: 0.1

--elasticsearchExecutorRam
      The amount of ram resource to allocate
         to the Elasticsearch executor
      (MB).
      Default: 32.0

--elasticsearchNodes
      Number of Elasticsearch instances.
      Default: 3

--elasticsearchPorts
      User specified Elasticsearch HTTP and
         transport ports. [NOT RECOMMENDED]
      Default: <empty string>
```

```
--elasticsearchRam
      The amount of ram resource to allocate
        to the Elasticsearch instance
      (MB).
      Default: 256.0

--elasticsearchSettingsLocation
      Path or URL to Elasticsearch yml settings file.
        [In docker mode file must be in /tmp/config]
        E.g. '/tmp/config/elasticsearch.yml' or
        'https://gist.githubusercontent.com/mmaloney/
        5e1da5daa58b70a3a671/raw/elasticsearch.yml'
      Default: <empty string>

--executorForcePullImage
      Option to force pull the executor image.
      [DOCKER MODE ONLY]
      Default: false

--executorImage
      The docker executor image to use. E.g.
        'elasticsearch:latest' [DOCKER
      MODE ONLY]
      Default: elasticsearch:latest

--executorName
      The name given to the executor task.
      Default: elasticsearch-executor

--frameworkFailoverTimeout
      The time before Mesos kills a scheduler and
        tasks if it has not recovered
      (ms).
      Default: 2592000.0

--frameworkName
      The name given to the framework.
      Default: elasticsearch

--frameworkPrincipal
      The principal to use when
        registering the framework (username).
      Default: <empty string>
```

```
--frameworkRole
      Used to group frameworks for
        allocation decisions, depending on the
      allocation policy being used.
      Default: *

--frameworkSecretPath
      The path to the file which
        contains the secret for the principal
      (password). Password in file must not have a newline.
      Default: <empty string>

--frameworkUseDocker
      The framework will use docker if true, or jar files
        if false. If false, the user must ensure that
        the scheduler jar is available to all slaves.
      Default: true

--javaHome
      When starting in jar mode, if java is
        not on the path, you can specify
      the path here. [JAR MODE ONLY]
      Default: <empty string>

--useIpAddress
      If true, the framework will resolve
        the local ip address. If false, it
      uses the hostname.
      Default: false

--webUiPort
      TCP port for web ui interface.
      Default: 31100

--zookeeperMesosTimeout
      The timeout for connecting to zookeeper for Mesos (ms).
      Default: 20000

* --zookeeperMesosUrl
      Zookeeper urls for Mesos in the format
        zk://IP:PORT,IP:PORT,...)
      Default: zk://mesos.master:2181
```

Logstash on Mesos

This section explains how to run Logstash on top of Mesos. Once Logstash is deployed on the cluster, any program that runs on Mesos can log an event that is then passed by Logstash and sent to a central log location.

We can run Logstash as a Marathon application and deploy it on top of Mesos with the following Marathon file:

```
{
  "id": "/logstash",
  "cpus": 1,
  "mem": 1024.0,
  "instances": 1,
  "container": {
    "type": "DOCKER",
    "docker": {
      "image": "mesos/logstash-scheduler:0.0.6",
      "network": "HOST"
    }
  },
  "env": {
    "ZK_URL": "zk://123.0.0.12:5181/logstash",
    "ZK_TIMEOUT": "20000",
    "FRAMEWORK_NAME": "logstash",
    "FAILOVER_TIMEOUT": "60",
    "MESOS_ROLE": "logstash",
    "MESOS_USER": "root",
    "LOGSTASH_HEAP_SIZE": "64",
    "LOGSTASH_ELASTICSEARCH_URL":
      "http://elasticsearch.service.consul:1234",
    "EXECUTOR_CPUS": "0.5",
    "EXECUTOR_HEAP_SIZE": "128",
    "ENABLE_FAILOVER": "false",
    "ENABLE_COLLECTD": "true",
    "ENABLE_SYSLOG": "true",
    "ENABLE_FILE": "true",
    "ENABLE_DOCKER": "true",
    "EXECUTOR_FILE_PATH": "/var/log/*,/home/jhf/example.log"
  }
}
```

Here, we used the Docker image for deployment, the configurations of which can be changed according to your cluster specification. Save the preceding file as `logstash.json` and submit it to Marathon with the following command:

```
$ curl -k -XPOST -d @logstash.json
  -H "Content-Type: application/json"
  http://MARATHON_IP_ADDRESS:8080/v2/apps
```

Logstash on Mesos configurations

Logstash and Elasticsearch are tested with the Mesos version 0.25.0 and later. We need to add Logstash to the list of roles on every Mesos master machine. This can be done with the following command:

```
$ sudo echo logstash > /etc/mesos-master/roles
```

If the purpose of Logstash is to monitor `syslog` (a message logging standard), then we need to add the TCP and UDP port `514` to the resources list in every Mesos node in the cluster. This can be done by adding the following entry in the `/etc/mesos-slave/resources` file:

```
ports(logstash):[514-514]
```

To monitor `collectd`, we need to add the TCP and UDP port `25826` to the resources for the Logstash role by adding the following line to the `/etc/mesos-slave/resources` file:

```
ports(logstash):[25826-25826]
```

Kibana on Mesos

If we run Kibana on Mesos, then each instance of Kibana will run as a Docker image in the Mesos cluster. For each instance of Elasticsearch, one or more instances of Kibana can be deployed to serve the users.

We can clone Kibana on the Mesos project from the following repository:

```
$ git clone https://github.com/mesos/kibana
```

Build the project with the following command:

```
$ cd kibana
```

```
$ gradlew jar
```

This will generate the Kibana JAR file (`kibana.jar`).

Once `kibana.jar` is generated, we can deploy it with the following command:

```
$ java -jar /path/to/kibana.jar
  -zk zk://zookeeper:2181/mesos -v 4.3.1 -es http://es-host:9200
```

Here, `-zk` represents the ZooKeeper URI and the `-es` points to the Elasticsearch endpoint, which we deployed in the previous section. Set them accordingly.

The following command-line options are also supported by the `kibana.jar` file:

Short keyword	Keyword	Definition
`-zk`	`-zookeeper`	This is the Mesos ZooKeeper URL (Required)
`-di`	`-dockerimage`	This is the name of the Docker image to be used (The default is `kibana`)
`-v`	`-version`	This is the version of the Kibana Docker image to be used (The default is `latest`)
`-mem`	`-requiredMem`	This is the amount of memory (in MB) to be allocated to a single Kibana instance (The default is `128`)
`-cpu`	`-requiredCpu`	This is the amount of CPUs to allocate to a single Kibana instance (The default is `0.1`)
`-disk`	`-requiredDisk`	This is the amount of disk space (in MB) to be allocated to a single Kibana instance (The default is `25`)
`-es`	`-elasticsearch`	These are the URLs of Elasticsearch to start a Kibana for at startup

Here are some references:

- `http://mesos-elasticsearch.readthedocs.org/en/latest/#elasticsearch-mesos-framework`
- `https://github.com/mesos/logstash`
- `https://github.com/mesos/kibana`

Kafka on Mesos

This section will introduce Kafka and explain how to set it up on Mesos while also discussing the problems commonly encountered during the setup process.

Introduction to Kafka

Kafka is a distributed publish-subscribe messaging system designed for speed, scalability, reliability, and durability. Some of the key terms used in Kafka are given as follows:

- **Topics**: These are the categories where message feeds are maintained by Kafka
- **Producers**: These are the upstream processes that send messages to a particular Kafka topic
- **Consumers**: These are the downstream processes that listen to the incoming messages in a topic and process them as per requirements
- **Broker**: Each node in a Kafka cluster is called a broker

Take a look at the following high-level diagram of Kafka (source: `http://kafka.apache.org/documentation.html#introduction`):

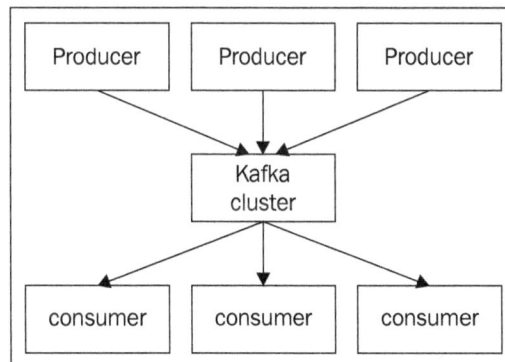

A partitioned log is maintained by the Kafka cluster for every topic, which looks similar to the following (source: `http://kafka.apache.org/documentation.html#intro_topics`):

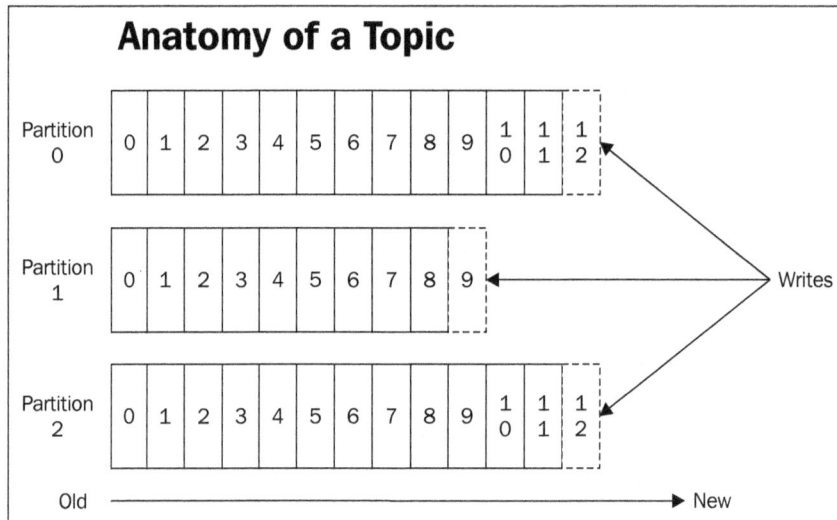

Anatomy of a Topic

Partition 0	0	1	2	3	4	5	6	7	8	9	1 0	1 1	1 2

Partition 1	0	1	2	3	4	5	6	7	8	9

Partition 2	0	1	2	3	4	5	6	7	8	9	1 0	1 1	1 2

Writes

Old ──────────────────────────► New

Use cases of Kafka

Some important uses of Kafka are described here:

- **Website activity tracking**: Site activity events, such as page views and user searches, can be sent by the web application to Kafka topics. Downstream processing systems can then subscribe to these topics and consume the messages for batch analytics, monitoring, real-time dashboarding, and other such use cases.

- **Log aggregation**: Kafka is used as an alternative to traditional log aggregation systems. Physical log files can be collected from various services and pushed to different Kafka topics, where different consumers can read and process them. File details are abstracted by Kafka, which enables faster processing and support for a variety of data sources.

- **Stream processing**: Frameworks, for instance Spark Streaming, can consume data from a Kafka topic, process it as per requirements, and then publish the processed output to a different Kafka topic, where this output can, in turn, be consumed by other applications.

Setting up Kafka

Before installing Kafka on Mesos, make sure the following applications are available on the machine:

- Java version 7 or later (`http://openjdk.java.net/install/`)
- Gradle (`http://gradle.org/installation`)

We can clone and build the Kafka on Mesos project from the following repository:

```
$ git clone https://github.com/mesos/kafka
$ cd kafka
$ ./gradlew jar
```

We will also require the Kafka executor, which can be downloaded with the following command:

```
$ wget https://archive.apache.org/dist/
  kafka/0.8.2.2/kafka_2.10-0.8.2.2.tgz
```

We will also need to set the following environment variable to point to the `libmesos.so` file:

```
$ export MESOS_NATIVE_JAVA_LIBRARY=/usr/local/lib/libmesos.so
```

Once these are set, we can use the `kafka-mesos.sh` script to launch and configure Kafka on top of Mesos. Before doing so, we need to create the `kafka-mesos.properties` file with the following contents:

```
storage=file:kafka-mesos.json
master=zk://master:2181/mesos
zk=master:2181
api=http://master:7000
```

This file can be used to configure the scheduler (`kafka-mesos.sh`) if we don't need to pass the arguments to the scheduler all the time. The scheduler supports the following command-line arguments:

Option	Description
`--api`	This is the API URL—for example, `http://master:7000`.
`--bind-address`	This is the scheduler bind address (such as master, `0.0.0.0`, `192.168.50.*`, and `if:eth1`). The default is `all`.
`--debug <Boolean>`	This is the debug mode. The default is `false`.

Option	Description
--framework-name	This is the framework name. The default is kafka.
--framework-role	This is the framework role. The default is *.
--framework-timeout	This is the framework timeout (30s, 1m, or 1h). The default is 30d.
--jre	This is the JRE zip file (jre-7-openjdk.zip). The default is none.
--log	This is the log file to use. The default is stdout.
--master	These are the master connection settings. Some examples are: - master:5050 - master:5050,master2:5050 - zk://master:2181/mesos - zk://username:password@master:2181 - zk://master:2181,master2:2181/mesos
--principal	This is the principal (username) used to register the framework. The default is none.
--secret	This is the secret (password) used to register the framework. The default is none.
--storage	This is the storage for the cluster state. Some examples are: - file:kafka-mesos.json - zk:/kafka-mesos The default is file:kafka-mesos.json.
--user	This is the Mesos user to run tasks. The default is none.
--zk	This is Kafka zookeeper.connect. Some examples are: - master:2181 - master:2181,master2:2181

Now, we can use the scheduler to run a Kafka scheduler via the following commands listed:

```
#Start the kafka scheduler
$ ./kafka-mesos.sh scheduler
```

The next thing we need to do is to start up one Kafka broker with the default settings. This can be done via the following command:

```
$ ./kafka-mesos.sh broker add 0
```

```
broker added:
  id: 0
  active: false
  state: stopped
  resources: cpus:1.00, mem:2048, heap:1024, port:auto
  failover: delay:1m, max-delay:10m
  stickiness: period:10m
```

At this point, our Kafka cluster will have one broker that is not yet started. We can verify this with the following command:

```
$ ./kafka-mesos.sh broker list
```

```
broker:
  id: 0
  active: false
  state: stopped
  resources: cpus:1.00, mem:2048, heap:1024, port:auto
  failover: delay:1m, max-delay:10m
  stickiness: period:10m
```

We can now start this broker with the following command:

```
$ ./kafka-mesos.sh broker start 0
```

```
broker started:
  id: 0
  active: true
  state: running
  resources: cpus:1.00, mem:2048, heap:1024, port:auto
  failover: delay:1m, max-delay:10m
  stickiness: period:10m, hostname:slave0
  task:
```

```
id: broker-0-d2d94520-2f3e-4779-b276-771b4843043c
running: true
endpoint: 192.168.25.62:31000
attributes: rack=r1
```

If the preceding output is shown, then our broker is ready to produce and consume messages. We can now test this setup with kafkacat.

The kafkacat can be installed on the system with the following command:

```
$ sudo apt-get install kafkacat
```

```
$ echo "test" |kafkacat -P -b "192.168.25.62:31000" -t testTopic -p 0
```

Now that we have pushed the test to the broker, we can read it back with the following command:

```
$ kafkacat -C -b "192.168.25.62:31000" -t testTopic -p 0 -e
```

```
test
```

Now, let's take a look at how we can add more brokers to the cluster at once. Run the following:

```
$ ./kafka-mesos.sh broker add 0..2 --heap 1024 --mem 2048
```

The preceding command adds three kafka brokers to the cluster with the following output:

```
brokers added:

  id: 0
  active: false
  state: stopped
  resources: cpus:1.00, mem:2048, heap:1024, port:auto
  failover: delay:1m, max-delay:10m
  stickiness: period:10m

  id: 1
  active: false
  state: stopped
  resources: cpus:1.00, mem:2048, heap:1024, port:auto
```

```
failover: delay:1m, max-delay:10m
stickiness: period:10m


id: 2
active: false
state: stopped
resources: cpus:1.00, mem:2048, heap:1024, port:auto
failover: delay:1m, max-delay:10m
stickiness: period:10m
```

We can start all the three brokers at once with the following command:

```
$    ./kafka-mesos.sh broker start 0..2


brokers started:

  id: 0
  active: true
  state: running
  resources: cpus:1.00, mem:2048, heap:1024, port:auto
  failover: delay:1m, max-delay:10m
  stickiness: period:10m, hostname:slave0
  task:
    id: broker-0-d2d94520-2f3e-4779-b276-771b4843043c
    running: true
    endpoint: 192.168.25.62:31000
    attributes: rack=r1

  id: 1
  active: true
  state: running

  id: 2
  active: true
  state: running
```

If we need to change the location of the Kafka logs where the data is stored, we need to first stop the particular broker and then update the location with the following commands:

```
$ ./kafka-mesos.sh broker stop 0
```

```
broker stopped:
  id: 0
  active: false
  state: stopped
  resources: cpus:1.00, mem:2048, heap:1024, port:auto
  failover: delay:1m, max-delay:10m
  stickiness: period:10m, hostname:slave0,
    expires:2015-07-10 15:51:43+03
```

```
$ ./kafka-mesos.sh broker update 0
  --options log.dirs=/mnt/kafka/broker0
```

```
broker updated:
  id: 0
  active: false
  state: stopped
  resources: cpus:1.00, mem:2048, heap:1024, port:auto
  options: log.dirs=/mnt/kafka/broker0
  failover: delay:1m, max-delay:10m
  stickiness: period:10m, hostname:slave0,
    expires:2015-07-10 15:51:43+03
```

Once done, we can start the broker back up with the following command:

```
$ ./kafka-mesos.sh broker start 0
```

```
broker started:
  id: 0
  active: true
  state: running
  resources: cpus:1.00, mem:2048, heap:1024, port:auto
  failover: delay:1m, max-delay:10m
  stickiness: period:10m, hostname:slave0
```

```
task:
id: broker-0-d2d94520-2f3e-4779-b276-771b4843043c
running: true
endpoint: 192.168.25.62:31000
attributes: rack=r1
```

Kafka logs management

We can get the last 100 lines of the logs (`stdout` -default or `stderr`) of any broker in the cluster with the following command:

```
$ ./kafka-mesos.sh broker log 0
```

If we need to read from the `stderr` file, then we will use the following command:

```
$ ./kafka-mesos.sh broker log 0 --name stderr
```

We can read any file in the `kafka-*/log/` directory by passing on the filename to the `--name` option. For example, if we need to read `server.log`, then it can be read with the following command:

```
$ ./kafka-mesos.sh broker log 0 --name server.log
```

Also, if we need to read more numbers of lines from the log, it can be read using the `--lines` option, as follows:

```
$ ./kafka-mesos.sh broker log 0 --name server.log --lines 200
```

An advanced configuration guide

The following are the configuration options available while *adding* broker(s) to the cluster:

```
$ ./kafka-mesos.sh help broker add
Add broker
Usage: broker add <broker-expr> [options]
Option          Description
--bind-address          broker bind address (broker0, 192.168.50.*,
                            if:eth1). Default - auto
--constraints           constraints (hostname=like:master,
                            rack=like:1.*). See below.
--cpus <Double>         cpu amount (0.5, 1, 2)
--failover-delay        failover delay (10s, 5m, 3h)
```

```
--failover-max-delay    max failover delay. See failoverDelay.

--failover-max-tries    max failover tries. Default - none

--heap <Long>           heap amount in Mb

--jvm-options           jvm options string (-Xms128m -XX:PermSize=48m)

--log4j-options         log4j options or file. Examples

                        log4j.logger.kafka=DEBUG\, kafkaAppender

                        file:log4j.properties

--mem <Long>            mem amount in Mb

--options               options or file. Examples:

                        log.dirs=/tmp/kafka/$id,num.io.threads=16

                        file:server.properties

--port                  port or range (31092, 31090..31100).
                          Default - auto

--stickiness-period     stickiness period to preserve same node
                          for broker (5m, 10m, 1h)

--volume                pre-reserved persistent volume id


Generic       Options
Option        Description
------        -----------
--api     Api url. Example: http://master:7000broker-expr examples:


  0       - broker 0
  0,1     - brokers 0,1
  0..2    - brokers 0,1,2
  0,1..2  - brokers 0,1,2
  *       - any broker


attribute filtering:
  *[rack=r1]           - any broker having rack=r1
  *[hostname=slave*]   - any broker on host with name starting
                           with 'slave'
  0..4[rack=r1,dc=dc1] - any broker having rack=r1 and dc=dc1


constraint examples:
  like:master      - value equals 'master'
  unlike:master    - value not equals 'master'
```

```
like:slave.*     - value starts with 'slave'
unique           - all values are unique
cluster          - all values are the same
cluster:master   - value equals 'master'
groupBy          - all values are the same
groupBy:3        - all values are within 3 different groups
```

We will now take a look at the options that are available when starting the broker(s):

```
$ ./kafka-mesos.sh help broker start
Start broker
Usage: broker start <broker-expr> [options]
Option      Description
------      -----------
--timeout   timeout (30s, 1m, 1h). 0s - no timeout


Generic  Options
Option   Description
------   -----------
--api    Api url. Example: http://master:7000


broker      - expr examples:
  0         - broker 0
  0,1       - brokers 0,1
  0..2      - brokers 0,1,2
  0,1..2    - brokers 0,1,2
  *         - any broker


attribute filtering:
  *[rack=r1]             - any broker having rack=r1
  *[hostname=slave*]     - any broker on host with name starting with
                             'slave'
  0..4[rack=r1,dc=dc1]   - any broker having rack=r1 and dc=dc1
```

The following are the configuration options available while *updating* broker(s) in the cluster:

```
$ ./kafka-mesos.sh help broker update
```

```
Update broker
Usage: broker update <broker-expr> [options]
```

```
Option                  Description
------                  -----------
--bind-address          broker bind address (broker0, 192.168.50.*,
                            if:eth1). Default - auto
--constraints           constraints (hostname=
                            like:master,rack=like:1.*). See below.
--cpus <Double>         cpu amount (0.5, 1, 2)
--failover-delay        failover delay (10s, 5m, 3h)
--failover-max-delay    max failover delay. See failoverDelay.
--failover-max-tries    max failover tries. Default - none
--heap <Long>           heap amount in Mb
--jvm-options           jvm options string (-Xms128m -XX:PermSize=48m)
--log4j-options         log4j options or file. Examples:

                            log4j.logger.kafka=DEBUG\, kafkaAppender

                            file:log4j.properties
--mem <Long>            mem amount in Mb
--options               options or file. Examples:

                            log.dirs=/tmp/kafka/$id,num.io.threads=16

                            file:server.properties
--port                  port or range
                            (31092, 31090..31100). Default - auto
--stickiness-period     stickiness period to preserve same node
                            for broker (5m, 10m, 1h)
--volume                pre-reserved persistent volume id
```

```
Generic Options
Option  Description
------  -----------
--api   Api url. Example: http://master:7000
```

```
broker-expr examples:
  0          - broker 0
  0,1        - brokers 0,1
  0..2       - brokers 0,1,2
  0,1..2     - brokers 0,1,2
  *          - any broker

attribute filtering:
  *[rack=r1]            - any broker having rack=r1
  *[hostname=slave*]    - any broker on host with name
                             starting with 'slave'
  0..4[rack=r1,dc=dc1] - any broker having rack=r1 and dc=dc1

constraint examples:
  like:master      - value equals 'master'
  unlike:master    - value not equals 'master'
  like:slave.*     - value starts with 'slave'
  unique           - all values are unique
  cluster          - all values are the same
  cluster:master   - value equals 'master'
  groupBy          - all values are the same
  groupBy:3        - all values are within 3 different groups

Note: use "" arg to unset an option
```

The following are the configuration options available while stopping broker(s) in the cluster:

```
$ ./kafka-mesos.sh help broker stop
```

```
Stop broker
Usage: broker stop <broker-expr> [options]

Option      Description
------      -----------
--force     forcibly stop
--timeout   timeout (30s, 1m, 1h). 0s - no timeout
```

```
Generic  Options

Option   Description
------   -----------
--api    Api url. Example: http://master:7000


broker-expr examples:
  0        - broker 0
  0,1      - brokers 0,1
  0..2     - brokers 0,1,2
  0,1..2 - brokers 0,1,2
  *        - any broker
attribute filtering:
  *[rack=r1]           - any broker having rack=r1
  *[hostname=slave*]   - any broker on host with name
                           starting with 'slave'
  0..4[rack=r1,dc=dc1] - any broker having rack=r1 and dc=dc1
```

The following are the configuration options available while adding a topic to the broker(s) in the cluster:

```
$ ./kafka-mesos.sh help topic add
Add topic
Usage: topic add <topic-expr> [options]


Option                  Description
------                  -----------
--broker                <broker-expr>. Default - *. See below.
--options               topic options. Example:
                          flush.ms=60000,retention.ms=6000000
--partitions <Integer>  partitions count. Default - 1
--replicas <Integer>    replicas count. Default - 1


topic-expr examples:
  t0       - topic t0
  t0,t1    - topics t0, t1
  *        - any topic
  t*       - topics starting with 't'
```

```
broker-expr examples:
   0        - broker 0
   0,1      - brokers 0,1
   0..2     - brokers 0,1,2
   0,1..2 - brokers 0,1,2
   *        - any broker
```

The reference for this is https://github.com/mesos/kafka.

Summary

This chapter introduced the reader to some important big data storage frameworks such as Cassandra, the ELK stack, and Kafka and covered topics such as the setup, configuration, and management of these frameworks on a distributed infrastructure using Mesos.

I hope that this book has armed you with all the resources that you require to effectively manage the complexities of today's modern datacenter requirements. By following the detailed step-by-step guides to deploy a Mesos cluster using the DevOps tool of your choice, you should now be in a position to handle the system administration requirements of your organization smoothly.

Index

future 29
reference link 28
hypervisor-based model
reference link 226

I

Image 249
Image Provisioner 249
installation
Playa 177
Vagrant 176
VirtualBox 176
internals, Mesos containerizer
about 236
pid namespace 236
pid namespace, advantages 236
Posix Disk Isolator 237
shared filesystem 236
IOperating system (OS) 225
IP Address Management (IPAM) Server 241
IPAM client 241
IP-per-container capability in frameworks
about 242
NetworkInfo Message 242
network requirements specification,
examples 243-245
isolator 235

J

Java version 7
URL 305

K

Kafka
about 112, 303
broker 303
consumers 303
key terms 303
logs management 311
producers 303
setting up 305-310
topics 303
use cases 304

Kafka, on Mesos
about 303
advanced configuration guide 311-317
Kibana
about 294
features 294

L

Linux Container (LXC) 228
load balancing 111
log analytics 293
Logstash
features 294
shard 294
Logstash, on Mesos
about 300, 301
configurations 301
long-running services
Aurora 6
Marathon 6
Singularity 6
SSSP 6

M

**machine, launching on Google Compute
Engine (GCE)**
about 78
Google Cloud Platform project,
setting up 78, 79
machine, launching on Microsoft Azure
about 85
Cloud Service, creating 85, 86
instances, creating 86-90
managed whitelist 184
manual whitelist 184
MapReduce
about 264
Map Task 264
Reduce Task 264
Marathon
about 111
installing 112, 113
launching, in local mode 114

REVIVE 199
SHUTDOWN 200
TEARDOWN 197
supported modules
allocator 54
authenticator 54
isolator 54
QoS controller 54
resource estimator 54

T

Terraform
about 170
cluster, destroying 172
installing 170
used, for configuring Mesos cluster 170
used, for deploying Mesos cluster 170
used, for spinning up Mesos cluster on
Google Cloud 171, 172
test environments
creating, Playa Mesos used 176-178
two-level scheduling 9-11

U

use cases, Kafka
log aggregation 304
stream processing 304
website activity tracking 304

V

vertical scalability 287
virtual machine (VM)
instances 67

X

xterm 93

Z

ZooKeeper
installation, for storing state 113
reference link 113

www.ingramcontent.com/pod-product-compliance
Lightning Source LLC
Chambersburg PA
CBHW080910220326
41598CB00034B/5536